Design at Home

Domestic advice literature is rich in information about design, ideals of domesticity, consumption and issues of identity, yet this literature remains a relatively neglected resource in comparison with magazines and film.

Design at Home brings together etiquette, homemaking and home decoration advice as sources in the first systematic demonstration of the historical value of domestic advice literature as a genre of word and image, and a discourse of dominance. This book traces a transatlantic domestic dialogue between the UK and the US as the chapters explore issues of design, domesticity, consumption, social interaction and identity markers including class, gender and age.

Areas covered include:

- the use of domestic advice by historians
- relationships between advice, housing and the middle class
- links between advice and gender
- advice and the teenage consumer

Design at Home is essential reading for students and scholars of cultural and social history, design history, and cultural studies.

Grace Lees-Maffei is a Reader in Design History at the University of Hertfordshire and the Managing Editor of the *Journal of Design History*. She researches the mediation of design, edited *Writing Design: Words and Objects* and co-edited *Made in Italy: Rethinking a Century of Italian Design* and *The Design History Reader*.

Directions in Cultural History
Series Editors: Gillian Swanson and Ben Highmore

The *Directions in Cultural History* series directs history towards the study of feelings, experiences and everyday habits. By attending to the world of sensation, imagination, and desire at moments of change, and by coupling this to the materials and technologies of culture, it promotes cultural history as a lively and vivid arena for research. The series will present innovative cultural history in an accessible form to both scholars and upper level students.

Print Culture: From steam press to ebook
Frances Robertson

Dreams and Modernity: A cultural history
Helen Groth and Natalya Lusty

Design at Home: Domestic advice books in Britain and the USA since 1945
Grace Lees-Maffei

Forthcoming titles:

Cultural History: Detail and intimacy
Gillian Swanson

Practicing Cultural History
Ben Highmore

Home Discontents
David Ellison

Design at Home
Domestic advice books in Britain and the USA since 1945

Grace Lees-Maffei

Routledge
Taylor & Francis Group

LONDON AND NEW YORK

First published in paperback 2024

First published 2014
by Routledge
4 Park Square, Milton Park, Abingdon, Oxon OX14 4RN

and by Routledge
605 Third Avenue, New York, NY 10158

Routledge is an imprint of the Taylor & Francis Group, an informa business

© 2014, 2024 Grace Lees-Maffei

Publisher's Note
The publisher has gone to great lengths to ensure the quality of this reprint but points out that some imperfections in the original copies may be apparent.

British Library Cataloguing in Publication Data
A catalogue record for this book is available from the British Library

Library of Congress Cataloging in Publication Data
Lees-Maffei, Grace.
Design at home: domestic advice books in Britain and the USA since 1945 / Grace Lees Maffei. — 1 [edition].
pages cm.—(Directions in cultural history)
1. Home economics—Great Britain—History—20th century. 2. Home economics—Great Britain—History—21st century. 3. Home economics—United States—History—20th century. 4. Home economics—United States—History—21st century. I. Title.
TX57.L44 2013
640.941—dc23
2013023399

ISBN: 978-0-415-65669-6 (hbk)
ISBN: 978-1-03-292605-6 (pbk)
ISBN: 978-0-203-06663-8 (ebk)

DOI: 10.4324/9780203066638

Typeset in Sabon
by Book Now Ltd, London

For the generations:
Sylvia and Peter Lees
Mildred Lees, Rosemary Jankowska
and, in memoriam,
James Lees and Stanislaw Jankowski.

Contents

Illustrations

Tables

Acknowledgements

Ian Bell's use of a letter-writing guidebook in an undergraduate seminar on the eighteenth century epistolary novel at the University of Wales Aberystwyth made me laugh. I remembered it when developing my doctoral research: sincere thanks to my supervisors Tim Putnam and Valerie Swales and my examiners Christopher Breward and Esther Sonnet. In writing this book, I was supported by an Arts and Humanities Research Council research leave award, 'Designing Domesticity' (2007), through funding from the Design History Society and the University of Hertfordshire, where particular thanks are due to the School of Creative Arts, Michael Biggs and Steven Adams.

Colleagues within the design history community who have contributed to my thinking on domestic advice literature include Nic Maffei, Emma Ferry, Anne Massey, Penny Sparke, Trevor Keeble, Fiona Fisher, Patricia Lara-Betancourt, Jeremy Aynsley, Jessica Kelly, Paul Atkinson, Jill Seddon and Judy Attfield. For gifts of domestic advice books I am grateful to Phil Gray, Michael Biggs, Stephen Hayward, Dennis Kelly, Sylvia Lees, Joan Maffei, Sean O'Connell, Linda Sandino, Jo Turney, Bren Unwin and Melanie Unwin. Thanks to Elizabeth Darling for help decoding the identity of 'Hugh Anthony' and to Reggie Blaszczyk for information about Dow paints.

My thanks are due to convenors, chairs and delegates at the conferences at which I have spoken about domestic advice literature, including: the University of California, Berkeley; Istanbul Technical University; Bowling Green University, Ohio; the Centre for Contemporary British History, Institute of Historical Research, University of London; the AHRC Centre for the Study of the Domestic Interior, Royal College of Art and Royal Holloway, University of London; the Association for Research in Popular Fictions at Liverpool John Moores University; the Social History Society annual conferences at Trinity College, Dublin and UMIST, Manchester; the Women's Library, London and the Centre for Studies of Home/Geffrye Museum, London. Various articles and chapters generated in the course of this project are referenced in the book. Thanks to the team at Routledge, and particularly series editors Ben Highmore and Gillian Swanson. Finally, I am immensely grateful to my family, Nic Maffei, Jay and Laurel Lees-Maffei for their patient support during the writing of this book.

Permissions

The following material has been reproduced with kind permission. While every effort has been made to trace copyright holders and to obtain permission, this has not been possible in all cases. Any omissions brought to our attention will be remedied in future editions.

Figures

1.1 Cover, Lady Troubridge, *The Book of Etiquette*, Cedar Edition, Kingsworth, Surrey: The World's Work, [1926] 1958.

1.2 IPC Media for kind permission to reprint Portrait of Lady Troubridge, *Etiquette and Entertaining*, London: Amalgamated Press, 1939. Reprinted with permission of IPC Media, a Time Warner company www.ipcmedia.com

1.3 IPC Media for kind permission to reprint Cover, Lady Troubridge, *Etiquette and Entertaining*, London: Amalgamated Press, 1939. Reprinted with permission of IPC Media, a Time Warner company www.ipcmedia.com

1.4 Photoshot Ltd for permission to reprint Portrait of Lady Elizabeth Anson, Universal Pictorial Press, Back Cover, Lady Elizabeth Anson's *Party Planners Book: The Complete Guide to Entertaining Stylishly and Successfully*, London: Weidenfeld & Nicholson, 1986. ZB21_221761_0001. Lady Elizabeth Georgina Shakerley. Credit: Photoshot

1.5 Orion for permission to reprint Jacket design by Anita Turpin for Lady Elizabeth Anson's *Party Planners Book: The Complete Guide to Entertaining Stylishly and Successfully*, London: Weidenfeld & Nicholson, 1986.

1.6 'Disguising' an 'intimidating room', plate between pp. 60–61, Anson, 1986.

1.7 'Efficient grouping of kitchen equipment' Christine Frederick, *Scientific Management in the Home*, London: G. Routledge & Sons, 1920, 22.

2.5 Endpapers, The Good Housekeeping Institute's *Book of Good Housekeeping*, London and Chesham: Gramol Publications Ltd., 1946 (1944, 1945).

2.6 Orion for permission to reprint Cover, Adrienne Spanier, *Furnishing and Decorating in Your Home*, London: Arthur Barker Ltd., 1959.

2.7 The eight Betty Crocker official portraits, 'Who Was Betty Crocker?' Center for History and New Media, George Mason University. Courtesy of General Mills Archives.

2.8 Cover, *Betty Crocker's Guide to Easy Entertaining: How to Have Guests - And Enjoy Them*, New York: Golden Press, copyright © 1959 by Random House Children's Books. Used by permission of Random House Children's Books, a division of Random House, Inc. Any third party use of this material, outside of this publication, is prohibited. Interested parties must apply directly to Random House, Inc. for permission.

3.1 The Estate of Osbert Lancaster for permission to reprint 'Should be addressed H. E.', drawing by Osbert Lancaster in Nancy Mitford, ed., *Noblesse Oblige*, Oxford: OUP, [1956] 2002, 8. With permission of Clare Hastings.

3.2 Illustration facing John Betjeman's poem 'How to Get On in Society', drawing by Osbert Lancaster in Nancy Mitford, ed., *Noblesse Oblige*, Oxford: OUP, 2002 (1956), 104. With permission of Clare Hastings.

3.3 Getty Images for permission to reprint HGE:168522069 Woburn Abbey Open To Visitors, Photographer/Artist: William Vanderson. 'It is a tremendous pleasure sharing one's treasures with others', Fox Photos, John, Duke of Bedford, *A Silver-Plated Spoon*, London: Cassell, 1959, plate between pp. 198–199.

3.4 Peter Owen Publishers for permission to reprint 'The Raw Material of One's Contempt', Nicolas Bentley, Bedford, *The Duke of Bedford's Book of Snobs*, London: Peter Owen, 1965, 17.

3.5 Peter Owen Publishers for permission to reprint 'Do not make a joke of the hired help', Nicolas Bentley, in Bedford, *The Duke of Bedford's Book of Snobs*, London: Peter Owen, 1965, 75.

3.6 Carlton Books for kind permission to reprint 'Are only interested in the commonplace things', ffolkes, *How to Run a Stately Home*, Bedford in collaboration with George Mikes, London: Andre Deutsch, 1971, 51.

3.7 University of Brighton Design Archives for permission to reprint Utility B2 metal bedstead, introduced May 1945, in *Utility Furniture and Fashion 1941–1951*, catalogue of an exhibition held at The Geffrye Museum, London:

4.5   Seymour Chwast for permission to reprint Illustration
       by Seymour Chwast, *Esquire Party Book*, London:
       Arthur Baker, [1935] 1965.

4.6   Little, Brown Book Group for permission to reprint
       'Pyrosil Ware Consort Skillets in plain white. Can be used on top
       of a cooker. Detachable handles. James A. Jobling & Co. Ltd
       Photographer: Steve Hielt' in Elizabeth Good, *Tableware*, London:
       MacDonald & Co. (Publishers) in association with the Council of
       Industrial Design, 1969, 13.

4.7   IPC Media for kind permission to reprint 'Electric plate-warmer
       for the sideboard by English Electric with translucent china in
       plain white', *Woman's Own Book of Modern Homemaking*,
       London: George Newnes, 1967. Reprinted with permission of
       IPC Media, a Time Warner company www.ipcmedia.com

4.8   Little, Brown Book Group for permission to reprint
       'Possible design for a service trolley...', illustration by
       K. Baker in George Salmon, *Storage: A Design Centre
       Publication*, London: Macdonald & Co. in association
       with the Council of Industrial Design, 1967, 36.

4.9   Patrick Dickson, Director of Licensing, Russel Wright
       Studios LLC for kind permission to reprint 'Room divider/
       peninsular unit from the Walker Art Center's Idea House II – built
       in Minneapolis, Minnesota, USA', Mary Wright and Russel Wright,
       Guide to Easier Living, New York: Simon & Schuster [1950] 1954.

4.10   Little, Brown Book Group for permission to reprint
       Ilana Henderson, revolving kitchen, Elizabeth Good,
       Tableware: A Design Centre Publication, London:
       Macdonald & Co. in association with the Council
       of Industrial Design, 1969, 57.

4.11   Back cover, Sarah Maclean, *The Pan Book of Etiquette and Good
       Manners*, London: Pan, 1962.

4.12   Jacket Cover copyright © 1966 by Doubleday, a division of
       Random House, Inc., from *Phyllis Diller's Housekeeping Hints* by
       Phyllis Diller. Used by permission of Doubleday, a division of
       Random House, Inc. Any third party use of this material, outside
       of this publication, is prohibited. Interested parties must apply
       directly to Random House, Inc. for permission.

4.13   Cover, *The Art of Being a Woman* by Amabel Williams-Ellis,
       published by The Bodley Head. Used by permission of The
       Random House Group Limited.

4.14   'How to Get Hold of the Men in Your Life',
       illustration by Jan Mitchener for Shirley Conran, *Superwoman*,
       London: Penguin, [1975] 1977, 190.

5.1   'Don't grab your favorite page and go into seclusion', Betty Allen
       and Mitchell Pirie Briggs, *If You Please! A Book of Manners for*

        Young Moderns, rev. ed., J. B. Lippincott Company, [1942] 1950, 191.

5.2   Linden Artists Ltd for permission to reprint 'This does not mean, of course, that a teenager should arrive home every evening with a starving crowd', illustration by Belinda Lyon, in Pam Lyons, *Today's Etiquette*, London: Bancroft and Co. Ltd, 1967, 31.

5.3   Ryland Peters & Small Ltd for permission to reprint Cover, *Teen Zone: Stylish Living for Teens* by Judith Wilson, published by © Ryland Peters & Small Ltd, London and New York, 2007. Photographer Winfried Heinze.

5.4   Rosie Fisher, 'Teenage Room', *Rooms to Grow Up In*, London: New Burlington Books, 1984, 11.

5.5   'Chimneybreast before and after conversion', Joyce Lowrie, *Practical Homemaking*, London: Oldbourne, 1965, 89.

5.6   Linden Artists Ltd for permission to reprint 'Clothing suitable for the country', illustration by Belinda Lyon in Lyons, *Today's Etiquette*, London: Bancroft and Co. Ltd., 1967, 135.

Tables

2.1   Narrative analysis of The Good Housekeeping Institute's *Book of Good Housekeeping*, London and Chesham: Gramol Publications Ltd., 1946 (1944, 1945).

2.2   Narrative analysis of Agnes Miall, *Modern Etiquette*, third edition, 1961.

5.1   Life course narrative analysis of Pam Lyons, *Today's Etiquette*, 1967.

Text

Chapter 4, *Easier Living? Lady Behave!*: Gender and domestic advice literature, is adapted from Lees-Maffei, G. 'Accommodating "Mrs Three in One": Homemaking, Home Entertaining and Domestic Advice Literature in Post-War Britain', *Women's History Review* 16, no. 5 (2007): 723–754. Extracts are reprinted with kind permission of Taylor & Francis, Ltd. Copyright © 2007 Routledge.

Introduction
Defining a genre: domestic advice literature

Marianne, an American woman of a certain age, sits at a dining table in a living/dining room interior and tells us how to use a napkin. While Marianne is talking about the basic facts of napkin use, in one of a series of video etiquette guides posted by expertvillage.com (2006) to YouTube, there is time to take in the interior she occupies: the colour scheme, the sofa, the side tables, the accents. Marianne presents an accessible, straightforward screen persona. However, her effectiveness in delivering the simplest information is thrown into question by the vitriolic comments of YouTube's typically uncompromising respondents. Cut to a seasonal special of the home makeover show *Changing Rooms* made by Bazal Productions (1999): British celebrity interior designer Linda Barker is in Tenerife, talking with Paul and Louise about how to decorate neighbours Joanne and Richard's front room. 'Cool, minimal, quite contemporary' Barker says, to which Paul responds 'Cherub-free at last!' We already know that Joanne likes a 'cosy', 'cottage' feel, rather than what Richard calls the 'show house' taste of Paul and Louise, so the scene is set for discord.

Whether you type 'dinner party advice' into YouTube, or watch a rerun of the erstwhile TV series *Changing Rooms*, advice about homemaking has never been more abundant. Moreover, with the introduction of Web 2.0, the read-write web, internet users have begun to publish a vast array of online content, from Facebook profiles and family snaps on Flickr, to home movies on YouTube, opinions on blogs and product reviews on Amazon. Notwithstanding unresolved issues about privacy and archiving, an immense resource has been created, at once intimate and widely seen, which allows unparalleled access into the homes and lives of a billion web users.

The extent to which homes have been regarded as private or public has altered over time. Today, homes are largely perceived as private refuges from the public world: family and friends are allowed in, of course, and occasionally public meetings or business transactions may be conducted in domestic spaces (Tupperware party, anyone?) Due to its privacy, the home has been, to borrow feminist historian Sheila Rowbotham's phrase, 'hidden from history' (1973). However, feminist work proclaiming that 'the personal is political', to use Carol Hanisch's 1969 rallying cry (Hanisch, 1970;

Humm, 1995: 204), and work in cultural studies demonstrating that every-day life repays analysis (Highmore, 2002a, 2002b) have produced a surge of interest in domesticity and the domestic interior, to which this book contributes.

Defining domestic advice literature

Advice books are published on a vast range of aspects of life, from the relatively familiar, such as cleaning and maintaining a home, conduct at work and sports, to experiences that are separated from our everyday lives, either spatially, such as foreign holidays or business, or temporally, with infrequent rites of passage, such as weddings and funerals (McCracken, 1990: 104–117). The advice that readers consult depends on the point they occupy on the life course. Events such as puberty, marriage and bereavement perennially occupy advice writers. Here, I explore advice about that most familiar, and yet hidden, space: the home. I propose 'domestic advice literature' as a term for books of advice concerning the social and material home, specifically etiquette, homemaking and home decoration – and use this material as a resource through which to construct a history of the home. While there are explicit studies of etiquette, for example by Norbert Elias ([1939] 1994), Jorge Arditi (1998) and Cas Wouters (2007), and cultural histories of homemaking and home decoration sources (Leavitt, 2002; Morley, 1990), there has been no comparative study of etiquette, homemaking and home decoration discourses which understands them as related through a shared concern for the home, constituted both socially and materially. Here, I bring together the discourses of etiquette, homemaking and home decoration books to illuminate the relationship between the social aspirations of ideal domestic practices and the environments designed for their material manifestations.

Advice literature needs careful handling. It cannot be taken as direct evidence of past experience; it is not a record of what people actually did in their homes or of how they decorated or used their domestic interiors. But, to disregard advice literature as unreliable, and to prefer primary unpublished sources such as diaries and letters as having a closer relation to actual historical practice, is to miss out on its value. Sociologist Cas Wouters (1995: 109) has pointed out that etiquette books circulate what I term 'real ideals' (see chapter two). The normative ideals shared by members of a society prescribe desirable behaviours and consumption practices. Domestic advice literature is, therefore, a richly useful genre of constructed ideals offering insights into the social and material histories of the home (Lees-Maffei, 2003).

The learned code of etiquette and the behaviours called manners share a twofold function: they regulate social interaction to achieve a smooth and considerate result, and they provide a framework within which to judge others. In pursuing the interpersonal aims of courtesy, ease and hospitality, etiquette writers have much to say about the things with which we surround ourselves, from the clothes we wear to the way we decorate our homes, and the accoutrements of home entertaining, whether setting a table or furnishing a guest room. Etiquette writers therefore share some concerns with the authors of a large swathe of didactic literature, including the decorating and lifestyle books which help us to express our identities through a particular assemblage and use of consumer goods, and the guides to home entertaining which aim to assist us in opening our homes, even our kitchens, to others with the minimum of stress. Etiquette books treat the home as a social entity, advising readers about situations in which friends, associates and extended family are invited inside, sometimes with guidance on family interaction, too.

'Homemaking' is a verb and may be seen to point to domestic practices rather than things, but it also invokes the fabrication ('making') of a home as object, or space. Homemaking books treat the home holistically, telling readers how to make, manage and maintain their homes, with advice on decoration, cleaning, entertaining, etiquette and cooking. Cookbooks are not the focus of this study, because the general blend of advice provided in early examples has given way to a focus on recipes, albeit sometimes combined with information about entertaining and family dining. Homemaking books are the most likely of the domestic advice literature group to be arranged alphabetically, like an encyclopaedia, which organisational device lends coherence to their diverse content, from sewing with taffeta to maintaining drains.

Home decorating books help people make interior design decisions for their homes, albeit of an everyday, amateur kind. While they focus on domestic design, they sometimes include advice on architecture and building matters. DIY books have been excluded from the sample for this study because they are primarily technical, and less discursive. In providing guidance on the assemblage of goods and the arrangement of spaces to accommodate family life, home decoration books have embedded within them assumptions about the behaviours that are likely to take place in the home.

Etiquette, homemaking and home decoration discourses may each be seen as occupying different points on a notional continuum between the social and the material. Each may be read for gratification as much for instructions to be applied in action. Etiquette and homemaking books are given as gifts, as the poignant or wry inscriptions found in second-hand copies testify. An etiquette book is a gift which anticipates potential home entertaining, whether or not the advice given is applied. Readers of homemaking books are primed for domestic life, whether or not they ever get to grips with cleaning linoleum or constructing a mini-bar. However, much as US domestic doyenne Martha Stewart – figurehead of a 'Dreamers into Doers' campaign (Martha Stewart Living Omnimedia, 2012a, 2012b) – might wish it weren't so, consumers of home decorating books may be dreamers as well as doers, as they consume real ideals.

Defining a genre: from the 'ephemeral' to the 'influential'

How to choose which books to examine from the abundant quantities of published advice? In their history of sex advice, Roy Porter and Lesley Hall (1995: 5) ignore works they deem 'ephemeral' and focus instead on those they regard as 'influential', meaning best-sellers, or works by noted authors, or both, such as Marie Stopes' *Married Love* (1918). Influence is gauged by a combination of biographical information about authors, documentary evidence of reception (sales figures, critical notices) and bibliographic evidence concerning editions and re-editions. Focusing on notable examples avoids the difficulties associated with an absence of information on little-known or anonymous authors, but it also effaces the catholic nature of the advice genre and misses an opportunity to promote otherwise disregarded examples.

Porter and Hall's approach contrasts with US cultural historian Sarah Leavitt's pleasure in naming and championing unknown writers alongside those of note: 'Most of the authors of this advice never became famous', she observes, and their books 'rest today in the rare book rooms of libraries and archives, their strong opinions muted by time' (Leavitt, 2002: 7). Here, I selected texts for discussion initially using keyword searches of the catalogues of comprehensive deposit libraries, the British Library, the University of Cambridge Library and the Library of Congress, plus the Harry Ransom Humanities Research Center at the University of Texas, Austin and The Women's Library, London. Many writers of domestic advice are women. By examining the work of lesser-known, unknown and even anonymous writers alongside that of well-known domestic advisors, I contribute to the feminist project of valuing women's cultural achievements.

The authorship of domestic advice books can be complicated. For example, some aristocratic advice writers have maintained their anonymity by using pen names which only refer to their status – such as 'A Lady' – because they wished to conceal their engagement in paid employment. Others, however, such as the Duke of Bedford and Lady Elizabeth Anson, have capitalised upon their status, as communicated through their titles, to promote their publications, and have been criticised for so doing. Authorship is complicated, too, by the collaborative nature of much advice, as demonstrated by the work of magazine writers, and related ventures such as the Good Housekeeping Institute, and in the fact that some advice writers have associated companies, including the Emily Post Institute and Constance Spry Ltd. Finally, advice is sometimes purportedly given by entirely imagined branded authors, such as Betty Crocker, whose image and signature convey authenticity in spite of her fictional status, as discussed in chapter two.

Re-editions and revisions further complicate the categorisation of domestic advice literature as either ephemeral or influential. For example, an ostensibly anonymous 1834 work by 'Agogos' (the pseudonym of

Charles William Day) was published in various editions over more than a century. Successive re-editions exemplify the popularity and longevity of certain titles and the function of advice in responding to and mediating changing manners. Although it responds to social changes, advice literature can appear to be a rather static, normative discourse. Its dynamism is best seen at the level of genre – that is, through a study which regards its focal texts as *representative* rather selecting them on the basis of their influence. Domestic advice literature is a remarkably coherent genre, in that it emphasises both behavioural and literary precedents. It is pre-eminently self-reflexive: even books which are not themselves revised or reissued refer directly or indirectly to earlier examples of the genre. Domestic advice books closely resemble one another and contain a high level of intertextuality. This is mostly unacknowledged, but some advice books explicitly reference the work of others. In Betty Allen and Mitchell Pirie Briggs's *Behave Yourself! Etiquette for American Youth*, readers are told, with reference to a leading American etiquette expert of the twentieth century: 'Those who gobble and grab are not Emily Posted' ([1937] 1945: 7).

In this book, I demonstrate how advice literature bore witness to changes in class, gender and age in the second half of the twentieth century in the UK and the USA. Existing studies of published advice have focused principally on nineteenth-century examples, or on magazines. More recently, twentieth-century lifestyle TV and self-help books have received attention from sociologists and cultural studies scholars. Twentieth-century domestic advice books remain relatively neglected by comparison. I explore what domestic advice literature can reveal about ideals of domesticity since 1945 in Britain and the USA. After the Second World War, continued social developments in both of these countries related to issues of class, gender and age necessitated reconfigured designs for, and uses of, the home, such as open-plan interiors and multi-function rooms. Finally, previous studies of domestic advice literature have been bounded by national borders. Advice literature has been regarded as a tool for inscribing national identity and as an aid to international relations. But, domestic advice books have routinely been published in the USA and the UK simultaneously, or with only a short delay. The same books have been published under slightly different titles. The domestic advice genre is characteristically self-referential, and British advisors are as likely to refer to US sources as they are to the output of their own nation, and vice versa. For these reasons, in this book I examine US and UK domestic advice books together and I posit an Anglophone transatlantic domestic dialogue, in which domestic advice as a genre in the UK and the USA has developed as a result of an exchange of knowledge between these nations. (Here, the terms UK and Britain are used interchangeably for variety, although it is acknowledged that the term 'Britain' does not include Northern Ireland.)

A guide to this book

Part I examines the use of domestic advice literature in writing history, in two chapters: the first historiographic and the second methodological. Domestic advice literature is historically revealing because it is historically constructed. Chapter 1 traces the roots of contemporary domestic advice literature in guides to courtly life, books on husbandry and housewifery, and recipe books. Domestic advice literature is situated within a wider context of instructional discourses, including self-help books, magazines, lifestyle television and advertising. This chapter traces the development of domestic advice literature in the twentieth century as characterised by two complementary tendencies: first, advice literature became more specialised over the course of its development and therefore its constituent categories have multiplied, and second, more advice has been published in an increasingly wide range of formats so that domestic advice literature can be seen to have fractured both in form and content.

Chapter 2 critiques some of the ways in which advice literature has been used for understanding the past. While some writers have dismissed advice literature as unimportant or unreliable, others have marshalled it as direct evidence of historical practice. I propose, instead, that the most effective approach to domestic advice literature entails analysis of the narrative techniques employed by domestic advice writers in promoting their ideal solutions persuasively, including intertextuality and self-referentiality, stock characters, recurrent motifs, subtexts, relationships between text and image and 'before and after' stories.

Part II comprises three case studies of the solutions promoted in books of domestic advice for diverse markets – a newly enlarged middle class, the newly unassisted hostess and (parents and) the teenage consumer, in addition to lacunae surrounding, for example, men's roles. Chapter 3 explores modernism and the newly expanded middle class. During the twentieth century, the aristocratic influence upon domestic taste – which had emphasised luxury and grandeur – gradually ceded to attempts to cater to the extensively theorised growing middle class, through practical, economical solutions expressed in modernist designs and informal social practices. Notwithstanding its purported egalitarian practicality and concern for efficiency and thrift, domestic advice literature has essentially functioned to train new consumers through engendering desire for lifestyle expressed in consumer goods.

Chapter 4 considers the impact of social and economic changes of the second half of the twentieth century on women, and men, as homemakers. Women accustomed to the assistance of staff received advice on managing alone, while women new to running a middle-class household were also addressed. Rather than recommending that assistance be sought from other family members, including men, domestic advisors confined themselves to suggesting ways that women might manage their burden alone.

The final chapter examines the responses of domestic advisors to the challenge of the teenager. In 1945 – as an established figure in the USA and a newcomer in the UK – the teenager was both criticised for antisocial behaviour and emulated stylistically. The teenage bedroom was a microcosmic home – equipped to accommodate sleeping, grooming, studying and entertaining – within the larger adult home. It removed the teen from the remaining shared, and therefore adult, domestic spaces. The voices of children and teenagers are largely absent from advice on manners and home life; these discourses are remarkably consistent, nostalgic and conservative, rather than fulfilling their vaunted transforming potential. The book concludes by considering advice in the internet age, in which consumers themselves publish domestic advice.

In each case study, domestic advisors are seen offering solutions based to a greater or lesser degree on modernist design values, including utility, economy, flexibility and modularity, in the belief that these novel material forms would better accommodate post-war social practices. However, close reading reveals ambiguity and fault lines in the advice, which is shown ultimately to serve existing dominant groups, privileged by class, gender and age. While modernism in design does not live up to the claims made for it by domestic advisors, domestic advice literature itself appears compromised by the advisor's necessary authority, which produces inherently ideological hegemonic discourses. Class, gender and age, along with ethnicity, nationality and sexuality, have been crucial determinants of identity, social opportunity and the distribution of power in the home. Resultant tensions are visible within the pages of domestic advice literature – just as they have been within actual homes – in two key ways. The first is preponderance: domestic advice writers responded to the problems associated with social, cultural and economic developments in the post-war period and, in so doing, articulated three new cultural characters – the new middle-class householder, the newly unassisted hostess and the teenage consumer – consistent with the recurrent preoccupations in domestic advice of class, gender and age. These are examined in turn in chapters three, four and five. The second is absence: men are largely absent from mainstream domestic advice literature, whether as hosts or husbands, fathers or friends. Other lacunae identifiable in domestic advice literature include ethnicity and sexuality. Advice writers purported to cater for a range of newly identified groups, but close textual and visual analysis reveals some ways in which domestic advice functioned as a discourse of dominance.

Part I

1   The roots of domestic advice literature

In order to explore the historical value of domestic advice literature, it is essential to understand how the form and content of advice books is constituted by, and reflective of, historical, cultural and social changes. Domestic advice literature is here defined as a genre of advice concerning the social and material home, mediated through etiquette, homemaking and home decoration books. This genre has developed from a number of earlier, parallel, discourses, and therefore French historical sociologist and philosopher Michel Foucault's notion of genealogy is apt. Following German philosopher Friedrich Nietzsche ([1887] 1996), Foucault rejected a history reliant on linear causality in favour of genealogy, which models historical development as a multifarious series of intertwined branches ([1969] 1972). Foucault examined institutions of power and control as they relate to the interrelationship of self and society, and emphasised the role of discourse in conditioning material experience and historical preoccupations. He proposed that knowledge and power have in common their possession by the few and their exertion over the many, especially in the case of writings on technical knowledge by specialists using a specialised vocabulary. His 'science of discipline' examined institutions such as schools, prisons, asylums or hospitals and families, each of which forms its individual inhabitants through repetitive exercises, detailed hierarchies, 'normalizing judgment' or laws and timetables (Foucault, 1979).

Domestic advice literature similarly functions as a discourse that forms identity and history, and as a disciplinary institution. The advice writer assumes an authority based on the possession of knowledge, as do other 'experts'. This chapter traces the roots of contemporary domestic advice literature in a concise genealogy, before examining twentieth-century domestic advice literature in terms of various modes of authority, based on Max Weber's tripartite model of legitimisation. It closes by examining related channels, such as magazines and television, through which advice is mediated.

Specialization: from the courtly tradition to middle-class morals

Some of the earliest advice books were addressed to children and behaviour at court. Elias's *History of Manners* acknowledges that etiquette emerged before

'Greco-Roman antiquity, and doubtless also of the related, preceding "civiliza-tions"'. He mentions the Latin precepts for behaviour produced by 'learned ecclesiastics', such as *De institutione novitarium* by Hugh of St. Victor, who died in 1141 ([1939] 1994: 48). However, for Elias the most significant point in the history of manners was the development of the concept of *civilité* 'at a time when chivalrous society and the unity of the Catholic Church were disintegrating'. Elias explains that: 'Its individual starting point can be exactly determined. It owes the specific meaning adopted by society to a short treatise by Erasmus of Rotterdam, *De civilitate morum puerilium* (on civility in chil-dren), which appeared in 1530' (Elias, [1939] 1994: 42–43). Elias notes the relative popularity of this text, based on its several re-editions. In Britain, early published domestic advice was offered in general texts, such as Thomas Twine's *The Schoolemaster or Teacher of Table Philosophie* (1576).

Early cookery books are important forerunners to the domestic manuals of the twentieth century. Texts dealing with domestic economy, which concerned recipes for food, drinks and toiletries and appeared from 1500 to 1700, divided in the mid-seventeenth century into those dealing with husbandry – farming and agriculture, and the management of country houses – and housewifery ('the invisible labour of domestic women'), as well as books of 'secrets' offering information on 'arcane alchemical experiments' along with more straightforward recipes and hints (Hunter *et al.*, 1999: 276–280). Lynette Hunter observes the coalescence from 1600 of three distinct types of advice text aimed at women: the cookery book with recipes; the 'gentry housewife's book related to household activities, cookery and domestic medicine', exemplified in the work of Gervase Markham; and 'the aristo-cratic, or aspiring, lady's book concerned with preservation and conservation, [...] medicines, experiments and some specialized cookery', such as Sir Hugh Platt's *Delightes for Ladies* (1602). Further specialisation catered to women who made a living from domestic labour, and those who oversaw domestic work carried out in their homes. The work of Hannah Wolley, for example, including *The Gentlewoman's Companion* (*ca.* 1670), shifted 'the focus firmly from the self-sufficient community of the country house to the private home of the urban middle class' (Hunter *et al.*, 1999: 277).

Cookery books flourished in the eighteenth century in both Britain and the USA. Waldo Lincoln (1849–1933), American Antiquarian Society president from 1907 to 1927, compiled a bibliography of American cookery books from his collection of more than 800 examples in 1929 (American Antiquarian Society 2004, 2005). Revised and enlarged by Eleanor Lowenstein ([1954] 1972) and William Woys Weaver (1983), his bibliography shows the extent of publishing activity in this area in the eighteenth and nineteenth centuries in the USA. Britain was equally active. Although the trend in cookery books was for an increasing focus on recipes rather than general advice, works on both sides of the Atlantic combined 'moralizing advice' with 'receipts for nourishing soups' and enabled 'the charitable lady to fulfil her obligations without excessive expense' (Hunter *et al.*, 1999: 279).

Writing on the development of manners across the *longue durée*, Andrew St. George (1993: 5) observed that: 'In a world before specialisation, (or where generalism *was* the specialisation) [...] a certain type of society was preserved by courtesy and humanity'. The sixteenth century, he notes, 'saw a march of courtesy books which were to divide over the succeeding centuries into books of parental advice, polite conduct, policy and civility' (St. George, 1993: 3). However, St. George is only interested in early texts, such as Henry Peacham's *The Compleat Gentleman* of 1622, for the extent to which they prefigured or differed from the Victorian books that form his focus: 'the Victorians sought, by means of codes of manners and behaviour, to re-establish the boundaries which had been eroded by the relatively fluid society of the seventeenth and eighteenth centuries with their gentlemen, courtiers, lawyers, poets and merchants' (ibid. 6). With the development of print culture, published domestic discourse shifted from general works offering guidance for the Renaissance man, to expert guides on discrete, albeit related, subjects written for the specialist of the industrial era.

The novel, advice literature and the middle classes in the long nineteenth century

Several converging factors influenced the development of domestic advice literature in the eighteenth century. Elias ([1939] 1994) based his analysis of etiquette books on the structural understanding that industrialisation necessitated interaction between the aristocratic elite and growing groups of merchants, manufacturers and professionals. Ian Watt ([1957] 1987) notes that the conditions which led to the development of the novel as a specific literary form also produced Protestantism, capitalism and the middle class, each of which, like the novel, was anchored in individualism. The development of print culture was partly based on the expansion of literacy among those in middle-class occupations and, to a lesser extent, among those members of the working class who read technical, vocational material. Another catalyst was increased affluence among the growing numbers of retailers and office workers, who could afford a greater range of available printed materials, while the working classes chose from a limited selection of cheaper publications. As a new group of retailers, booksellers offered an alternative to the system of patronage in publishing. A third enabler for the growth of print culture was increased leisure, significantly for women in the middle and at the lower end of the social spectrum. Household servants, particularly, are likely to have enjoyed the (albeit limited) leisure, money, privacy, light to read by, access to reading matter and example set by their employers, necessary to engage in print culture.

Like the novel, advice literature has roots in the epistolary form. The fourth Earl of Chesterfield, Philip Dormer Stanhope (1694–1773), began writing letters to his five-year-old son in a mixture of English, French and Latin in 1737. The letters were not intended for publication, but following

Chesterfield's death they were sold to a publisher by his daughter-in-law, Eugenia Stanhope, and were published as *Letters to His Son*, together with some letters Chesterfield wrote to his godson (Ward and Waller, [1907–1921] 2000). Chesterfield's *Letters* became a representative example of English manners both at home and abroad. Thirty-one editions were printed in the USA from 1775 to 1798, and six more editions appeared in the decade 1806 to 1816, usually with the 'improprieties' edited out. American historian Arthur Schlesinger notes that 'in 1827, the work completed the final formality of naturalization by being offered to the public as *The American Chesterfield*' ([1946] 1968: 13).

The literary developments of the eighteenth century paved the way for the expansion of advice literature in the nineteenth century as a means for disseminating Victorian values to a growing readership. A widening of the reading public resulted in a middle-class hegemony preferring the realism and narratives of social mobility found in the novel over the literature of the fantastic, abstract or general (Watt, [1957] 1987: 48). Richard Ohmann has noted that: 'Together, manners and material culture partially unveil for our contemplation a style and an ethos well suited to the aspirations of middle class people in growing industrial and commercial cities' (1996: 153). New styles of life were communicated to newly middle class consumers via a range of mediating channels. Social historian Bill Lancaster has described the growth of the department store as 'almost a mirror image of the emerging middle-class household' (1995: 13) and, just as the department store emerged in Britain and the USA, domestic advice literature mirrored and managed the development of the middle class.

Several best-selling advice books appeared in their first and successive editions during the second half of the nineteenth century. American domestic advice books by Catharine Beecher and Harriet Beecher Stowe, discussed below, enjoyed regular reprintings. In Britain, Samuel Smiles' *Self-Help* of 1859 became a best-seller by encouraging hard work and self-control in the virtuous working class, selling 20,000 copies in its first year and 250,000 copies in Smiles' lifetime (Sinnema, 2002: vii). The current editor of *Self-Help*, Peter W. Sinnema, has described Mrs Beeton's landmark homemaking text *Beeton's Book of Household Management* as part of '*Self-Help*'s Legacy', a 'companion-piece to that of Smiles' for a specifically female audience'. Yet, Beeton's book appeared in the same year as *Self-Help*, as a serial in her husband's periodical *The Englishwoman's Domestic Magazine*, before it was published in a single volume two years later (Beeton, 1859–1861). And, *Household Management* sold more than three times as many copies as *Self-Help* in its first year, and two million copies in its first decade, as compared with the quarter of a million copies of *Self-Help* sold during the 45 years between its first publication and Smiles' death (Humble, 2000: vii–xxx). *Household Management* eclipsed *Self-Help* to become the pre-eminent nineteenth-century advice book.

By combining recipes with general household advice, Beeton's book continued a typically eighteenth-century amalgam of advice. There was a continued market for such titles in both Britain and the USA; Beeton's American contemporary Eliza Leslie, who wrote literature, cookbooks and advice on domestic economy, found the latter to be her most profitable publications (Longone, 1999: 15–17; 1998–1999: 450–451). But, while English readers from the fifteenth to early eighteenth centuries found information on etiquette, homemaking and cookery in their advice books, nineteenth and twentieth century readers in the UK and the USA increasingly consulted discrete volumes for advice on these topics. American historian Sarah Leavitt's assertion that 'Domestic advice manuals originated in the 1830s' (2002: 9) is based on this pattern, although it is of course only accurate as a description of the US case, not the British or wider European markets. The effects of specialisation are seen, for example, in the first culinary advice books written specifically for working-class readers, which appeared in the nineteenth century. Early examples by Mrs Rundell (1807, 1815) and Eliza Acton (1845) were followed in 1852 by Charles Francatelli's *Plain Cookery Book for the Working Classes* ([1852] 1862). If Francatelli's role as Queen Victoria's chef did not directly inform his advice to working-class readers, his celebrity certainly helped him attract a mass readership. Macmillan's 'Art at Home' series (Ferry, 2003) provides an instructive case study for the marketing of advice to middle-class readers.

Domestic advice literature in the twentieth century

As general works developed into the specialised literature of domestic advice, so they have increasingly invoked an authority based on the author's practical expertise and qualifications. The progressively more specialised discourses of twentieth-century advice can therefore be understood with reference to founding sociologist Max Weber's work on authority as being based on traditional, rational and charismatic processes of legitimisation (Weber, 1964: 328; 1968: 212–245; Gerth and Wright Mills, 1946). Within a model of traditional legitimisation, followers accept long-standing power structures and the right of those who have ruled to continue to do so. Under the influence of rational legitimisation, followers accept the existence of certain rules or laws upon which the authority of their leaders is based and therefore accept the right of their leaders to rule. Charismatic legitimisation depends upon followers being persuaded by the particular individual characteristics of a leader that she or he has the right to rule. Weber's tripartite model of legitimisation may be seen at work in etiquette, homemaking and home decoration books alike. However, the following analysis examines traditional legitimisation principally in relation to etiquette, rational legitimisation at work in homemaking literature and charismatic legitimisation bolstering the literature of home decoration.

Traditional legitimisation and the decline of aristocratic authority

Advice literature fulfils a number of functions, one of which is to manage social change through the proffering of solutions informed by existing social and material possibilities. The precepts promoted in etiquette, homemaking and home decoration books are derived to some extent from tradition, longevity and precedent, what is 'done' and 'not done'. Domestic advice is, therefore, reliant on traditional legitimisation, and works to maintain and reinforce it.

Prior to the twentieth century, a key mode of legitimisation for advice literature was that of aristocratic authorship. Lord Chesterfield's *Letters to His Son* (1774) was enormously influential in defining the terms and scope of etiquette discourse and prompted many imitations. Those members of the aristocracy or upper classes who were moved to write published advice often obscured their identities in pen names, possibly to avoid being seen as working for financial gain, yet their pseudonyms communicated elite status as a legitimating technique. Examples include *A Manual of Etiquette for Ladies: or, True Principles of Politeness. By a Lady* (1856) and *The New Book of Etiquette. By a Lady in Society* (1907). This trend was not restricted to the UK; see, for example, *Etiquette for Ladies: A Manual of the Most Approved Rules of Conduct in Polished Society for Married and Unmarried Ladies* (1894) by A Lady of New York and *In True Politeness: A Hand-Book of Etiquette for Gentlemen by an American Gentleman* of 1847, based on an 1840 London edition and reissued annually until 1853 (Aldrich, 1991: 202). It continued well into the twentieth century in such texts as *The A. B. C. of Etiquette by a Society Lady* of 1923. Of course, some authors leveraged aristocratic authorship without the cloak of anonymity, such as Gertrude Elizabeth Blood, who became Gertrude Elizabeth Campbell, Lady Colin Campbell: her *Etiquette of Good Society* (1893) enjoyed numerous reissues and had sold 92,000 copies by 1911.

In the middle of the twentieth century, 'all forms of authority faltered'; 'parents, politicians, priests and police as well as scoutmasters and schoolteachers all became less trusted, less popularly admired as the century wore on' (Halsey, 2000: 18). Chapter 3 explores in more detail the social and economic context which impacted upon aristocratic authority, but suffice it here to note that domestic advisors maintained the authority of their texts by changing the voice and content of their work during the post-war period, from traditional to rational and charismatic appeals, as the work of Laura, Lady Troubridge, shows.

Lady Troubridge's *The Book of Etiquette*, published in 1926 and successively reissued, epitomises traditional legitimisation. Touted as 'the complete standard work of reference on social usages', according to its 1958 cover, it was lauded by the bibliographer F. Seymour Smith (1956: 24) as 'perhaps the most comprehensive English book on the subject' and its re-editions suggest that many readers agreed (Figure 1.1). While the foreword cautions that 'Books of etiquette

THE BOOK
OF
ETIQUETTE

THE COMPLETE STANDARD
WORK OF REFERENCE
ON SOCIAL USAGES

10/6 net
A CEDAR BOOK
Compiled from the most authoritative sources
BY LADY TROUBRIDGE

Figure 1.1 Cover, Lady Troubridge, *The Book of Etiquette* [1926] 1958.

Figure 1.2 Portrait of Lady Troubridge, *Etiquette and Entertaining*, 1939.

are guides, not regulations to be followed blindly' (Troubridge, [1926] 1958: v), the first chapter explains 'The Need for Etiquette' and chapter two, on engagements, begins with a formal register: 'There is perhaps no time when the rules of etiquette need to be so strictly observed as during the period of courtship' (ibid. 6). The author, Laura, Lady Troubridge, née Gurney, married Sir Thomas Troubridge, fourth baronet, and become a writer for the romantic genre imprint Mills and Boon (Figure 1.2). Traditional legitimisation is found here not only in the titled author, whose status recalls the dominance of court etiquette on wider manners, but also in her formal language and strict advice. Reputations were at stake, hence Troubridge's firmness, but this approach contrasts sharply with the informality of a later book bearing her name.

Etiquette and Entertaining by Lady Troubridge (Figure 1.3) was published in 1939 by Amalgamated Press, which had also published Sir John Alexander Hammerton's edited *Home-Lovers Encyclopedia* (1933) and homemaking texts for *Woman* magazine (1938). Here, the authorial voice differs from that of Troubridge's 1926 book. After an opening chapter, 'The New Etiquette is Informal', 'All About Engagements' reassures: 'So let me help you, my dear engaged girl, by giving you a few hints on how to tread that primrose path towards the altar' (Troubridge, 1939: 12). This book contains American idioms

Figure 1.3 Cover, Lady Troubridge, *Etiquette and Entertaining*, 1939.

such as 'movies' and cute phrases such as: 'I just hate to think of people worrying themselves into fiddlestrings over all sorts of little points of social conduct' (ibid. 9). The writing implies that this 1939 book is drawn from syndicated advice: 'Are you engaged? If so, this article is for you' (ibid. 12). The 1939 Troubridge exercises charismatic authority in her friendly, informal text, while retaining traditional legitimisation through the use of an aristocratic title. Published in the year the Second World War commenced in Europe, the book's closing words are 'Never be afraid'.

Weber's techniques of legitimisation coexist in Troubridge's oeuvre: a named author possesses distinct, even contradictory, qualities in two discrete volumes as social shifts differentiated domestic discourse of the middle and end of the interwar period. Another 1939 text, Norbert Elias's *The Civilizing Process*, explains the changes in manners of the early part of the twentieth century as resulting from the increasing interdependence of individuals throughout society, and the development of an internal code of good behaviour applicable in everyday life, which replaced court conduct as the principal influence. This shift provides the context for Troubridge's later style of advice, although the subsequent re-edition of the 1926 text complicates that conclusion.

Another example of an aristocrat invoking traditional legitimisation is Lady Elizabeth Anson (Figure 1.4), with her *Party Planners Book* of 1986. Anson exploits her aristocratic lineage in the author profile:

Figure 1.4 Portrait of Lady Elizabeth Anson, Back Cover, Lady Elizabeth Anson's *Party Planners Book: The Complete Guide to Entertaining Stylishly and Successfully*, 1986.

Lady Elizabeth Anson, who was born in Windsor in 1941, is the daughter of the late Viscount Anson and the late H.R.H. Princess Anne of Denmark. A cousin of the Queen and a sister of photographer Lord Lichfield, she was educated in England and France.

(Anson, 1986: inside cover)

The fact that Anson broke with family tradition to support herself financially through the founding, in 1960, of a successful party planning company is mentioned only after her family connections. The book's cover iconography communicates quality (Figure 1.5). An elaborate script typeface sits on a marbled background, with pink to connote femininity. Instead of the crossed swords of heraldry and chivalry, a crossed 'P' motif signifies Anson's Party Planners business, with the initials strewn with roses and apparently made from grosgrain ribbon. The surrounding cartouche includes symbols of hospitality (grapes, a glass of wine) and entertainment (bugle and mask) and the fruits of

Figure 1.5 Jacket design by Anita Turpin for Lady Elizabeth Anson's *Party Planners Book: The Complete Guide to Entertaining Stylishly and Successfully*, 1986.

Figure 1.6 'Disguising' an 'intimidating room', *Party Planners Book: The Complete Guide to Entertaining Stylishly and Successfully*, 1986.

the land and sea (flowers, pears, mushrooms, carrots, fish), topped with organic rococo forms. This luxurious imagery echoes the aesthetic of Anson's party interiors. Here, she describes her approach to a 'rather intimidating room' (Figure 1.6): 'I disguised ugly dark curtains with draped muslin, tied white balloons to tree branches set in quick-drying cement and put a huge flower arrangement on the mantelpiece to break up a long expanse of bare wall' (Anson, 1986: caption for plate between pp. 60–61). Clearly, Anson's aesthetic needs to be understood within the context of 1980s fashions in interior design, but this does not obscure the fact that her temporary interventions within an already relatively ornate interior illustrate her preference for elaborate applied decoration in environments used for entertaining, rather than design marked by modernist design principles, such as honesty and simplicity. Anson employs a visual and material language drawn from a long tradition of aristocratic dominance of taste and splendour.

Although Anson's book declares itself to be 'eminently practical', it is most useful as a guide to using the services of a party planning company, and is something of an advertisement for her company's services. First in Anson's 'ten-point plan' is 'Delegate. Hired help should be a high priority' (Anson, 1986: 149). Anson's book has not been republished: its advocacy of hiring staff and its emphasis on emulating – albeit using temporary means – an aesthetic of splendour mean that it is out of step with the advice sought by the majority of readers. Anson's charismatic legitimisation, such as it was, did not offset her emphasis on traditional legitimisation sufficiently to give her book longevity.

These two examples each suggest a shift from traditional to charismatic legitimisation. A general trend throughout the twentieth century saw aristocratic influence on taste and domestic practices decline so that domestic advisors were increasingly pedagogues from the disciplines of domestic science and home economics, or from the charismatic world of celebrity. But while traditional legitimisation gave ground to professional expertise, meritocracy and, latterly, celebrity, in practice these modes of authority coexisted within the genre across the century.

Rational legitimisation and the professionalisation of domesticity

In the nineteenth and twentieth centuries, domestic advisors and home economists worked to professionalise domesticity and promote women as expert producers of domestic advice, as well as being its primary market (Matthews, 1987; Robertson, 1997). In so doing they have shown home-making to be as much a form of production as consumption (Cowan, [1983] 1989). Women's authorship of published domestic advice is a dem-onstration of the accepted credibility of their domestic expertise as a result of conventional divisions of labour according to gender. The gender of the producers of etiquette has been explored by, for example, Jorge Arditi, who generalises that 'before the 19th century virtually none of the manuals on behaviour were written by women' whereas from 1880 to the beginning of the twentieth century half of advice writers were women. Arditi presents this 'emergence of a women's discourse on manners' as 'a chapter, however ambiguous, in the history of women's empowerment' (1996: 417). In this he follows Michael Curtin, who regards etiquette books as a feminine form: 'Powerless in most ways, ladies found in manners a means by which they could assert themselves and create effects in their interest' (Curtin, 1985: 419). However, etiquette was not the only advice discourse in which women predominated: the other literatures of domestic advice – homemaking and home decoration – were similarly associated with women, in terms of authorship as well as presumed readership.

Catharine Beecher's 1841 *Treatise on Domestic Economy, For the Use of Young Ladies at Home, and at School* had its greatest impact in the twen-tieth century, as 'a forerunner the "home economics movement"' (Delgado, 1995: 400–401). It was reprinted and revised many times, for example in 1845 and 1970, and appeared with a critical introduction in 1977 (Beecher, [1841] 1977). Here, Christian ideology combines with the pragmatic appli-cation of scientific principles to homemaking, cooking and childcare. This mixture derives from Beecher's upbringing: she was a daughter of Presbyterian preacher Lyman Beecher and, following her mother's death, when Beecher was sixteen, she took on the care of her twelve siblings. This latter practical experience underpinned her subsequent expertise in exemplary homemaking (a situation echoed, incidentally, in the life of con-temporary homemaking powerhouse Martha Stewart, who is discussed below). In 1823, Beecher used money inherited upon her fiancé's death to set up a school for women (she also set up another, short-lived, school in

Cincinnati in 1832). She wrote textbooks (for example, Beecher, 1832) and developed her expertise in the education of women. Beecher published a number of moral and didactic works (for example, Beecher, 1845, 1857), as well as collaborating with her sister, Harriet Beecher Stowe (1811–1896), abolitionist and author of the anti-slavery novel *Uncle Tom's Cabin* (Beecher Stowe, [1852] 1992), on *The American Woman's Home* (Beecher and Beecher Stowe, [1869] 1991). She also published other domestic works ([1846] 2001, 1873) and a guidebook for servants (1842). Beecher's books adopt a practical, analytical approach to domestic work; she is willing to dispense with conventions where necessary in order to improve domestic labour practices and the lot of the people who work in the home. Beecher is considered to be an important figure of American history, hence the scholarly editions of her works (Cross, 1965) and biographical interest (Sklar, 1976). The fact that Beecher worked as a pioneer of women's education while opposing women's suffrage (Beecher, 1871) epitomises the contradiction implicit in the teaching of the subject she prefigured: home economics is both emancipatory and conservative, in that it professionalises the domestic roles traditionally performed by women.

The home economics movement emerged in cooking schools set up in the 1870s, such as the New York Cooking Academy, founded by Professor Pierre Blot in 1865, and with teachers such as Sarah Corson in Philadelphia, and Fannie Farmer and Mary Lincoln in Boston (Longone, 1999: 16; Shapiro, 2001: 44). The Boston Cooking School's cookbook was advanced in its address to a broad general audience (Lincoln [1884], 1996); its popularity and utility are exemplified by the numerous reissues throughout the century following its initial publication. In 1862, the Morrill Act led to the setting up of land grant colleges and the Agricultural and Mechanical Universities across the USA, such as that at College Station, Texas. Homemaking skills were taught to women as potential farmer's wives, with the label 'domestic science' being adopted at the end of the nineteenth century. Vassar and MIT alumnus Ellen Richards organised a series of conferences which led in 1908 to the founding of the American Home Economics Association (Albert R. Mann Library, 2012). Home economics became a widely taught subject in girls' schools and colleges and in adult education curricula at the turn of the twentieth century and some women pursued academic careers as chairs of home economics. Cornell University was an early training centre for home economics, and maintains an interest in the history of the subject. Richards was one of a group of feminist supporters of domestic science (Ehrenreich and English, [1978] 1989: 141), along with Charlotte Perkins Gilman, who promoted the kitchenless house and communal solutions (Scanlon, 2004). Not only did these more radical solutions challenge the American dream as taking place in a single-family detached home (Hayden, 1978), they were also incompatible with the commercial constraints placed on domestic advisors by a publishing industry intent on addressing a mass readership.

Domestic advice literature responded not only to changes in homemaking discourses wrought by the moves to professionalise it as home economics or domestic science, but also to the spreading influence of the Efficiency Movement and, particularly, scientific management as applied to the home.

Frederick Winslow Taylor (1856–1915) based *The Principles of Scientific Management* on his experience of developing time-and-motion studies in steel manufacturing: observing working patterns and redesigning them for ultimate efficiency (Taylor, 1911; Haber, ([1964] 1973). While Taylor's ideas were popular with manufacturers and managers keen to maximise the output of their staff and plant, they were controversial, especially among trade unionists and Marxist analysts (Braverman, 1974). However, when scientific management and time-and-motion studies were applied to the home, they were presented as beneficial to homemakers themselves (Hoy, 1995; Sivulka, 2001). Frank Gilbreth (1868–1924) and Lillian Gilbreth (1878–1972) collaborated on a number of books about scientific management and time-and-motion studies. Lillian, in particular, applied scientific principles to the work of homemaking, in titles such as *The Home-Maker and Her Job* (1927) and, with Orpha Mae Thomas and Eleanor Clymer, *Management in the Home: Happier Living through Saving Time and Energy* ([1954] 1959). Gilbreth went on to produce advice for disabled homemakers, including educational films (Gilbreth, 1998; Lancaster, 2006). However, notwithstanding her towering career, Lillian Gilbreth is best remembered as a mother of twelve, as depicted in a book by two of her children, Frank Jr. and Ernestine, *Cheaper by the Dozen* (1948), and in Walter Lang's film adaptation (1950) (rather than Shawn Levy's 2003 adaptation and Adam Shankman's 2005 sequel, both starring Steve Martin).

Developer of the 'New Housekeeping', Christine Frederick (1883–1970) was influential in the USA and internationally for applying Taylorist ideas of scientific management to the home (on her influence in Germany, for example, see Bullock, 1998). Frederick learned about scientific management from her husband, a Taylorist mechanical engineer, and set up a product testing centre in her home before joining the staff of the *Ladies' Home Journal* as household editor in 1912, where her column, 'The New Housekeeping', appeared until 1919 (Rutherford, 2003). In 1913 she published *The New Housekeeping: Efficiency Studies in Home Management* with an early 'bibliography of home economics'. *Household Engineering: Scientific Management in the Home* was published in Chicago in 1919, and in London the following year as *Scientific Management in the Home*. Frederick's other publications include *Selling Mrs. Consumer* (1929), on marketing to women, and *The Ignoramus Book of Housekeeping* of 1932. As well as refining behavioural processes, such as saving steps (Figure 1.7) and time management, Frederick took an early interest in what later became known as ergonomics, encouraging manufacturers to tailor household equipment to female proportions (Scanlon, 1995: 66; Rabinbach, 1992; Dreyfuss, 1960;

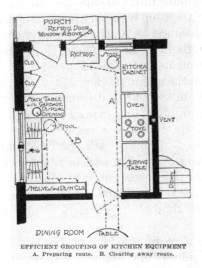

EFFICIENT GROUPING OF KITCHEN EQUIPMENT
A. Preparing route.   B. Clearing away route.

Figure 1.7 'Efficient grouping of kitchen equipment', Christine Frederick, *Scientific Management in the Home*, 1920.

Flinchum, 1997). By applying scientific methods to housework, Frederick hoped to make women's lives easier, while also making housework more serious, joining the home economists in professionalising domestic processes. But like Beecher before her, Frederick has been criticised for her ambiguity in relation to women's roles (Rutherford, 2003). As Scanlon notes: 'Although she supported suffrage, Frederick was committed to liberating women only from the inefficiency of the household, not from the household altogether' (1995: 62).

Partly due to Frederick's efforts, rational 'scientific' approaches to homemaking attracted a wider general audience in popular magazines, with both the number of titles and circulation figures growing consistently during the early decades of the twentieth century. Businessman Clark W. Bryan launched *Good Housekeeping* in 1895, and five years later the Good Housekeeping Institute opened as the magazine's 'experiment station' for testing consumer goods. By 1911, when the Hearst Corporation purchased the magazine, circulation had reached 300,000, and by 1966, readers numbered 5.5 million (Library of Congress, 2011). The Good Housekeeping Institute's seal of approval therefore functioned as a guarantee of quality and reliability for millions of homemakers. In 2002, the editor of *Good Housekeeping* admitted that the Good Housekeeping Institute 'costs a fortune but [...] is key to what *Good Housekeeping* stands for' (Ryle, 2002). Similar initiatives include the *New York Herald Tribune* Home Institute and the Cleanliness Institute, set up in 1927 through the collaboration of Lever Brothers, Palmolive, Procter &

Gamble, Colgate and other soap manufacturers to capitalise on and promote increased awareness of the relationship between hygiene and health.
These forays into public welfare education by American industry complicate a commitment to objective authority that the Good Housekeeping
Institute defended so staunchly (Sivulka, 2001: 229–231).

The influence of scientific management for the home upon domestic
advice published subsequently in both the USA and Britain is formative,
whether in recommendations for appropriate time management, as seen in
The Housewife's Book (*Daily Express*, 1937), or maps for saving steps,
such as the 'ideal kitchen arrangement' in Emily Post's *The Personality of
a House* ([1930] 1948), both of which are discussed in Chapter 4. An
ironic dimension to debates about the time management of housework was
offered retrospectively in *Wasting Girls' Time* (Attar, 1990), a critique of
the curtailing of women's horizons through a pedagogic emphasis on
homemaking, however scientific.

Discourses of domestic economy were informed by the development of
the consumer movement on both sides of the Atlantic. It grew, in part,
out of unease about the spread of consumerism fuelled by mass production, which led to manufacturing and marketing tactics such as planned
obsolescence, whether technical or stylistic (see Hilton, 2003; Daunton
and Hilton, 2001). Consumer Reports, in the USA, and the Association
for Consumer Research, later known as the Consumers' Association, in
Britain, each aimed to empower consumers with knowledge about the
strengths and weaknesses of the products on offer in the marketplace.
Techniques included challenging the claims of advertisers by subjecting
goods to typological comparative testing. Susie McKellar has described
the North American Consumer's Union publication of *Consumer Reports*
(from 1936) as a project by 'left-wing ideologues' to inform 'the "consum-
erized worker"', noting, however, that in response to post-war affluence,
it addressed a new readership of wealthier urban middle-class consumer
'keen to shop in the post-war consumer boom' (McKellar, 1999: 86;
2002). The first issue of the Consumers' Association' magazine *Which?*
was published in Britain 'for the person who wants to know what he is
buying' in autumn 1957, according to the cover of the bound edition of
the first six numbers (Figure 1.8). *Which?* was initially quarterly, then
monthly; each issue explained the aims and methods of consumer
research and justified its objectivity. This approach has been seen as an
attempt to rationalise the irrational act of consumption. While the
American consumer movement has suffered difficult associations with
manufacturers, in Britain the Consumers' Association and the Board of
Trade have similarly experienced tense relations (Hilton, 2001: 252 ff.).
Expertise, which needs to appear to be objective to be trusted, and the
different, even opposed, constraints of commercialism clashed in the history of the consumer movement, as they did in the pages of domestic
advice books.

Figure 1.8 Cover, *Which?* Autumn 1957.

From the innovations of Catharine Beecher and the early home economists, through the scientific management applied by Christine Frederick and Grete Lihotsky (which we will return to in Chapter 4), to the Good Housekeeping Institute and the Consumer Movement, the rational legacy of the professionalisation of domesticity, household efficiency and the kitchen as laboratory continues as an ideal in contemporary domestic advice literature. Yet, persuasive discourses rely on irrationality as much as rationalism. In the same year that *Which?* first appeared, Theodor Adorno's analysis of astrology 'The Stars Down to Earth' ([1957] 2002) was published. Adorno analyses the rhetorical techniques used in the *Los Angeles Times* astrology column to show how columnists have *cultivated* ambiguity in their writing, in order to appeal to the concerns of the widest possible group of readers. Adorno describes astrological forecasts as a 'discourse of irrationality'; they pander to readers' emotions rather than containing any scientific merit. Domestic advice literature, too, depends for its success on anticipating and articulating the needs and problems of its potential readers. While one branch of the genre has turned to scientific knowledge for its authority, and appealed to readers' pragmatism, others have played upon readers' social and material *desires*, and used a type of authority based on charisma.

Charismatic legitimisation in domestic advice literature

Charismatic legitimisation is achieved through the use of compelling personae capable of persuading an audience. In examining domestic advice literature, Weber's 'charismatic legitimisation' may be transmuted from a style of leadership into an emphasis on authority derived not only from the professional status and domestic or design philosophies of authors, but also from their personal style, aesthetics and charismatic appeal. Domestic advice literature is populated with authors who have exploited the power of their own personalities in order to incite emulation and offer something akin to brand reassurance.

As well as publishing works of design philosophy or polemic, designers have published domestic advice books dependent upon charismatic authority. A tradition of decorating advice books by interior designers includes texts by Candace Wheeler (1903), Elsie de Wolfe (1913), Dorothy Draper (1939) and Derek Patmore (1945). J. L. Martin and Sadie Speight's *The Flat Book* (1939) is just one example from the large group of domestic advice books written by architects. Industrial designer, journalist and promoter of European modernism George Nelson and Henry Wright's *Tomorrow's House* (1945) functions as a contribution to the genre, as does ceramicists Mary and Russel Wright's *Guide to Easier Living* (1950), and the public education volumes based on the design broadcasts of furniture designer Gordon Russell (Russell, 1947, 1964; Jones, 2003). While the department store itself offers a kind of education, retailer and designer Terence Conran's reforming zeal has found additional expression in his books, such as *The House Book* (1974), to the extent that Conran set up the Conran Octopus imprint with Paul Hamlyn in order to publish lifestyle books (for example, Conran and Wilhide, 2003). These diverse authors have in common with one another, and with professional domestic advice writers, the cultivation of a public persona based on an authority, whether developed through direct experience in design practice or education, or through vision and the ability to communicate it convincingly.

Books on home decorating draw on their authors' design expertise and confer it. Lisa Tiersten has suggested that while home decorating literature (largely written by men, she asserts) professionalised the role of the housewife as decorator, the correlative role of women as 'guardians of aesthetic value' confined women to the status of decorative homemakers, and indeed women themselves were presented as decorative objects in these sources (1996: 19). However, the not inconsiderable body of home decorating literature written by women has assisted in the ascription of professional status to women as decorators, designers and advice writers, and to the professionalisation of interior design and domesticity more widely (Lees-Maffei, 2008). Elsie de Wolfe is one example. In his account of 'arbiters of twentieth-century taste', Philip Core describes de Wolfe as 'a woman doing a man's job' with a professionalism that replaced 'the weapons of previous arbiters: authority, aristocracy and amateurishness' with 'the whole concept of Taste as a career' (Core, 1984: 49, 61; Sparke, 2003, 2005; Kirkham and Sparke, 2000). De Wolfe herself started out as an actress, a reminder that expertise in etiquette, homemaking or home decoration has not always been a prerequisite for the authority upon which advice is based. Some very successful domestic advice books have been written by public figures known for other pursuits, such as Director of the National Gallery, Charles Eastlake's *Hints on Household Taste* of 1868, and novelist Edith Wharton's *Decoration of Houses* (with Ogden Codman Jr, 1897).

Figure 1.9 Foreword by Anna Neagle, *How to be a Good Hostess, ca.* 1950.

Charismatic legitimisation is perhaps seen most clearly in those domestic advice books which employ celebrity endorsement. Advertising cookbooks began to appear in the USA in the 1880s (Gartrell, 2000). As the genre developed, manufacturers often sought the endorsement of qualified experts such as home economists, exemplifying Weber's rational legitimisation. However, *How to Be a Good Hostess* (Spillers Flour, *ca.* 1950) eschews traditional and rational processes of legitimisation in favour of the charismatic appeal of popular British film actress Anna Neagle (1904–1986) (Figure 1.9). Born Florence Marjorie Robertson, Neagle began her career as a dancer before marrying director/producer Herbert Wilcox. From 1930 to 1959, Neagle's film career included acting and producing and she was made a Dame of the British Empire in 1969 (Neagle, [1974] 1979). Possessing no other qualification than celebrity, Neagle offered the reassurance of a recognisable face and helped to glamorise the act of baking on behalf of the Spiller's flour brand, which published *How to Be a Good Hostess*. Neagle's endorsement extends only as far as the cover and the foreword, but it is powerfully personalised. The foreword is autographed and graphically framed as though it were a letter, beginning 'How lovely to see you' and ending with the celebrity autography 'Yours sincerely, Anna Neagle'. The book therefore borrows techniques designed to create an impression of intimacy with a famous film star from the numerous film magazines of the era.

Domestic advice books can also exhibit charismatic legitimisation when a domestic advice writer achieves celebrity status. Examples include Emily Post and Amy Vanderbilt (Fletcher, 1963), British cook Fanny Craddock and her US counterpart Julia Child (Beck, Bertholle and Child, 1961) and – more recently – British cookery writer Delia Smith and interior designer Linda Barker (1997, 2000). However, the persona and brand of Martha Stewart, particularly, combines not only all the strands of domestic advice literature I discuss here, but also all three of Weber's processes of legitimisation. Like Beecher, Stewart's credentials as a domestic advisor were rooted in personal experience and parental influence during her childhood (Drachman, 2005: 150). Stewart's varied professional experiences also inform her domestic advice. Stewart's degree is in history and architectural history. She worked as a model and then as a Wall Street stock trader, before leaving to restore a house in New England. She subsequently set up a catering business, which led to the publication of her first book, *Entertaining* (1982).

In the first of nearly 100 subsequent titles, Martha Stewart placed herself in a tradition of domestic advice:

> When the Emily Post etiquette book was rewritten in 1965, it asserted that a strict code of social behaviour was as obsolete as the old social pyramid. I still shudder with a sympathetic case of nerves when I read the pompous little book of entertainment advice written in 1888 by Ward McAllister, Mrs. Aster's famous advisor, or see in Edith Wharton's fiction the severe and detailed instructions for the handling of social habits and rituals – the gardenia in the lapel, the proper time for after-dinner calls, and the proper drinks to serve the guests. But there is no such cause for anxiety today, for there is no longer any one proper behavior, or one taste (to be offended), but many to celebrate.
>
> (Stewart, 1982: 12)

Emily Post has been the absolute authority on etiquette in North America, and well-known in the UK, since 1922, and her appeal is proven and extended by the continuance of her publishing activity and, to some extent, her persona by younger members of her family (Lees-Maffei, 2012). Like Emily Post, who was an advisor, author and broadcaster on etiquette, home decoration and child-rearing, as well as a writer of novels and travel literature, Stewart has worked across media ('Omnimedia', indeed) to deliver advice on a range of subjects. In the passage above, Stewart presents herself as the solution to the problem Ward McAllister, Edith Wharton and Emily Post have created. In this, she follows Mary and Russel Wright, who wrote in 1950 of 'that able Evangelist Emily Post' subtly preaching a 'Dear Old Dream', which 'dominates writing and merchandising connected with the home, haunts domestic architecture across the country, and tyrannically rules American family life' ([1950] 1954: 2; Lees-Maffei, 2011).

Martha Stewart represents the zenith of the professionalisation of domesticity; she professionalises every activity in which she engages, from the crafting of handmade party favours to the maintenance of garden furniture upholstery. Stewart's success depends on her reach, in terms of both content (entertaining, cooking, gardening, interior design) and form; her Martha Stewart Living Omnimedia (MSLO) company spans her magazine, television and radio shows, several product lines and her extensive use of social media. Martha the woman is almost indistinguishable from the brand:

> a leading provider of original 'how-to' information, inspiring and engaging consumers with unique lifestyle content and beautifully designed, high-quality products. MSLO is comprised of Publishing, Broadcasting and Merchandising businesses, the combination of which enables the Company to cross-promote content and products.
> (Martha Stewart Living Omnimedia, 2011)

Stewart leverages traditional, rational and charismatic forms of legitimisation, so that during her trial and imprisonment for criminal dealing of stock in 2004–5, MSLO's profits dipped, the online retailing arm of her website closed, there was a hiatus in the production of her television programme and the base rate advertising fees for her publications were lowered. Stewart's release from prison coincided with a revival in the fortunes of her company; her persona had been renewed and enriched with a new dimension of resilience and redemption.

Specialisation and fracture: form, content, readership

In his *Genealogy of Manners,* Jorge Arditi follows Foucault in arguing that the form of advice, as well as its content, has been ideologically shaped. Arditi asserts that prior to the twentieth century, etiquette books took the narrative form of reasoned treatises based around an organising metaphor – grace – whereas the 'decentred social reality' of twentieth century North America is embodied in the reference-book format of listing 'rules without principles' (1999: 35; 1998). He attributes the popularity of Lillian Eichler, and later Emily Post, in the early decades of the twentieth century to their use of the reference book format rather than the treatise. Arditi proposes that changes in identity attendant upon the development of modernity led to a preference for the quasi-neutrality of the reference format rather than the personalised and closely argued treatise which requires time and empathy to consume. Arditi is only concerned with etiquette, not the broader category of domestic advice. In the latter, a shift from treatise to reference book is less easily discerned as volumes comprising discursive arrangements of thematic chapters coexist not only with alphabetically organised encyclopaedias and dictionaries but also with the proliferation of magazines and marketing literature, which make an appearance in advice books in modified forms.

The definition of domestic advice pursued here has necessitated a broadly based exploration of its genealogy. This genealogy demonstrates how the form and content of advice literature, as a discourse that mediates between society and the individual, have been shaped in response to social and cultural changes throughout the late modern period. Domestic advice literature has developed from its roots in guides to courtly life, books on husbandry and housewifery and recipe books, to holistic texts on domestic economy, akin to the catch-all nature of the almanac, and into specialised and differentiated subgenres of etiquette, homemaking and home decoration, with a common concern for the material and social home. Twentieth century domestic advice literature displayed two complementary tendencies: it became more specialised, and therefore its constituent categories have multiplied, *and* more advice has been published in an increasingly wide range of formats. During the post-war period, domestic advice literature has fractured both in form and content, as it has specialised and expanded across the cultural and literary landscape, aided by increased literacy and affluence, cheaper books, such as paperbacks, increased choice in consumer goods as a result of developments in manufacturing, distribution, marketing, advertising and retailing, social developments that engendered an extended market for advice and cultural developments attendant upon the aesetheticisation of everyday life and lifestyles. At the beginning of the twenty-first century, the various modes of authority or legitimisation which advice literature employs – traditional, rational and charismatic – have been overturned by the online availability of peer advice, in which personal experience and testimony take the place of a hierarchy of authority between giver and receiver of advice; examples run the gamut from TripAdvisor.com, for peer reviews of travel destinations, to webMD.com, where patient testimonies are exchanged.

Channels of social mediation

Although concerned with what happens inside the home, domestic advice literature is by no means private. Characterised by Geoff Eley as mediating 'between society and state', as a sphere 'in which the public organizes itself as the bearer of public opinion' ([1993] 1995: 186), Frankfurt School theorist Jurgen Habermas's notion of the public sphere depends on a mediating discourse: 'for transmitting information and influencing those who receive it. Today newspapers and magazines, radio and TV are the media of the public sphere' ([1962] 1974: 49–55). The public sphere has developed from the growth of literacy and print media, increased organised social interaction in growing urban centres and the development of new social centres, from coffee houses to youth clubs. Domestic advice literature is a tool of the public sphere in several ways: as a discourse of mediation between the state and society, as a conduit for the expression of commonly held ideals, as a constituent part of print culture and as a discourse of sociability. Domestic advice literature shapes private domesticity through public discourse.

In this regard, domestic advice literature forms part of a wider group of instructional and entertainment artefacts, including magazines, advertising, lifestyle television and self-help books. Here, I focus on domestic advice literature published in book form, partly because twentieth-century advice books have been neglected in favour of their nineteenth-century fore-bears, and because other twentieth-century channels of advice, such as magazines, have been much more extensively mined by cultural historians. Domestic advice literature shares many concerns and techniques with these related media, with two significant distinctions: first, while serial forms such as magazines, advertising campaigns and television series need to keep their readers and viewers coming back for more, domestic advice books, by contrast, attempt to be definitive; and second, domestic advice books appear to aspire to an objective authority incompatible with commercial endorsement and direct advertising, but *indirect* advertising is common across the genre.

Magazines: serial advice

Like domestic advice books, magazines function within the public sphere to mediate between society and the individual, inscribing norms and negotiating social change, and each attracts a large female readership. Indeed, the close relationship between magazines and domestic advice is exemplified by the fact that digests of magazine content have regularly been published as standalone domestic advice books, gaining their markets from the authority and trust that the magazine title has accrued amongst its readership. *Harper's Bazaar* was published in the USA from 1867 to 1900, with Robert Tomes' *The Bazaar Book of Decorum: The Care of the Person, Manners, Etiquette, and Ceremonials* appearing in 1872. *Esquire Etiquette: A Guide to Business, Sports and Social Conduct by the Editors of Esquire Magazine* was published in New York in 1953 and in London and Sydney by Angus & Robertson the following year. Other examples include *Vogue's Book of Etiquette* (1934; see also Fenwick, 1948), *The Good Housekeeping Annual* (Robinson, 1960), *Good Housekeeping Kitchens* (Austen and Davies, 1976) and the *Woman's Own Book of Modern Homemaking* (1967).

But, these two mediating channels also display critical differences. The first of these is historiographic: magazines have been subject to extensive academic analysis, from Barthes ([1967] 1985), Winship (1987) and Farrell (1998) to Aynsley and Forde (2007) (see also Lees-Maffei, 2009: 368–369, n. 92, 93), while domestic advice books – those published in the twentieth century, at least – have not.

Second, although magazines conform to a formula, they are able, through their serial status, to respond more quickly to social change than books; the ephemeral form of magazines offers piecemeal advice geared to the here and now. Serials balance 'the fostering of anxiety that draws readers to seek out advice and the offering of positive messages that encourage them to return the following month', as Scanlon found in her study of *The Ladies' Home*

Journal (1995: 5; Leman, 1980). Domestic advice books, however, are more time-consuming and expensive to produce; they aim to be definitive and promote the values of continuity and tradition.

Third, and related to their series format, magazines are mutually the product of reader and writer in a relationship built up over successive issues and based on forums such as the letters page. This collaboration is evident not only in the content of magazines, but also in their expression. Laird O'Shea Borrelli has examined the editorial voice in American *Vogue* as exemplifying 'a popular parlance used by readers and consciously invoked by editors to broaden the appeal of their messages', 'while readers imitate the language of fashion as a source of pleasure in its own right' (1997: 255). Some advice books are published in revised editions which take account of reader input, such as Doris Webster and Mary Alden Hopkins' *Mrs. Grundy is Dead* (1930), discussed in Chapter 5. However, most domestic advice books do not interact explicitly with their readers in this way.

Finally, magazines are shaped by their dependence on advertising revenue. They feature advice as part of a mixed diet, combining articles on a range of subjects with advertisements, provide a blend of instruction and entertainment and depend on a balance of editorial and advertising. Conversely, domestic advice books usually operate without advertising in order to maintain an appearance of objectivity and authority (although this has changed over the history of publishing, as we will see in the case of Dr Spock, below). Nevertheless, writers of domestic advice books, like those of magazines, need to negotiate a fine line between objective, neutral authority and advertising.

The *Woman Week-End Book* (*Woman*, [1949a] 1950) provides an instructive case study. It comprises 'a selection of popular short stories, many interesting and instructive hints on beauty, housewifery, and personal problems, cookery, knitting, and useful things to make', excerpted from *Woman* magazine (Figure 1.10). The fly leaf explains that 'Every feature merits the enduring status that a bound book provides' while the editor's foreword warns 'This is not a collection of *all* the best of WOMAN over recent months – we couldn't get that into a book which would be handy to hold and convenient to slip into a week-end suitcase.' However, she admits that:

> This book is really a compromise. It includes many features and stories which received notable welcome from our readers, and it also includes recipes, articles, stories and other features which the staff of WOMAN think worth re-publishing in book form. This anthology of the best of WOMAN is, therefore, chosen jointly by the readers and ourselves.
>
> (*Woman*, [1949a] 1950: 4)

The editor aims that the reader should often return to the book, 'like dropping in for a talk with a good friend'. The formula was successful and was

Figure 1.10 Cover, *Woman Week-End Book*, [1948] 1950.

repeated the same year in *Woman Week-End Book Number Two* ([1949b] 1950), with a consistently similar identity expressed in Esmé Eve's cover design (Figure 1.11). Eve was born in 1920 and studied at the Royal College of Art from 1941 to 1944 before working as a lecturer and freelance designer (Horne, 1994). Nearly a decade later, publisher Odhams Press transferred this same identity across genres, from the *Woman Week-End Book*'s emphasis on leisure and entertainment to *The 'Creda' Housecraft Manual* (Patten *et al.*, 1958) (Figure 1.12). The content of the latter book ranges from recipes to household management tips about cleaning materials and is determined by its purpose of promoting a household appliance brand, meaning it is related to the 'advertising cookbooks' discussed above. This repurposed cover design is a reminder of advice's commodity status: advice, too, is bought and sold, functioning in the service of a variety of companies from magazine publishers to electrical appliances manufacturers, and recommending to readers the consumption of yet further commodities.

Figure 1.11 Cover, *Woman Week-End Book Number Two*, 1949.

Figure 1.12 Cover, *The 'Creda' Housecraft Manual*, 1958.

Advising and advertising

Advising and advertising are related practices, with the latter having an educative as well as commercial function, but the border between them is guarded by those interested in trust, authority and objectivity. Christine Frederick is a case in point. By engaging in product endorsement, for example for the Whirlpool brand, Frederick shifted the role of the domestic advisor towards 'the marketing of specific products rather than of general ideas' (Scanlon, 1995: 69). Frederick's editor at *The Ladies' Home Journal*, Theresa Walcott, upheld a 'distinction between the editorial and advertising domestic science and household writers' (ibid. 70). Frederick left *The Ladies' Home Journal* in 1920 and continued to endorse products through her Applecroft Home Experiment Station on Long Island. She also influenced advertisers' methods through her 1929 book, *Selling Mrs. Consumer*; copywriters used entertainment and comedy to wrest reader attention from the 'reams of advice' in the editorial pages (ibid. 72). Frederick's case shows that advice writers who succumb to the lucrative lure of product endorsement are seen by some as irretrievably compromising their authority. However, like her twenty-first-century counterpart Martha Stewart, whose domestic authority has not suffered from extensive commercial exploitation (or from her imprisonment for financial misconduct and a corresponding hiatus in her role at MSLO), Frederick maintained her mantle of expertise after her dismissal. Frederick's case is notable because she accepted payment to promote specific brands, but tension between authoritative guidance (which should be neutral and objective) and commercial persuasion (in which a vested interest is the *raison d'être*) is common across the advice genre (Cook, 1994: 1–31).

In contrast to Frederick's energetic product endorsement, Dr Benjamin Spock's *The Common Sense Book of Baby and Child Care* (1946) provides an example in which the author strenuously seeks to avoid any commercial taint, albeit on a topic adjacent to domestic advice literature. By 1967, under the shortened title *Baby and Child Care*, Spock's book was a bestseller, having sold twenty million copies and reached its one hundred and seventieth printing. Yet, notwithstanding the book's obvious profitability, the 1967 edition outlines a dispute between Spock and his publisher about the inclusion of a central 'advertising and record-keeping section':

> Dr. Spock has expressed his opposition to the inclusion of advertising of any kind; he feels very strongly that, particularly in a work by a doctor, regardless of any disclaimer, there may be created an impression that he is in some way associated with the products advertised. Dr. Spock is not in any way associated with any commercial products, nor does he endorse any such product, and he wishes to be free of even the slightest implication of any commercial affiliation or endorsement. The Publisher, on the other hand, has felt that the inclusion of a publisher's advertising section has been of substantial value to every reader [...]

> The Publisher is conscious of its responsibility to bring to the public the best quality of reading matter at the lowest practicable price; indeed it considers that it is under a duty affirmatively to seek ways and means of achieving that objective.
>
> (Spock, [1946] 1967: i)

The unnamed author of this 'joint prefatory statement' places the dispute within a specific moment in the history of publishing:

> The last word is yet to be said as to what will ultimately be the format of mass-market books, and in the Publisher's judgment including advertising (as in magazines) will be one important way by which the price of books can be kept low.
>
> (Spock, [1946] 1967: i)

In fact, paperback book publishers have avoided recourse to advertising revenue through economies of scale, combining the populism necessary for high unit sales with relatively low production costs. So the relationships between form and content, advising and advertising, are historically contingent.

Spock sought to preserve the 'power of the expert', which American sociologist Talcott Parsons thought was based on an exchange of professional advice and client trust (Parsons, 1977). This exchange rests on the ability of the expert to:

> induce in the client a rational and responsible calculation of individual self-interest in the face of problematic circumstances, the expert's superior skill and knowledge, and recognition of the latter's ethical commitment to serve the client's best interest and well-being. The power of the expert is dependent upon his or her ability to persuade the client to realize self-interest by delegating that self-interest to the care of another.
>
> (Eide and Knight, 1999: 540)

Parsons' model may be compared with Foucault's notion of 'pastoral power', involving care, guidance and leadership in the exercise of government, whether of a nation or in 'techniques of the self' (Eide and Knight, 1999: 540; Foucault, 1990: 62). The power of the expert, based on the consumer's rational belief that the expert serves her or his best interests, is complicated by the aims and functioning of advertising. While advertising might play an important part in the infrastructure through which advice is delivered, it may equally be perceived by readers as existing to promote particular products and services for reasons of financial gain, and may therefore undermine their trust.

Yet, whatever the mandate for textual authority and objectivity, indirect advertising abounds in domestic advice literature through the use of manufacturers' and retailers' publicity images. For example, the advice in the *Woman's Own Book of Modern Homemaking* (1967) on flooring solutions is accompanied by two images, both of which feature products by Marley, a British company founded in 1948 (Figure 1.13). The images are captioned: 'Entrance hall floor with the look of marble is a clever arrangement of vinyl asbestos tiles in tones of grey (Marley Tuscan Marble)' and 'Hall floor that looks like parquet but is hard-wearing Marley Consort, inexpensive and easy to lay. The tough vinyl surface takes a lot of punishment.' Marley's products are specifically identified and praised, and no other companies are mentioned. While this may be seen to compromise the objective authority of the domestic advisor, it is common practice throughout the genre. The use of marketing materials was cheaper and easier than photographing especially staged rooms and objects. Notwithstanding its quasi-scientism, the Good Housekeeping Institute has also engaged in product promotion. For example, in *It's Your Party: A Book of Successful Entertaining*

Entrance hall floor with the look of marble is a clever arrangement of vinyl asbestos tiles in tones of grey (Marley Tuscan Marble)

Figure 1.13 Vinyl flooring by Marley, *Woman's Own Book of Modern Homemaking*, 1967.

'prepared by *Good Housekeeping* in association with Smith's crisps' (1961) product endorsement occurs on the cover, in the preface, 'From Smith's to You' and in the recipes, which features Smith's crisps as an ingredient (Figures 1.4–1.16).

Figure 1.14 Cover, *It's Your Party: A Book of Successful Entertaining*, 1961.

Figure 1.15 'From Smith's to You', Preface, *It's Your Party*, 1961.

GUY FAWKES PARTY
If possible, have a large bonfire, well clear of trees or buildings, and light it a short time before the party starts.

Supply plenty of fireworks, ranging from rockets and Catherine wheels to sparklers for the younger children. (Make sure that the box of fireworks is in the safe keeping of a grown-up.)

Treacle toffee and parkin are traditional foods. If a cake is wanted, make a Victoria sandwich and decorate to resemble a bonfire, using marzipan and chocolate biscuits.

Potatoes baked in their jackets around the fire are good, especially if served with grated cheese and butter. Hot dogs, toasted chestnuts and toasted marshmallows are fun—but provide plenty of long forks. Hot drinks are essential, and soup is popular.

PARKIN
6 oz. wholemeal flour
6 oz. fine oatmeal
1½ tsps. mixed spice
2½ tsps. ground ginger
2 tsps. cinnamon
2 tsps. cream of tartar
1 tsp. bicarbonate of soda
4 oz. margarine or lard
3 oz. brown sugar
8 oz. syrup or treacle
1–2 eggs
Put dry ingredients into a bowl and mix well. Warm fat, sugar and treacle. Beat the eggs, pour into a well in the flour, etc., and mix well, gradually adding liquid mixture. Pour into a prepared square or oblong tin, and bake in a slow oven (325° F., mark 2) about 1½ hours.

Wrap parkin in greaseproof paper when cold, and store in an airtight tin until it becomes softer and slightly sticky.

TREACLE TOFFEE
1 lb. brown sugar
½ pint of water
A pinch of cream of tartar
3 oz. butter
4 oz. black treacle
4 oz. golden syrup
Dissolve sugar in water, and add remaining ingredients. Bring to boil and heat to 270° F., then pour into an oiled tin, mark with a knife, and break into squares when cold.

115

Figure 1.16 Party recipes featuring Smith's Crisps, *It's Your Party*, 1961.

Television

Radio and television are consumed, principally, in the home to the extent that they can be seen to *constitute* the domestic, both as conduits of domestic advice and as symbols of home (Andrews, 2012). Although commercial television relies on advertising revenue for the production and purchase of programmes, it educates as well as entertains, and can be seen as functioning in the same way as domestic advice literature in traversing 'the public/private distinction by airing private problems in a public forum' (Eide and Knight, 1999: 536; Barbatsis, 1983). Television and domestic advice literature both offer representations of the world that may be consumed either as catalysts to action in the practice of life, or as pure entertainment, without any ensuing emulation or action (see

O'Sullivan, 2005; Palmer, 2008). Yet, television has been theorised in a way that distinguishes it from advice literature. Television is predominantly visual with a textual element, while domestic advice literature is a predominantly textual form accompanied by images. Theories of television dwell on the way in which it puts the public sphere literally inside the private world of the home, in a way that print media, and indeed advice books, do not (Morley, 1992; Spigel, 1992). For sociologist Keith Tester, following Georg Simmel, television is both a 'window on the world' – a portal for entering a 'broader space of moral responsibilities and solidarity' – and, conversely, 'a door on to a world from which the viewer has exited (by the spatial and imaginative movement into the private and domestic sphere of television consumption and out of the spatial and imaginative spaces of public life)', 'a literal and metaphorical screen between the viewer and all that is outside' (1999: 481). Of course television does not represent 'all that is outside', but rather only a tiny, highly mediated fraction of it. Nevertheless, theories of television dwell on its superabundant polyvocality. We see this tendency even in a study of how the BBC and the Council of Industrial Design defined a specifically visual mode of educating public taste in design in post-war Britain:

> While other components of mass communication such as radio, books, magazines and newspapers were also admitted into the private sphere, they operated through a process of conscious selection, a regulated influence in comparison with what was seen as the pervasive visual presence of 'The Box'.
>
> (Jones, 2003: 307)

Even the relatively limited broadcast options of the post-war period are seen here as pervasive. Advice literature is a reference medium regardless of the format adopted. Readers actively seek out advice when they need it; accounts of television in the period before online delivery, by contrast, have emphasised it as something that enters the home practically unbidden, and with little choice on the part of viewers. That view of television cannot account for the contemporary situation, in which it is subject to a high degree of viewer selectivity, not only in terms of the increased number of channels competing for their attention, but also as a result of the expanding number of platforms through which television is delivered, including digital, satellite and online channels. Viewers can seek out etiquette advice from the Emily Post Productions' YouTube channel just as they can from the Emily Post Institute books.

Self-help

Didactic texts, including domestic advice literature, can be purchased and read as a way of furthering a sense of self, of who we are and who we *want* to be. The emphasis on social ease and harmonious relations which under-pins etiquette is related to the focus of self-help writers upon emotional intelligence. Although self-help shares with etiquette and other works of domestic advice literature a concern for self-improvement and the mechanics of advice-giving (issues of authority and expertise, for example), recent attempts to better understand the significance of self-help have largely ignored etiquette literature and other forms of domestic advice. One exception analyses etiquette, lifestyle and sex-education books as 'interpersonal manuals' (Miller and McHoul, 1998: 101–102). Some analyses of self-help discourses appear in recent work on lifestyle discourses (for example, Bell and Hollows, 2005; Lewis, 2008).

As we have seen, the popularity of contemporary works of self-help and lifestyle expertise has a long history. While Samuel Smiles' *Self-Help* of 1859 became one of the best selling books of the second half of the nineteenth century by encouraging the virtuous working class to aspire to join the middle class through hard work, auto-didacticism and self-control, F. Seymour Smith notes that publishing on 'How-To and Know-How started in real earnest in the 1890s' (1956: v). Self-help publishing grew fast in the second half of the twentieth century, especially in the USA (Simonds, 1992: 234–237). Between 1972 and 2000, the percentage of self-help books (broadly defined to include etiquette among other fields of expertise) listed in R. R. Bowker's *Books in Print* more than doubled, from 1.1 per cent to 2.4 per cent (Whelen, 2004). *American Bookseller* data show that 'self-help book sales rose by 96% in the five years between 1991 and 1996. By 1998, self-help book sales were said to total some $581 million' (McGee, 2005: 11). McGee notes the scale of the self-improvement industry, with 'one-third to one-half of Americans [having] purchased a self-help book in their lifetimes'.

The self-help genre has been regarded as a primarily American phenomenon, both within the USA and externally, with Sandra K. Dolby noting that 'Many people seem embarrassed by the fact that self-help books are so popular in America' (2005: 56; also Starker [1989] 2002). Self-help has been criticised as a tool for educating servants of capitalism, primarily during the Great Depression, both within and beyond the USA, but also in developing economies such as India (Currell, 2006: 131–144), yet self-help has been posited as a route to 'self-fulfilment and self-improvement', qualities which are antidotes 'to economic uncertainty' (McGee, 2005: 191). The buoyancy of the self-help industry is regularly cited as evidence of self-help's inefficacy; if self-help books worked, the afflicted reader would only need to buy one book, and not the succession of titles typically consumed by the self-help habitué (Salerno, 2005; Rimke, 2000). Business studies professor Paul Damien argues that self-help authors manipulate buzzwords for profit and misrepresent research findings (2008; also Paul, 2001). A more positive account suggests that self-help readers keep on reading to 'reinforce their optimism': 'In their desire for self-education, people engage personally with each self-help book they read, and they allow these books to mediate between the values of the culture [...] and their personal values' (Dolby, 2005: 158–159; also Simonds, 1992; Lears, 1983). Like magazines, then, self-help guides market constantly updated solutions, while also asserting their authoritative status, like domestic advice books.

Conclusion

This chapter began with a genealogy of domestic advice which revealed a process of specialisation and shifts in the mode of authority upon which such works are based, with increasing emphasis on the practical expertise and qualifications of advice writers. Domestic advice literature is both constituted by and reflective of broad cultural and social changes as shifting sites of authority affect both its form and content. The final part of the chapter examined how domestic advice literature compares in form, content and technique with the other didactic channels. Domestic advice is not a homogenous discourse, and the medium through which advice is delivered is important in determining the content. There is a need, therefore, for this discrete study of domestic advice books.

2   Real ideals
Advice and fiction

While sociologists have long recognised the uses of etiquette literature in understanding relations between the self and society, and have more recently documented the significance of lifestyle media for the same purpose, the broader category of domestic advice literature has been relatively neglected by sociologists and historians alike. There are several reasons for this neglect. First, domestic advice literature has been associated with women, both as authors and readers. Men have dominated the cultural canons in the patriarchal west, while women have been marginalised. Second, the study of domesticity has been neglected, until recently, in favour of a history of great men and great events. Domestic advice literature concerns the everyday, rather than the notable, spectacular or lauded. Third, domestic advice literature is dismissed as a published, mediating discourse, rather than being accorded the status of 'primary', unpublished source material. However, domesticity, the everyday, cultural mediation and advice discourses are all commanding greater interest, along with a wider interest in the history and sociology of intimacy and the emotions. This book therefore contributes to an ongoing reassessment of what is worthy of historical analysis.

This chapter examines how domestic advice literature has been used in some existing historical studies, from being dismissed as unimportant or unreliable by some writers, to being used straightforwardly as historical evidence by others. I approach domestic advice literature as a discourse of ideals and subject examples of the genre to close reading, revealing the narrative techniques used by domestic advice writers in promoting their ideal solutions persuasively. These techniques include the use of narrative patterns, 'before and after' stories and recurrent themes and motifs. The following chapters explore more techniques employed by advice writers, including stock characters, gaps, subtexts and meanings generated from the juxtaposition of text and image. Through intertextuality and self-referentiality, domestic advice writers display their concern for precedents from earlier advice books. I treat advice books as problem solving, and pursue the analysis so that the solution is the problem addressed.

Advice and change

Domestic advice literature is useful for understanding the past precisely because, in presenting shared ideals of conduct and consumption as models for readers to emulate, it mediates between the old and the new, traditional and modern, precedent and the unprecedented, and the individual and society. It is a convention of advice literature to depict the present as a moment of unprecedented social change. Domestic advice literature is a highly self-reflexive discourse and its authors consistently reflect in their texts on their role in managing change. Elias quotes from diplomat and printer William Caxton's *Book of Curtesye*, a verse primer for children of 1477–1478, on the changing nature of social habits:

> Thingis somtyme alowed is now repreuide
>
> And after this shal thines up aryse
>
> That men set now but at lytyl pryse.
>> (Elias, [1939] 1994: 66, quotes Caxton [1477–1748] 1868: 45)

A similar sense of the period occupied as one of unprecedented social change is found in advice literature of the twentieth century. *Cassell's Book of Etiquette* (A Woman of the World, 1922: v) comments that the First World War has 'changed many of our long-cherished conventions. In certain respects very much more freedom is allowed now than was considered permissible up to the opening of the present reign.' Three decades later, Edith Barber opens her *Short Cut to Etiquette* ([1953] 1956: vi) with the assurance that 'In this book you will find that old-fashioned and outmoded manners are treated only historically. Teenagers to-day are fortunate that the old formalities of "society" have been replaced by simple informalities.' By 1968, Mary and John Bolton's *Complete Book of Etiquette* (1968: 7) admits that 'although manners change with the years, some observance of the conventions and the unwritten rules of conduct are still required of those who wish to be accepted and to move with confidence even in today's more free-and-easy society.' Logically, not all moments can exceed all others in their extent of change, but this sense is constant throughout the history of the genre. Advice literature does not agitate for change. Rather, it responds to, and mediates, change, while its dominant trope is past precedent: the tried and tested.

Each of the statements above exemplifies a perception of informalisation, in opposition to Elias's idea of the increasing self-control and restraint of what he termed the 'civilizing process', meaning the process through which we have become more interdependent and therefore have internalised more civilised behavioural codes. Elias ([1939] 1994: xiv) argues that the civilising process is only seen over several centuries of change (five in his study). He adopts a structuralist model in recognising as significant the *variations* in the basic pattern (Elias, [1969] 1983: 10). In order to gain perspective on such variations and avoid historical relativism, long-term social change needs to be shown as the result of social figuration rather than individual action (ibid. 14). A shorter period of study, based on the length of an individual life, would reveal counter tendencies and a decivilising process. Elias prefigured Marc Bloch and the Annales School in their critique of an emphasis in contemporary historiography on political and military national histories, later termed by Fernand Braudel (1969) as *histoire événementielle* (event history), and their belief in the superiority of an evolutionary history based on the *longue durée*. Following Elias, Talcott Parsons explored civilisation through 'the processes of modernization (especially secularization, differentiation and growing complexity)' (Turner and Robertson, 1991: 255).

Elias's long-term approach has been influential but, with the exception of Arditi (1998), it is not replicated in the few subsequent academic studies of advice. Those studies dwelt on what has been regarded as the genre's apogee, the nineteenth century (St. George, 1993; Davidoff, 1973; Morgan, 1991, 1994), perhaps because during this period European manners were flamboyantly visible and specifically American manners are deemed to have flowered. This emphasis implicitly consigns advice literature to a notional past, apart from contemporary culture. Wouters (2007) exploits the relative abundance of material available for a shorter and more recent period to examine the dynamic relations between various classes, and between the sexes, across several nations in his account of informalisation in the twentieth century.

Here, I take the end of the Second World War as my starting point. Both World Wars engendered changes in manners in Britain and the USA, but British domestic advice literature in particular displays greater levels of change after the Second World War, exemplifying its characteristic cultural lag, to use a term popularised by Chicago sociologist William F. Ogburn (Fischer, 1992: 8). During the Second World War, British middle- and working-class women had tasted the independence attendant upon performing traditionally male working roles, and as the daughters of suffragism and the mothers of second-wave feminism, post-war women negotiated a new range of conditions. The post-war period saw developments in the ethnic composition of British society (resulting partly from government recruitment strategies in the West Indies, for example) and the influence of the social freedoms claimed by African Americans through the civil rights movement. The British Empire and aristocracy were being dismantled and British advice writers, who had recommended modes of living derived from upper-class models, modified their advice to suit middle- and working-class readers. The pervasive influence of North American culture in the UK, disseminated initially through Hollywood films and then through commercial television, suggested new lifestyles to British consumers, in a continuation of a transatlantic domestic dialogue.

On both sides of the Atlantic, the shortages of materials, labour and housing resulting from the war galvanised architects and planners into implementing modernist solutions on an unprecedented scale. While home economics had thrived as a thriving subject of study in the first two decades of the twentieth century in both the USA and Britain, its effects on domestic advice literature for the general market were clearly seen in the 1950s, when post-war consumerism was buoyed by the end of rationing and an increase in disposable income. The post-war period formed the bedrock for the social, political and cultural developments of the 1960s in Britain and the USA, such as the raft of liberalising acts that underpinned the permissive society with enormous changes in the lives of women, young people and homosexual men and women, black Americans and black Britons.

Advice literature as historical evidence

As a didactic, published discourse, advice literature has a complex relationship with historical practice, between fact (that which is verifiably known about the past) and fiction (that which is either known to be untrue or unverifiable), and is considered to be, variously, both primary and secondary source material. In asserting that 'All serious historical work must be based on primary source material', popular historian Arthur Marwick defined primary source material as 'material originated, within the period studied, by individuals and groups pursuing their own particular purposes, rather than consciously striving to provide comprehensive accounts for posterity', which includes statistics, acts of parliament, social surveys, personal records, newspapers, films, novels, television programmes, paintings, buildings and 'the plethora of miscellaneous printed sources', such as political party conference reports, polemics and 'major seminal works' (Marwick 1996: 488). Domestic advice literature fits this model of primary source material and, indeed, some historians have used advice literature more or less as direct evidence of historical practice.

Elias promoted advice literature, specifically etiquette books, as a useful historical resource, symptomatic of social practice, revealing the interdependent relation between 'personality structures' and 'social structures' ([1939] 1994: 184):

> If we wish to observe changes in habits, social rules and taboos; then these instructions on correct behaviour, though perhaps worthless as literature, take on a special significance. [...] They show precisely what we are seeking – namely, the standard of habits and behaviour to which society at a given time sought to accustom the individual.
> (Elias, [1939] 1994: 67)

Elias believed that when read historically, etiquette texts allow historians to ascertain the moment at which a particular point of etiquette was adopted by the readership because it is omitted from subsequent texts. Conversely, public resistance to the adoption of certain points of behaviour is exemplified by their repeated appearance in successive texts. This schematic approach does not allow for a variety of readings of these texts.

Advice literature has been regarded as unreliable evidence by historians who are suspicious of the validity of ideal representations for understanding life *as it was lived*. So while Lawrence Stone's use of late sixteenth- and early seventeenth-century Protestant advice sources to talk about a 'remarkable change' in the theory and practice of child-rearing (1977) has been criticised for 'turning prescription into practice, without adducing any primary evidence', so Linda Pollock's *Forgotten Children* (1983), for example, is praised for its use of diaries and autobiographies to reveal a continuous narrative of four centuries of affection, rather than a shift from harshness to permissiveness (Fletcher and Hussey, 1999: 3). Some historians have classed domestic advice literature as secondary material and used it as an auxiliary to sources which are more easily distinguished as primary, such as oral testimony, letters, diaries and probate inventories. Of course, conclusions are shaped by sources consulted.

American historian Susan Strasser recommends approaching advice literature 'in conjunction with information about technical change and economic development':

> Because I was eager to know what women in the past actually *did*, not just what they were told to do, I used advice literature carefully, mindful that it is intended to prescribe, not describe. Nineteenth-century manuals, magazine, and cookbooks tell neither more nor less about reality than the current issue of *McCall's* or the latest edition of *The Joy of Cooking*. Women do not necessarily believe everything they read, and the advice – a kind of reform literature – often contradicted their own experience, presented inconsistent ideas, or offered doctrines that were at variance with their cultural backgrounds. Fortunately the literature is shaped by these realities as much as it shapes them, and considerable information can be read between the lines.
>
> (Strasser, [1982] 2000: x)

Domestic advice literature, as a genre of women's cultural production, should not always need validation through recourse to the principally masculine discourses of technology and economics. Strasser's distinction between domestic advice literature and what women 'actually *did*' sits oddly with her recognition of the active, critical nature of reading: reading has long been one of the things women actually *did*. Strasser is right to use advice literature 'carefully', but as well as recognising that 'considerable information can be read between the lines' it is important to analyse the lines of domestic advice directly.

Because academic studies of domestic advice literature are few, it is useful to look at other advice discourses to understand how advice can be used as an historical resource. Prompted by an interest in authority and ethics, the history of medicine has produced several studies of advice literature (Cook, 1994), including sex advice (Gordon, 1971; Ross, [1980] 1981; Garner, Sterk and Adams, 1998), also termed 'marriage', 'courtship' or 'romance' advice (Spurlock, 1998; Shumway, 1998), and analyses of advice on specific conditions such as menstruation (Murray, 1988; Strange, 2001), pregnancy (Longhurst, 1999) and maternity (Mechling, 1975). Writing about sex advice books, Rosalind Brunt acknowledges their limitations:

> With adequate resources, using the methods of interview question-naire and personal account, it would of course be possible to test the permissively phrased 'ought' of the advice books with the 'is' of people's own experience. Without those resources, I would not claim that the 'ought' of proposed sexual conduct, however permissively expressed, automatically coincides with the 'is' of sexual practices.
> (Brunt, 1982: 146–147)

Historians have used published advice to overcome a lack of direct testimony about these private and potentially embarrassing subjects. Brunt recalls Foucault's 1979 discussion of sex as both secret and a discursive obsession. She sees advice books as 'agenda-setters and worth examining seriously as ideological "texts" in their own right' as they exemplify a shift in sex advice books 'from the realm of ethical considerations' to 'the arena of lifestyle and etiquette'. Sex advice discourses break the silence surrounding a repressed aspect of life: 'given the social invisibility of sexual activity in our culture, the manuals' power-to-define will be a particularly forceful and authoritative one' (Brunt, 1982: 146; see also Hochschild, 1994).

Sex advice is produced publicly and, typically, consumed privately. For Roy Porter and Lesley Hall (1995), this privacy confers authenticity on sex advice. They describe their sources as anti-authoritarian and populist: sex advice books are commercially published, written by a heterogeneous group of authors, challenge medical orthodoxy, enlighten the public and require readers to overcome social barriers in order to purchase and read them (ibid. 219). Evidence of the influence of such sources may be found in readers' letters to authors, and archival material such as that collected by Mass Observation (ibid. 220–223, 225–226). Porter and Hall make the deceptively simple observation that individuals read different sorts of advice differently at different times and in different contexts and may even hold contradictory opinions about it at the same time (ibid. 279–282). Their book was criticised for its 'mistake in pretending that ideas about sex can be separated from sexual practices' (Gillis, 1996: 1210), but an opposing argument suggests that no association between prescription and practice should be inferred. Jay Mechling proposes that historians should not use manuals to 'make the qualitative, inferential leap to talking about [shared] values in the culture'; rather, they should 'make these manuals the primary sources which they really are rather than the secondary sources which they seem to be' (1975: 56). He discounts the imaginative impact of advice discourses upon actual practices of everyday life.

Jennifer J. Popiel demonstrates the benefits of a complex understanding of the relationship between advice literature and practice. 'While this rhetoric of domesticity may appear manipulative and demeaning to a modern eye', she says of her focal material of child-rearing manuals published from 1760 to 1830, they 'demonstrated the ways in which compliance would be greatly to a woman's advantage' through 'the enunciation of a seemingly repressive refrain of "separate but equal"' which 'may have helped to pave the way for the modern enunciation of equality *tout court*' (Popiel, 2004: 345–346). Similarly complex is Andrew Singleton's approach to the subtexts of 'Christian Men's Self-Help Literature', which 'constructs and addresses men as a collective who are "oppressed" and under siege' thereby marginalising 'competing social conversations about men's status in society, especially feminist critiques of male privilege' (2004: 154; also Paul, 2001). Singleton offers a critical, post-structuralist close reading, which allows for ambiguity and multiple interpretations.

By recognising domestic advice literature as a mediating discourse with a highly complex relation to practice, we see its historical value. Like all didactic discourse, domestic advice literature cannot simply be used as direct evidence of historical practice due to the impossibility of ever tracing the extent to which published advice was followed, using either the subjective accounts of letters, diaries and oral history, the wider data offered by the book trade or the meta-discourse of critical reception. However, neither should domestic advice literature be ignored, because it is written and published with a view to mass appeal and communicates ideals which are '"real"; that is, they are not constructed by social scientists' (Wouters, 1995:109). By making domestic advice literature a focus of analysis, we see it as a group of real ideals consumed – whether humorously or seriously – as representations of what has been possible or desirable, socially and culturally.

Literature and domestic advice

Domestic advice literature does not fit current definitions of 'literature'. A nineteenth-century definition meaning 'a totality of written or printed works' ceded to the use prevalent from the mid-twentieth century based on 'imaginative, creative or artistic value, usually related to a work's absence of factual or practical reference' (Baldick, 2008: 189). Advice writing is imaginative: the etiquette writer *imagines* the settings in which social interactions will be performed just as the home decorating advisor *imagines* patterns of behaviour in need of accommodation. Yet, 'factual or practical reference' is the purpose of domestic advice literature. Domestic advice books appear in a limited number of formats: as encyclopaedia or dictionary with short entries arranged alphabetically; in the dialectical form, as questions and answers or FAQ (frequently asked questions) which integrate an imagined reader; and as authorial polemic, arranged into thematic chapters. If literature must be autotelic, then what are we to make of the fact that not all readers of domestic advice literature seek direct guidance on their domestic practices? Readers may go to advice literature for pure entertainment rather than guidance; they may wish to encounter an imagined social world that is more or less plausible as a substitute or alternative to the life they actually lead. Some advice books are evidently intended as pastiche (Birnbach, 1980), while online forums about domestic advice literature exemplify the variety of reader responses, from the serious to the humorous (Miss Abigail, 2012; Peril, 2002).

The qualities of 'imaginative, creative or artistic value' imply originality, but advice literature is not expected to be innovative; it functions to manage norms and, in so doing, refers to earlier examples from the genre. Mrs Mary Cole, in *The Lady's Complete Guide; or, Cookery in All its Branches* of 1788, criticised the practice of plagiarism:

> If all the writers upon Cookery had acknowledged from whence they took their Receipts, as I do, they would have acted with more candour by the public. Their vanity to pass for Authors, instead of Compilers, has not added to their reputation.
>
> (Cole, [1788] 1791, cited in Davidson, 1999: 203)

Offenders included John Farley and Hannah Glasse; Glasse's *Whole Art of Cookery Made Plain and Easy* ([1747] 1974) heavily plagiarised earlier cookery books, including *The Whole Duty of a Woman* (A Lady, 1695; Stead, 1983; Bain, 1986; Lucraft, 1997).

J. Hillis Miller has articulated three benchmark characteristics of narrative: first, 'beginning, sequence, reversal'; second, 'personification [...] bringing protagonist, antagonist, and witness "to life"'; and third, 'some patterning or repetition of elements surrounding a nuclear figure or complex word'. He goes on, 'Even narratives that do not fit this paradigm draw their meaning from the way they play ironically against our deeply ingrained expectations that all narratives are going to be like that' (1990: 75). Miller does not specify originality as a criterion for narrative. Popular narratives include genre fiction, such as 'chicklit', which shares various concerns with advice literature, even as it parodies self-help discourse and domestic competence in works such as Helen Fielding's Bridget Jones novels (1996, 1999, 2001; see Smith, 2005 and Hoeller, 2007). Therefore, the term 'literature' in 'domestic advice literature' is more accurately described as narrative.

'Narrative' provides more appropriate contexts for examining the form and function of domestic advice books, with one exception: domestic advice is delivered in images as well as words, and it therefore demands visual, as well as textual, analysis. Historical research has preferred documentary sources over images and objects. Even design historians examine objects through a variety of sources including texts, from promotional literature to biographies. Here, I am attentive to the interplay of word and image in domestic advice literature. I position the material and social worlds as mutually constitutive: the ways in which the material world is organised result from social needs and desires and they, in turn, condition behaviour. Representations of table settings, suggested flatware, glassware and serving equipment, flower arrangements, gadgets and appliances, room decorations, furniture, and storage solutions abound in domestic advice books. While some domestic advice books are heavily illustrated, most examples feature at least five to ten line drawings; in others, black and white illustrations and photographs are accompanied by a series of colour plates. I here analyse domestic advice literature, both text and image, as a genre of popular narrative.

Didactic techniques: stories and lists

The formal composition of domestic advice texts varies in relation to broader trends, as a comparison of two domestic primers for schoolgirls from the beginning and middle of the twentieth century shows. The distinction between textbooks for school use and advice texts intended for the extra-curricula consumption of the same audience of girls, and sometimes boys, is not clear cut. Sometimes the authors are the same, and such sources work together to offer domestic education.

In 1913, in 'First Attempts', the first of a four-volume 'Domestic Subject Reader' *The Little Housekeeper*, Florence Tapsell delivered domestic guidance through narrative episodic chapters about two well-meaning young girls, Milly and Hilda, who are keeping house while their mother is away (Tapsell, 1913–1914) (Figure 2.1). Initially, the prospect of running a home excites Milly, but her mother cautions: 'You will find that you still have much to learn, even though it may not be lessons out of a book' (ibid. 4). Mrs Peters is right: Milly gets into debt, and she burns her arm badly while trying to light a fire. The book ends with her mother's return: 'next week you and I will do the housekeeping together, and that will teach you better than any amount of telling' (ibid. 67). Although the book is apparently designed so that readers develop domestic competence along with Milly as they read the story, these two framing statements from Mrs Peters, at the beginning and end of the book, ironically emphasise learning through doing.

Published almost four decades after Tapsell's narrative guidebook of 1913, Margaret Nicol's *Homecraft and Homemaking* (1952) displays

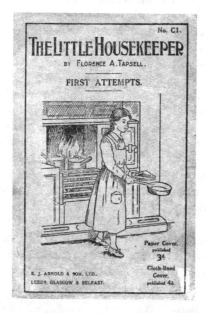

Figure 2.1 Cover, Florence A. Tapsell, *The Little Housekeeper: First Attempts*, 1913.

the growing influence of home economics and domestic science (Figure 2.2). Part of the 'McDougall's Modern Homecraft' series, the back cover blurb explains that the book is 'up-to-date in conception and presentation, with concise instructions and clear explanations. Notetaking is eliminated and self reliance encouraged.' *Homecraft and Homemaking* contains a section 'Time and Motion Study' which recommends reconfiguring the house, and especially the kitchen, according to time-saving principles (Nicol, 1952: 12):

> Note over a period of a few days the time you take to do a specific job, e.g. cleaning a grate, or peeling potatoes. Each day note where you can reduce time. By doing this carefully you will ultimately get on much more quickly and have more leisure and more time for social life and recreation.

(Nicol, 1952: 13)

Nicol, who was examiner in theory for various colleges of domestic science in Scotland, recounts examples of 'domestic science' through a series of numbered lists as memory aids for girls who will be tested:

1. If you have a vacuum cleaner, use it at least once a week, working systematically over the whole carpet.

Figure 2.2 Cover, Margaret Nicol, *Homecraft and Homemaking*, 1952.

2. If you do not have a vacuum cleaner, protect furniture by dust sheets, and sprinkle the carpet with well washed damp tea leaves.
3. With either a long- or a short-handled switch go carefully over the whole carpet, doing a width at a time.
4. Sweep towards the hearth or the window.
5. Turn back edges and sweep carefully underneath.
6. Sweep dust and tea leaves into dust pan and burn.

Note. It is an excellent plan, whether carpet is done by vacuum or by hand, to go carefully over the whole surface with a clean duster after sweeping

(Nicol, 1952: 54)

Homecraft and Homemaking is illustrated with technical drawings depicting plumbing, heating systems and the interior of a cleaning cupboard (Figure 2.3). There, nails on the door hold a 'Housewifery (Duster) Bag' with separate spaces for cloths for dusting, silver, other metals, polishing, rubbers and two spares. The cupboard also contains brushes, which are treated in their own chapter, with detailed information about their materials, manufacture, care and use.

The textual differences between Tapsell's *The Little Housekeeper* and Nicol's *Homecraft and Homemaking* are indicated in their cover designs. *The Little*

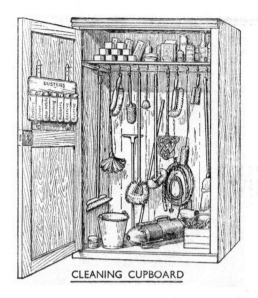

CLEANING CUPBOARD

Figure 2.3 Cleaning Cupboard, Margaret Nicol, *Homecraft and Homemaking*, 1952.

Housekeeper features a line drawing of its protagonist, Milly, while the cover of *Homecraft and Homemaking* is purely typographical, combining a sans serif typeface with a script face indicative of the author's signature and a circular motif to emphasise the word 'modern' in the series name 'McDougall's Modern Homecraft'. Nicol's book is also distinguished by the use of a bright primary red field, as opposed to the grey paper covers for Tapsell's volume, and the paper is coated to make it resistant to stains and wear. This is not unique: *America's Housekeeping Book* of 1947 trumpets from a banner headline across the cover 'This cover is washable' (*New York Herald* Home Institute, 1941).

These two homemaking books also exemplify the shift from treatise to encyclopaedia formats that Arditi has observed in etiquette books as evidence of an increasingly decentred personality (1996, 1998, 1999). However, such a shift was never more than a tendency, and narrative or treatise-type examples have always been present in domestic advice literature. A backlash in the USA against rational discourses of domesticity in which theory outweighs action is seen in, for example, Beulah Schenk and Gladys Denny Schultz's *The House That Runs Itself* (1929), which, according to Celeste Fraser Delgado, distinguished between 'theoretical "home economics" and practical "home-making" – it became not so important to wash the dishes the scientific way, as to see that they got washed at all' (1995: 401). In teaching readers how to write for homemakers, Richardson and Callahan noted in 1962 that 'Current practice is to put home economics facts and procedures into simple home language instead of the stilted, impersonal scientese so long considered the correct way to write a textbook' ([1962] 1970: 136). Subsequent domestic

Figure 2.4 Cover, Heather Barrie, *Practical Homecraft*, 1950.

advice books commonly adopt discursive formats, sometimes with a degree of narrative, or a blend of discursive and list formats.

Like Tapsell's *Little Homemaker*, Heather Barrie's *Practical Homecraft* of 1950 is enlivened by a sympathetic but inept female protagonist (Figure 2.4). Each chapter is introduced with a scene from the lives of Heather and her neighbour Belinda, 'the bride next door, who has so often brought her household problems to me that I was given the idea of compiling a fact-packed book on the subject of homecraft' (Barrie, 1950: 5). Chapter 1, 'Change from Gas to Electric Cookery', begins:

> A cry of despair came from Belinda. I swing myself over the low fence. "That electric stove – I could see it far enough," she stormed. Then, "Look at my nice dinner," she ordered [...] a chill crept up my spine. It was fully half past twelve, yet Belinda's dinner was uncooked and I knew Belinda's John was due back for his meal at one.
>
> (Barrie, 1950: 9)

The advice that follows is presented as a conversation between the two neighbours followed by a list of pointers. Each chapter provides a similar micro-narrative, in which an initial dramatic scene is resolved through domestic advice. The overarching narrative of the book closes when Belinda has attained sufficient domestic expertise to articulate imperatives for the education of others: 'Belinda believes in sandals for absolute comfort. "Happy feet mean a happy housewife," she declares. And she hopes every reader of this book is as happy as she is' (ibid. 167). So the myth of the happy house-wife is maintained. The third person usage in the final sentence denotes the narrator's – Heather's – voice, implying her insight into Belinda's thoughts and avoiding direct address to the reader from her fictional alter ego Belinda, because they are functionally united as each undergoes a domestic education during the course of the narrative. The vivid character of Belinda thereby enhances the didactic power of the text. In combining narrative with the rational techniques of home economics (for example, lists), Barrie presents a highly effective selection of imaginative and rational worlds.

Alphabetically arranged reference books, which are not discursive and sometimes dictate without explanation, are (happily) in the minority of twentieth-century domestic advice books. Although this study spans a period in which the scientism of home economics was strongly felt in domestic advice literature, I focus the analysis on texts which are organised into discursive, thematic chapters. Some use bullet points, sidebars, dia-grams and other typographical techniques for translating prose advice into action plans, but the majority retain a narrative format. The selection is therefore based on the internal structural coherence of the sources.

Domestic drama: *The Book of Good Housekeeping* (1946)

We have seen how the form of an advice book can bear evidence of its approach to domesticity. Now we turn to an example of dramatisation in domestic advice. The Good Housekeeping Institute's *The Book of Good Housekeeping* was first published in 1944, before the end of the Second World War, and was reprinted in 1945 and 1946 (Table 2.1). It's foreword to the third edition is entitled 'Take Ten Eggs...', in reference to the rhe-torical conventions of cookery books, and comments upon the impact of two wars on homemaking and the prospect of better living standards. Section 1, 'The Home Itself', covers choosing a home, decorating the com-ponent rooms, heating, lighting, plumbing and pet care. Section 2, 'Running the Home', explores budgeting, planning housework, domestic help, household tools, cleaning, entertaining, cookery, laundry, sewing, home maintenance, the telephone, law, insurance, safety, pests, leaving home, post-war materials and technologies. This arrangement allows for several narrative sequences. The first is the frame provided by the editors' fore-word, which locates the text immediately after the Second World War, with the deprivations of war still very much in evidence, and the book's conclud-ing chapter, 'Some Aspects of the Postwar Home', which discusses the prospect of post-war housing shortages. Stepping through this frame, the narrative pivots around the home, from its selection and purchase (Chapter 1, 'Choosing a Home') to homemaking – including an initial scene-setting phase of decoration, followed by maintenance of both home and family – to the penultimate chapter, 'Leaving Your Home'. *The Book of Good*

Table 2.1 Narrative analysis of The Good Housekeeping Institute's *Book of Good Housekeeping*, London and Chesham: Gramol Publications Ltd., 1946 (1944, 1945)

	Contents	Page	
	Foreword to the third edition: 'Take Ten Eggs…'	3	} Frame – present
SECTION 1: THE HOME ITSELF			
1	Choosing a home	17	} Frame – arrival
II	Choice of decoration	33	⎫
III	Home decoration	41	⎪
IV	Furnishing your home	51	⎬ Establishing – scene setting
V	Soft furnishings	65	⎪
VI	The nursery	77	⎪
VII	Rooms with a purpose	83	⎪
VIII	The kitchen	105	⎭
IX	Heating methods	125	⎫
X	Domestic hot-water systems	136	⎬ Establishing – fuel
XI	Cooking stoves	141	⎪
XII	Lighting	152	⎭
XIII	The storage problem	161	⎫
XIV	Planning the garden	177	⎬ Establishing – husbandry
XV	Care of domestic animals	191	⎭
SECTION II: RUNNING THE HOME			
XVI	Home budgeting	204	
XVII	Planning the housework	214	
XVIII	The problem of domestic help	223	} Antagonist
XIX	Selection of household tools	233	⎱ Maintenance –
XX	House care and cleaning	241	⎰ cleaning
XXI	Entertaining	260	} Externality
XXII	Catering	279	⎫
XXIII	First lessons in cookery	288	⎪
XXIV	Cakes, pastries and pudding	308	⎬ Maintenance – food
XXV	The preparation and cooking of vegetables	330	⎪
XXVI	Home preserving	337	⎭
XXVII	Household laundrywork	359	⎫ Maintenance – textiles
XXVIII	Clothes care and home valeting	379	⎪
XXIX	Home needlework	389	⎬
XXX	Simple dressmaking	399	⎭
XXXI	The home 'handyman'	412	⎫ Externality
XXXII	The telephone in your home	423	⎪
XXXIII	The householder and the law	426	⎬
XXXIV	Insurance, banking and you	441	⎭
XXXV	Home safety	453	⎱ Antagonists
XXXVI	Household pests	478	⎰
XXXVII	Leaving your home	486	} Frame – departure
XXXVIII	Some aspects of the postwar home	491	} Frame – future

Housekeeping therefore follows Miller's formula for narrative; it has a beginning (choosing a home), a sequence (decorating and maintaining the home) and a reversal (leaving the home), with the final chapter broadening the discussion to new materials and technologies and the future of housing, including, it is implied, the next home.

In terms of Miller's further criterion, personification, the house is both protagonist and antagonist, depending on whether we are considering the warm, cosy and welcoming shelter of the well-run, ideal home, or the succession of problems which punctuate the narrative sequence of establishment and maintenance, including 'The Problem of Domestic Help' (chapter 18), potential disasters (in chapter 35, 'Home Safety') or the live threat of 'mice, beetles or moths' (in chapter 36, 'Household Pests') (Good Housekeeping Institute, [1944] 1946: 478). The structure of *The Book of Good Housekeeping* makes explicit the capacity of the dwelling to shape human experience. The fictive time of the book is delimited by arrival at and departure from a single dwelling, and advice on the establishment and maintenance of the material home precedes discussions of the activities occurring within. Activities such as home entertaining are discussed in the section entitled 'Running the Home'. The ideology of the text is embedded in the relation of the component parts to one another.

Other important personae include the house's imagined inhabitants, and the readers, as witnesses. The foreword identifies the intended audience:

> Thousands of young people will have left or will soon be leaving the Services and setting up their homes: and these pages have been written in an effort to help them. We do not attempt to conceal the fact that the next year or two may still be a period of shortage and improvisation in home-making. But shortages can be treated with patience and improvisation with zest, and we hope to help to show you how.
>
> (Good Housekeeping Institute ([1944] 1946): 3)

The antagonists threatening ideal domesticity include – in addition to the laziness or ignorance underlying the poorly maintained home – post-war housing shortages and the lack of basic items under rationing, which extended almost a decade beyond the war years. Miller's reversal is found in the solutions offered: household pests are met with cleanliness, maintenance and vigilance; shortages are met with patience, thrift and ingenuity. The responsive reader is therefore cast as potential protagonist if she or he adopts the recommended practices.

The Good Housekeeping Institute itself functions as a character in *The Book of Good Housekeeping*. The Institute's reputation will have helped sales of its books. The title page attributes authorship to the Institute as a singular entity – 'Compiled by the Good Housekeeping Institute' – with the foreword written by an anonymous group, 'The Editors'. The Institute is capable of holding views, as in the phrase 'Good Housekeeping does not deal in fantasies of all-plastic houses' (the capitalization denotes a proper name) (Good Housekeeping Institute, [1944] 1946): 3). The Institute was a mainstay of rational authority in homemaking, mediating between the professionalising scientism of home economics as a discipline and the amateur, domestic realm of consumer magazines, as here:

> Permanganate of potash is an inexpensive and convenient stain, but it does not possess very lasting qualities, particularly on wood which is subjected to strong sunlight [...] It destroys brushes, and stains anything with which it comes into contact. The crystals should be dissolved in some earthenware receptacle, such as an old jam jar or basin.
>
> (Good Housekeeping Institute, [1944] 1946: 49)

This recommendation is not attributed to a named author: it represents the voice, and authority, of the Institute. Its narrative qualities derive from the interaction of the protagonist (the Institute), the antagonist (the permanganate of potash) and the witness (the reader). The scene implied is the Institute's Test Centre.

Miller's final stipulation is that a narrative should offer 'some patterning or repetition of elements surrounding a nuclear figure or complex word'. *The Book of Good Housekeeping* is about a house that becomes a home. Early on in the book, the term 'house' is used in chapters describing the processes before occupation – 'When you buy a house', 'When you build a house' – but by the penultimate chapter, 'Leaving Your Home', the house has been transformed through habitation. The central importance of the home in this narrative is exemplified in the division of the text into two sections, 'The Home Itself' and 'Running the Home'. The narrative shows 'home' to be a complex word through the extended treatment, over 512 densely printed pages, of its component regions, qualities and affordances. The 14 plates and numerous line drawings illustrate the variety of what home could be in 1946, as do the book's illustrated endpapers. They show modern flats with curtain windows and curving stuccoed walls; a curvilinear modern house, in which the fenestration emphasises horizontality, with a balcony, sun terrace and tennis court; a small, simple, thatched farm cottage; a grand half-timbered house; a contemporary bay-fronted suburban detached house; a Georgian house; and an Arts and Crafts style manor house in manicured grounds (Figure 2.5). Whether the endpapers are read as a diachronic stylistic history of British domestic architecture or as a synchronic representation of architectural heterogeneity, the homes shown are typologically connected. Home is both individuated and collective.

Figure 2.5 Endpapers, The Good Housekeeping Institute's *Book of Good Housekeeping*, 1946 (1944, 1945).

Etiquette books and the life cycle: Agnes Miall's *Modern Etiquette* (1950)

Narrative analysis of domestic advice books can reveal core value to wider social trends. Readers turn to advice books at times of need during their lives, from specific rites of passage such as weddings to broader stages of life. In giving advice on personal situations the assumed readership will encounter – such as courtship, friendship, furnishing a home, giving gifts and grooming – domestic advice books are sometimes structured around the life course, a convention which enables sensitivity to age-related matters while also attracting criticism for normalising diverse experiences and ignoring variables such as gender and ethnicity. Domestic advice books can therefore be read as life stories, ideal biographies or *picaresque*. Titles such as *Today's Etiquette* (Lyons, 1967), discussed in Chapter 5, are notable for the extent to which liberal, progressive and expansive opening statements about the options available to young women and men gravitate towards a conventional progression from dress and grooming through dating to marriage, homemaking and home entertaining undercut with fashionable and subversive illustrations.

Agnes M. Miall's *Modern Etiquette* of 1950 (Table 2.2) has an opening chapter entitled 'Hatched, Matched and Dispatched!', in which the reader is reminded that 'Etiquette plays such a vital part in our lives that a baby is no sooner born than it comes into operation', before going on to treat engagements, weddings and funerals (1950: 1). The subject coverage of this first chapter therefore constitutes a micro-lifecycle. Miall's next chapter, on the importance of manners at home, is followed by discussions of guests, mealtime manners, 'social life in general' – on introductions, calling cards and conversation – transport and travel, and tips and tipping. The sequence here is not one of time elapsing, but rather of widening horizons, from the family

Table 2.2 Narrative analysis of Agnes Miall, *Modern Etiquette*, third edition, 1961

	Content	Page	
	Foreword	vii	} Direct address, author to reader
I	"Hatched, matched and dispatched!"	1	} Life cycle: birth, life and death [time]
II	Family and everyday life	36	
III	Host and guest	48	
IV	Good manners at meals	57	Widening horizons: from familiar to
V	Social life in general	74	unfamiliar [space]
VI	Transport and travel	97	
VII	Tips and tipping	122	
VIII	Boy meets girl	131	
IX	Clothes for all occasions	150	Life cycle: from adolescence to
X	When you give a party	166	courtship and employment [time]
XI	Employer, guest and servant	184	
XII	The way you speak	190	
XIII	Letter-writing and modes of address	203	
			Widening horizons: from you to
XIV	In high society	223	them [space]
XV	Business, sport and miscellaneous matters	236	
	Index	249	

to the wider world. The next chapter, 'Boy meets girl', is followed by chapters on dress and parties, returning to the conventional life cycle arrangement, linking courtship with a heightened concern for self-fashioning and grooming. 'Employer, Guest and Servant' has a place in this part of the life cycle too, because the first job and the independence it confers are coterminous with courtship. After sections on speech, letter-writing, address and precedence, 'Business, Sport and Miscellaneous Matters' offer another micro-narrative of horizons widening from concern for the self to the external worlds of business, sport and royalty. Close reading of this complex structure reveals not one narrative sequence but five, alternately treating the life cycle and the widening geo-social horizons. The focus shifts from self to other throughout the text, reflecting Miall's concern that the reader shapes herself or himself according to the perceptions of others: 'Our manners are the first thing that strangers notice about us' (ibid. vii).

In the same year that Miall's book was published, sociologist David Riesman published his best-seller *The Lonely Crowd: A Study of the Changing American Character* (1950) in which he argues that between the Civil War and the end of the Second World War, Americans increasingly looked into themselves for 'inner-directed' behavioural guidance, while after the Second World War, a change of national character in the USA and Western Europe meant that people became increasingly other-directed, looking outward to their peers for approval. This echoes Elias's 'civilizing process', in which individuals internalise codes of conduct designed to aid harmonious interaction between disparate classes of people, and the dramaturgical model propounded by Erving Goffman in *The Presentation of Self in Everyday Life* ([1959] 1990). Richard Sennett has argued that Riesmann's 'sequence should be reversed': 'Western societies are moving from something like an other-directed condition to an inner-directed condition – except that in the midst of self-absorption no one can say what is inside. As a result, confusion has arisen between public and intimate life' ([1977] 1992: 5). Sennett has also criticised Goffman's dramaturgical construct as static, ahistorical and dependent upon simplistic conceptions of character and role (1973).

We have seen how domestic advice literature developed alongside the novel as a discourse of individualism. The narrative analysis of Miall's *Modern Etiquette* as a life story presented here shows the author to be concerned with the very issues of tradition-directed, inner-directed and other-directed personality models described by Riesman. Miall therefore encouraged readers to consider issues that occupied many sociologists at the same time. Miall's book aims to produce other-directed readers, seen as invaluable to society and its organisations.

Home decorating manuals and the domestic tour

Home decorating books conventionally comprise successive chapters on living rooms, dining rooms, kitchens, bathrooms and bedrooms. This narrative structure implies a journey around the home, instead of the journey through life adopted in etiquette books. Increasing degrees of intimacy are implied in the move from reception rooms to backstage regions (discussed further in Chapter 4). The idea of a domestic journey is rarely directly commented on by advice writers. An exception is provided by French author Adrienne Spanier, who was educated and published in the UK. Her *Furnishing and Decorating in Your Home* (1959) contains a chapter 'Round the House', which opens with the tantalising phrase: 'I think a tour of the house [...] might be amusing' (1959: 40) (Figure 2.6). But, the subsequent successive room treatments are not linked; Spanier simply invites an experiential reading of the chapter and leaves the imaginative labour to the reader.

As part of their promotion of European modernism in America (Nelson, 1934: 4), George Nelson and Henry Wright's book *Tomorrow's House* was simultaneously published in New York and London in 1945. Nelson's biographer Stanley Abercrombie describes the innovative approach of *Tomorrow's House*:

> *Tomorrow's House* did not concentrate on the practical problems of financing, site selection, service connections, and mechanical equipment, as other books of the time were doing, nor did it examine the house room by conventional room. Rather, it surveyed domestic activities and suggested sensible accommodations for them. ("You will not find a chapter

Furnishing and Decorating in your Home

ADRIENNE SPANIER

Figure 2.6 Cover, Adrienne Spanier, *Furnishing and Decorating in Your Home*, 1959.

on bedrooms ... but a great deal about sleeping.") These suggestions, of course, were unencumbered by tradition.
(Abercrombie, [1995] 2000: 68–9 cites Nelson and Wright, 1945: 9)

Following two introductory chapters, 'The Great Tradition' and 'Home is Where You Hang Your Architect', the narrative structure of *Tomorrow's House* adopts the conventional tour of rooms in a house, beginning with living rooms, 'Where Shall We Eat', 'Lighting' and a picture section 'Dining and Entertainment'. Chapters entitled 'The Work Center', 'The Room without a Name' and 'Heating' precede a picture section 'Kitchens and Baths' and another chapter 'Bathrooms Are Out of Date', then 'Manufacturing Climate', 'Sleeping' and a picture section 'Bedrooms and Closets'. Next come 'Organised Storage', 'Sound Conditioning', 'Windows', 'Solar Heating' and 'Putting the Pieces Together'. The last picture section 'Exteriors' is followed by 'How to Get Your House (or Remodel the One You Have)' and 'Projections'. The book closes with lists of architects, designers and photographers whose work is shown in the book. *Tomorrow's House* seeks to provide readers with a truly modern domestic arrangement, determined by function not convention (Forino, 2013: 105), but the book's arrangement adheres to the conventions of home decorating literature.

Abercrombie considerably overstates the originality of *Tomorrow's House* by comparing it to guidebooks by and for architects rather than domestic advice books. He cites F. R. S. Yorke's *The Modern House* (Architectural Press, 1934) as a 'pre-war British precedent' (Abercrombie, [1995] 2000: 68, n. 4) along with James and Katherine Morrow Ford's *The Modern House in America* (1940) and *Design of Modern Interiors* (1942); T. H. Robsjohn-Gibbings' *Goodbye, Mr. Chippendale* (1944); Elizabeth B. Mock's *Tomorrow's Small House* (1945) and *If You Want to Build a House* (1946); *Homes* by Thomas H. Creighton *et al.* (1947) and Catherine and Harold Sleeper's *House For You To Build, Buy, Or Rent* (1948). By failing to situate *Tomorrow's House* within the context of domestic advice literature and, more specifically, home decoration discourses, Abercrombie misunderstands its emphasis and genre conventions. The sales figures alone imply a wide readership: *Tomorrow's House* sold 3,000 copies a week on publication, and reached number nine in the *New York Times* best-seller list at the end of November 1945 (Abercrombie, [1995] 2000: 68, n. 4). Publishers Simon and Schuster advertised the book's sales figures in the April 1946 issue of *Architectural Forum*, a publication for which both Nelson and his co-author Henry Wright worked, and from which the material for *Tomorrow's House* was drawn.

Another title from the same publisher, Mary and Russel Wright's *Guide to Easier Living* ([1950] 1954) may be compared with *The Book of Good Housekeeping*, discussed above, in which the home is constructed before it is maintained; here, the Wrights suggest designs that foster easier living before detailing the practices of home. The Wrights' *Guide* offers a house tour sequence of increasing intimacy, beginning with 'Room to Relax' (the living room), 'The Vanishing Dining Room', and 'Private Lives' on bedrooms, bathrooms and children's rooms. 'All Around the House' examines transition spaces, such as entrances, stairs, halls, doors and windows, and 'Outdoor Living' considers the garden. Only then is the kitchen discussed, in 'The Housewife-Engineer', 'Today's Servants' and 'The New Hospitality'. The Wrights treat the reader like a guest: guests are received in the reception rooms, perhaps taking drinks before dinner in the living room and then moving on to the dining room for dinner. House guests staying for the night will then encounter bedroom and bathroom. The view of the kitchen as a backstage space, where entertaining did not occur, perhaps explains why the kitchen is discussed at the end of the *Guide to Easier Living*, along with servants, the 'New Etiquette' and cleaning.

Yet, the *Guide to Easier Living* is dedicated to unassisted entertaining, in which guests enter the kitchen to serve themselves directly from the oven at a buffet or help with the washing up. The authors distinguish their book from others in the domestic advice genre: 'Many etiquette and housekeeping books still promote an equally outmoded traditional way of keeping house, which is impossibly meticulous and far too laborious for our times' (ibid. 166, 155). The Wrights' emphasis on 'easier' living here is consistent with the informality of their tableware, including oven-to-tableware, available in mix and match and a series called 'Casual'. So the conventional narrative structure of the *Guide to Easier Living,* suggesting a separation of leisure and domestic work, persists in a book about refusing convention in favour of new patterns of living and thereby qualifies the informality prescribed. The mismatch between the progressive ideology of the text and images and the conventional nature of the narrative structure can be seen as symptomatic of a period of transition, away from traditional legitimisation.

Shortly after the *Guide to Easier Living* was reissued by Gibbs Smith in 2003, Beth O. Caldwell, a reader of the Wrights' manual, wrote about her experience of its continuing relevance:

> I bought this book when it had just come out and I was newly married. I've used it so much that it is in tatters, but I still treasure it. The information and illustrations of storage closets, kitchens, general home layouts, etc. are still as useful and inspiring today as they were back in the 1950s. [...] This book is like a dear old friend and has influenced my life for 50 some odd years. It is one of the 9 or 10 most influential and treasured books that I own.
>
> (Caldwell, 2004)

Notwithstanding the untrustworthy nature of online reader reviews, Caldwell displays a close connection with the text which is corroborated by other reviews claiming that *Easier Living* is still relevant today. Her enjoyment of the text appears to derive from the longevity of her relationship with it, ironic given its emphasis on offering readers innovative advice.

Manufactured characters: Betty Crocker as case study

Domestic advice literature has its stock themes, such as 'party flurry', and its stock characters, such as 'Mrs. Three-in-One' (see Chapter 4), but the fictional status of the domestic advice genre sometimes extends to its authors. Some domestic advice texts have uncertain authorship, such as Elsie de Wolfe's *The House in Good Taste* (1913), which is partly ghostwritten and recycled from magazine articles. Its complex authorship is compounded by lack of a distinction between pre-existing and staged arrangements in the objects and interiors presented in the illustrations (Sparke, 2003). In other cases, invented authors function as brand mouthpieces.

Betty Crocker exemplifies the invented advisor, as well as embodying both traditional and charismatic processes of legitimisation (see Chapter 1). As noted in Chapter 1, advertising cookbooks began to appear in the USA in the 1880s (Gartrell, 2000). As the genre developed, manufacturers drew on the consultancy and endorsement of qualified experts, such as home economists, consistent with Weber's model of rational legitimisation. In 1921, Washburn Crosby Co. invented a fictional expert, Betty Crocker, to 'sign' letters of reply to consumers' questions about baking. By manufacturing a fictional expert, the company retained complete control over its corporate identity and corporate literature and avoided ceding power to an imported authority. Washburn Crosby Co.'s decision may have been informed by a famous legal case in which the Franklin Mills flour company was sued by Abigail Roberson for using her portrait without her permission in a flour advertisement. Initial verdicts supported Roberson, but they were overturned in 1902 by the Court of Appeal (Banner, 2011: 143–147). In 1924 the 'Betty Crocker School of the Air' radio show was voiced by actors and in 1936 a commercial artist was commissioned to give Betty a face. Her face changed periodically to reinforce, rather than undermine, her appeal to consumers (Figure 2.7). The Library of Congress holds more than 200 books catalogued with Crocker as the author, beginning with *Vitality Demands Energy: 109 Smart New Ways To Serve Bread, Our Outstanding Energy Food* of 1934. By 1945, *Fortune* magazine reported that Betty Crocker had been voted the most famous woman

1936   1955   1965   1969

1972   1980   1986   1996

Figure 2.7 The eight Betty Crocker official portraits.

in America after Eleanor Roosevelt (Marks, 2008: 115). From 1954 to 1976, 'The Betty Crocker Search for the All-American Homemaker of Tomorrow' television programme was broadcast (*Advertising Age*, 1999). Crocker's signature is still used today, as seen in the Betty Crocker spoon logo.

Betty Crocker's Guide to Easy Entertaining of 1959 is typical of the Crocker oeuvre in offering a blend of recipes and etiquette for home entertaining. The titular reference to 'easy entertaining' echoes Mary and Russel Wright's 'easier living' ([1950] 1954). The book balances recipes with advice about entertaining and therefore fits the domestic advice literature genre. The recipes do not exclusively employ General Mills Crocker products, such as flour, Betty Crocker Quick Bread Sticks and Bisquick (General Mills was formed in 1928 when Washburn-Crosby merged with 26 other mills). By offering quality editorial content within an advertorial blend, General Mills accrued prestige for the brand.

The cover of *Betty Crocker's Guide to Easy Entertaining* is drawn to resemble needlepoint and mass reproduced through colour photolithography (Figure 2.8). The needlepoint here is domestic in three ways – not only

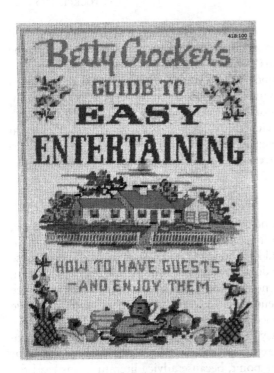

Figure 2.8 Cover, *Betty Crocker's Guide to Easy Entertaining: How to Have Guests – And Enjoy Them*, 1959.

is it a craft performed within the home, and typically applied to domestic soft furnishings and accessories, with associations of femininity and comfort, but also the imagery used here emphasises home comforts. It employs traditional legitimisation: a red-roofed home set in landscaped garden with a white picket fence is framed with a cartouche comprising a teapot and a roast turkey, a leg of ham, a pink iced celebration cake, pineapples – symbol of welcome – and other fruit, and the practical wire-binding is punctuated with rose motifs.

The book uses the Crocker signature and a possessive title, both exemplifying charismatic legitimisation. On the inside fly-leaf a letter from Betty begins: 'Dear Party Giver, Perhaps you are one of my many friends who has written asking about suggestions for special entertaining. Each week, I receive a growing number of letters asking for help.' 'Betty' explains of the book:

> In it are many of my own favorite party recipes, as well as anecdotes telling how my friends planned parties around specialities of their own. I hope you will enjoy them as much as I enjoy happy memories of the good times they bring back to me. Cordially, Betty Crocker.
>
> (Crocker, 1959: 2)

To enhance the verisimilitude, the letter is typeset in an irregularly spaced Courier-style typeface, as though written with a manual typewriter. On the title page, the small print reads '© Copyright 1959 by General Mills, Inc. [...] Betty Crocker is the trade name of General Mills.' Using textual and pictorial strategies, General Mills manufactured a mythical expert with friendly, familial appeal to soften its corporate identity (Marchand, 2001). Crocker's fictional status was key for General Mills, but it was apparently incidental to consumers. In order to engage with the Crocker myth, readers need to suspend their disbelief and overlook her fictional status.

Conclusion

Domestic advice books do not qualify as literature in the canonical sense; rather, they offer readers an imagined and improved future as 'a model to emulate and realize' (Eide and Knight, 1999: 531). The pleasure and purpose of domestic advice literature do not reside solely in its practical application, because advice may or may not be followed. While some books of advice employ ostensibly neutral encyclopaedic formats, other adopt narrative structures based on an imagined life story or a home tour as effective frameworks for the reader's fantasy engagement. These narrative formats make clear that questions about the extent to which the advice these books contain is followed therefore miss the point, because advice literature was read *for pleasure* (Mason and Meyers, 2001; Hollows, 2005). Advice literature is as useful in illuminating some of the ideals to which people in the past may have subscribed as it is unreliable as a source of information about how people lived. It can help historians to understand what people may have *thought*, but it cannot tell us what they *did*; advice literature exists between prescription and practice. Historians who wish to use domestic advice literature as a historical source material need techniques of both literary and visual analysis. Narrative analysis of domestic advice literature reveals textual and visual variance in relation to broader historical trends, which would be missed by analyses which look through advice texts for information about past actions. This chapter has shown how narrative analysis can reveal fault lines between the content and the structure of these books.

Part II

3 From *Decline and Fall* to *Rise and Sprawl*

Advice for the middle classes

Domestic advice literature is one channel through which class relations are articulated, negotiated and reinforced. As a discourse of social fluidity, it is prepared by those in possession of a particular form of knowledge for those who want it. Class is implicated in domestic advice literature, whether it is regarded as a tool for class conditioning, inculcating a mode of life that perpetuates the status quo and existing hegemony, or as tool of social mobility, in educating readers' tastes and consumption practices. Consumer societies do not only exchange goods, but also: 'the knowledge of how to discriminate within a world of goods is a further form of capital, this time symbolic, that generates equivalent or even more substantial rewards' (Chaney, 1996: 57; see also Simmel in Wolff, 1950; Baudrillard [1970] 1998: 75). Baudrillard recognised the function of glossy magazines such as *Maison Française* or *Mobilier et Decoration* in offering 'aristocratic models' which 'although they are high in "status" value, do impinge on sociological reality: they are not dream creations without commercial significance but, rather, models in the proper sense of the word' ([1968] 1996: 19). As we have seen in the previous chapters, while once aristocratic authors of conduct guides may have written with simple didacticism and unquestioned inherited authority – traditional legitimisation – after the Second World War, an author wishing to address matters of social distinction needed to gird her or his advice with humour and therefore to engage charismatic legitimisation. A material correlative is found in domestic advisors' promotion of emergent, modern design, which rewrote existing conceptions of status, luxury, comfort and hospitality and reified a new class formation based on entrepreneurial capitalism and class mobility. The title of this chapter uses phrases from Cannadine (1990) and Gunn and Bell (2003). Cannadine references two critiques of ruling power systems: Edward Gibbon's *Decline and Fall of the Roman Empire* (1776–1788) and Evelyn Waugh's novel *Decline and Fall* (1928), which heralded his successful career as a satirist of the aristocracy.

New order: the waning of aristocratic tastemakers and the growing middle classes

The aristocracy or social elite have long led taste, and aristocratic modes and manners have informed treatments of etiquette and home decoration alike in domestic advice literature. In post-industrial Western society, however, as the power base of aristocratic authority has diminished, so too has the role of aristocrats as tastemakers. Schlesinger ([1946] 1968) identified the decade from 1820 as pivotal in shifting American taste from a reliance on French and British courtly models to increasingly informal ideals of behaviour. Popular historian Russell Lynes has noted that Andrew Jackson's election as US president in 1828 heralded the '"age of the common man"', when 'Taste became everybody's business and not just the business of the cultured few' ([1949] 1980: 5). In Britain, the linkage of what American sociologist C. Wright Mills termed the 'power elite' ([1956] 1999) with the status elite and the wealth elite in the British aristocracy persisted until the 1870s (Cannadine, 1990: 18). Dispersal of the great estates between the 1880s and the 1930s unlocked the triangle of power, prestige and property (ibid. 343), while the sale of titles and honours allowed new money into high society. Plutocrats, such as the press barons Lord Beaverbrook and Lord Rothermere, satirised as Lord Copper (the name itself connoting plutocracy of a common kind) in Evelyn Waugh's novel *Scoop* (1938), were seen as undermining standards in public life. They 'lived far more loudly, lavishly, and luxuriously than the patricians, and [...] increasingly set the social tone' (Cannadine, 1990: 345). An influx into British high society of foreign brides, especially the tenfold rise in American peeresses between 1880 and 1914 (ibid. 347), functioned to relax conventions so that by 1938 Lady Londonderry complained that 'England has become Americanised' (Stewart, [1933] 1938: 251). The royal presentation of debutantes suffered a hiatus during the Second World War, to return for two more decades before ending for good (Lambert, 1989).

As the middle class expanded during the nineteenth and twentieth centuries, and presented new problems for advice writers to tackle, domestic advice books increasingly address the middle class reader on both sides of the Atlantic. However, neither class nor the readerships of domestic advice are clear-cut, of course, and advice ostensibly directed at middle-class readers will also have been read by the aspirational working class readers, and upper-middle-class readers in reduced circumstances following the Second World War. Since 1945, the authorial voice of domestic advice literature has been modified to enhance its accessibility and, as recommended entertainments and expenditure have contracted in scale and cost, material solutions have increasingly relied on modernist approaches to design.

Across British society, dissatisfaction with the austerity of war, the slow speed of post-war recovery (rationing remained in place in the UK until 1954) and increased taxes underpinned a Labour victory in the 1945 general election

(Kimber, 2010). Wartime coalition leader Winston Churchill unseated the Labour government in 1951; he resigned in 1955, but the Conservatives retained power until 1964, a fact which has been tied to middle-class aspiration by some contemporary commentators (Bedford and Mikes, 1965: 28). Thereafter, with the exception of one Conservative term from 1970, Labour retained power until 1979. From 1950 to 1980, the wealth of the top 5 per cent of British society declined from 70 per cent to 50 per cent (Edgell, 1993: 107, cites Atkinson, 1980 and HMSO, 1991). However, astute asset management led to legitimate tax avoidance and recovery in the 1950s, through schemes such as that administered by the National Trust to rescue the crumbling fabric of a displaced regime. Some aristocrats opened their homes directly to a paying public: cars and trains made the countryside and its stately homes accessible to city dwellers keen to encounter elite taste (Cannadine, 1990: 359). Aristocratic influence on taste was also maintained through involvement with expanding cultural institutions, such as major galleries and museums and the BBC, and civic engagements, such as mayoral roles and government committee work.

Class is historically contingent and industrialisation changed class structures. Max Weber's theory of status based on consumption better reflects the twentieth century situation, in which a class of white-collar workers expanded with the capitalist bureaucracy it serviced (1968; [1947] 1991; Coser, 1977: 228–230), than Marx's emphasis on production as determining class and his disregard of the middle class (which he believed would multiply to the extent that its labour was devalued and would then decline) (Marx and Engels, [1848] 1998). Marx's work is therefore largely of historical interest and, as communism declined, so post-Marxists pursued a Weberian culturalism focused on the subjective identities formed by discourse (Laclau and Mouffe, 1985: 84–85).

Definitions of classes are crucial in assessments of their growth, and relations between occupation and class are obviously complex. For example, a working class defined by manual labour declined in the UK 'from 75 per cent of the population in 1911 to [...] 64 per cent by 1961', but if defined more broadly as those who sold their labour – manual or otherwise – then it grew during that period (Hobsbawm, 1981: 17). Attempts to quantify class structures have attracted satire as well as criticism. While data have been marshalled to show that the proportion of white-collar workers in the UK rose from less than 14 per cent of the working population in 1911 to 43 per cent in 1981, and in America from 17.5 per cent in 1900 to 52 per cent in 1980 (Edgell, 1993, cites Routh, 1987 and Gilbert and Kahl, 1987), British sociologist John H. Goldthorpe *et al.* have pointed out that an inclusive definition of a new middle class as white-collar workers would include as much as 70 per cent of US society. Goldthorpe's own seven-part model of class (and later variants) rejects the proposition that affluent manual workers become culturally 'embourgeoisified' and therefore join a new middle class (Goldthorpe *et al.*, 1968–1969; see also Wright, 1979: 55). The issue was transatlantic: Goldthorpe's contemporary, the thirteenth Duke of Bedford wrote satirically in 1965:

> There are, if one comes to think of it, 623 different classes in Britain – definitions such as: lower-upper-middle class, upper-lower-upper-working class, middle-upper-middle-upper class are clear definitions for everyone to understand [...] But, whatever the class, snobbery is rampant in it.
>
> (Bedford and Mikes, 1965: 30)

Work on class structure is nevertheless revealing of historical change. Following C. Wright Mills' *White Collar: The American Middle Classes* (1951) and J. K. Galbraith's *The Affluent Society* ([1958] 1962: 279), which described a massively expanding 'New Class' that sought job satisfaction as well a financial reward from its white-collar labours (and which resonated on both sides of the Atlantic), Anthony Giddens (1981: 111–197) popularised the term 'new middle class' to describe the growing numbers of educated, white-collar salaried workers in the post-Second World War period to have enjoyed a relatively high degree of autonomy at work using technical or intellectual expertise. For Giddens, lifestyle choices have become increasingly central to the construction of social identities in 'high modernity' (1991: 50). In the USA and the UK alike, the twentieth century middle class was swelled by a newly affluent portion of the working class. Rather than being new, this newly enlarged middle class has constituted a new market for consumer goods, and for domestic advice, which disseminates ideal models of consumption.

If domestic advice has been associated primarily with a middle-class readership, the advice genre can, by extension, be seen as a middle-class cultural form. In May 1912, *Cassell's Saturday Journal* had lamented the lack of a clearly defined middle-class sensibility, complaining that it saw 'fiction dealing almost exclusively with the aristocracy' and pastimes which were 'a slavish and cheaper copy of the amusements of the upper ten' (*Cassell's Saturday Journal*, 1912; Waites, 1987: 50). Richard Ohmann acknowledged in his monumental study of magazines, *Selling Culture*, that 'the very profusion of etiquette books, their large sales, and the insistent flow of collateral advice in periodicals suggests a demand for and preoccupation with gentility among middle class people' (1996: 152–153). By 1941, George Orwell (1903–1950), who saw the upward and downward expansion of the middle class as rendering a Marxist social model of capitalists, proletarians and petit bourgeois redundant, noted that:

> in tastes, habits, manners and outlook the working class and the middle class are drawing together [...] the rich and the poor read the same books, and they also see the same films and listen to the same radio programmes. And the differences in their way of life have been diminished by the mass-production of cheap clothes and improvements in housing.
>
> (Orwell, [1941] 1962: 40–41)

A centralised education system with common curricula acted to reinforce a shared national consciousness across working- and middle-class constituencies (Bourke, 1994: 185), while new media disseminated education and entertainment across the population.

British television broadcasts had begun in 1936, but were abandoned for security reasons in 1939 (Robson, 2004), only resuming after the war. By 1947, 14,000 licences were held in Britain, but a rush to buy and rent televisions was prompted by the television broadcast of the coronation of Elizabeth II in 1953 (Andrews, 2012: 114), in which the head of the aristocracy performed a new kind of mass entertainment. As well as providing entertainment and information to an audience spanning the social classes, television broadcasting and ownership helped to create a more heterogeneous cultural environment in the UK, enhanced by the launch of commercial television channel ITV in 1955, and satellite broadcasts from the USA in 1962. By 1970, Britain followed the USA in terms of the penetration of television ownership, with 293 sets per 1,000 of the UK population and 412 per 1,000 in the USA. Adorno and Horkheimer (1979) and Marcuse (1972) theorised the role of the mass media in placating the working class:

> If the worker and his boss enjoy the same television programme and visit the same resort places, [...] then this assimilation indicates not the disappearance of class, but the extent to which the needs and satisfactions that serve the preservation of the Establishment are shared by the underlying population.
>
> (Marcuse, 1972: 21)

However, the 'Establishment' served by the changes in the mass media of the post-war period was not aristocratic but, increasingly, middle class. Bedford joked that 'Television is levelling out the speech barrier between classes and anybody who bothers about these things, can pick up the right accent and is free to speak like a BBC announcer. (Or an ITV one which is almost as good.)' (Bedford and Mikes, 1965: 10). Domestic advice literature bears evidence of a shift from following aristocratic tastemakers to the promotion of a pragmatic new aesthetic – modern design – driven initially by new elites but eventually adapted for the mainstream.

From traditional to charismatic legitimisation: the shifting voice of domestic advice literature

Domestic advice literature exemplifies the social and economic changes noted in a number of ways, one of which is a shift from traditional to charismatic legitimisation, seen most clearly in the advice books written by aristocratic authors. The use of humour, often satirical, and the re-presentation of the aristocrat as entertainer are both symptomatic of this shift, as shown in the writing of two British aristocrats, Nancy Mitford and the thirteenth Duke of Bedford. As Arditi has put it: 'instead of seeing etiquette books as mirroring the realities of a very small and obviously not representative minority of a population' they can be used 'as tools to study the emergence, structure and workings of what we might call the "cultures of dominance"' (1999: 42–44).

The Mitford family has been described by Cannadine as 'textbook declining gentry' who 'saw life and the world as one huge joke', but in Nancy Mitford's writing he finds 'a less naïve and more historically informed sense of aristocratic decline' (1991: 551, 550, 553). Mitford was one of six daughters of the second Lord Redesdale. Their brother, Tom Mitford, died at war in 1945 (Weisman, 1973). Deborah Mitford married Andrew Cavendish to become the Duchess of Devonshire. In 1950, Cavendish inherited Chatsworth and almost £7 million in death duties. One hundred and fifty staff members were made redundant, paintings were sold, and Hardwick Hall was passed to the National Trust. The Duke worked as a minister of state in the government of Harold Macmillan, his uncle (Anonymous, 2004). Another Mitford sister, Jessica, wrote seminal books on the US funeral industry (1963) and the prison service (1973). Unity Valkyrie (1914–1948) and Diana Mitford (1910–1996) were both fascists; Diana married Sir Oswald Mosley.

Diana Mosley's account of the genesis of her sister Nancy's book *Noblesse Oblige: An Enquiry into the Identifiable Characteristics of the English Aristocracy* (1956) noted that she 'preferred to be known as a novelist and a biographer rather than as an expert on etiquette or whatever it was' (Mosley, 1978: 1). The advice on language usage in *Noblesse Oblige* is given in the context of actions and environments to produce an ideal model of social engagement, therefore it functions in part as an etiquette book. Mitford's essay 'The English Aristocracy' was first published in the literary magazine *Encounter* – founded in 1953 under the editorship of Stephen Spender with contributors including C. P. Snow, Kingsley Amis and Sylvia Plath – and is based on an academic journal article, 'Linguistic Class Indicators in Present-Day English', which the author, Professor Alan Ross, had sent to Mitford following its publication the previous year (1954). In *Noblesse Oblige*, along with contributions by Evelyn Waugh, John Betjeman and Osbert Lancaster, Mitford dwells on distinctions between upper-class language usage and 'non-U' (non-us, non-upper-class) synonyms, such as 'looking glass'/'mirror', 'bag'/'handbag'. Mitford emphasises ease; upper-class linguistic sensibility is simple, and lacking in effortful formalities. In its refusal of superfluity, this approach represents a linguistic correlative for contemporary discussions about the less-is-more philosophy of modernist design.

In introducing the first American edition of *Noblesse Oblige*, Russell Lynes proposed that 'in some respects our Nancy Mitford is Emily Post, who has for many years occupied a quasi-official position as arbiter of U behavior in America' thereby underlining the etiquette function of Mitford's book and exemplifying the interplay between US and UK taste arbiters.

Lynes refers to Post's chapter 'The Words We Use and How to Choose Them' in *Etiquette: The Blue Book of Social Usage* in arguing that Post 'plays by the same rules as Miss Mitford' in preferring simple language to genteel formality ([1956] 1991). Lynes refers to the most recent edition of Post's book, but her list of approved 'Words, Phrases, and Pronunciation' appeared in the 1940 edition and therefore predates Mitford's essay by some years. Further, Lynes' comparison of Post and Mitford ignores the fact that Mitford's guidance was palliated with humour, whereas Post's was not (Post, 1940a: 87).

Writing from a US vantage point, Mosley criticised the publicity around *Noblesse Oblige* for erecting 'imaginary new barriers in England where there is a certain amount of rather absurd "class" feeling [...] the generation which has grown up since then would laugh at all these arbitrary and fiddling little rules' (1978: 2). While *Noblesse Oblige* may appear as wryly humorous social observation, the book is nevertheless an exemplar that was followed. As the Duke of Bedford jokily acknowledged:

> Anyone who cares may go out and buy that useful – indeed, indispensable – handbook by Professor Ross, Miss Mitford *et al.*, *Noblesse Oblige*, and learn the rules of U-speech. Since the publication of that renowned primer, many people would rather perish than [...] be seen wiping their mouths with a serviette: it must be a table-napkin and that's that. It is obvious from this that the secrets of the upper classes leak out and any person engaged in vulgar trade may pass as a peer of the realm if he is diligent in watching television and studying Miss Mitford's manual.
>
> (Bedford and Mikes, 1965: 10)

While some aspirational readers of *Noblesse Oblige* may have enjoyed seeing their own foibles satirised, other readers would have laughed at what they deemed to be non-U *outsiders*.

Osbert Lancaster illustrated *Noblesse Oblige* using humour to bolster an upper-class establishment threatened by the rise to dominance of a middle-class majority. In one image, a woman corrects the non-U title used in some graffiti: the humour here lies in the juxtaposition of propriety and vandalism (Figure 3.1). In another, 'Ancestors are no longer revered', furious-looking portraits are consigned to an unfurnished storage space; the humour is based on the subversion of dignity as the ancestors react to their reduced surroundings. The book's final image accompanies John Betjeman's poem 'How to Get On in Society', which satirises a pretentious hostess who calls dessert or pudding 'sweet' (Figure 3.2). The detailed rendering of the interior's fussy decoration – including a crinoline doll telephone cover – reminds us that as well as caricaturing English manners, Lancaster was known for his books on design and architecture, instigated by *Noblesse Oblige* contributor John Betjeman, who had himself

Should be addressed H.E.

Figure 3.1 'Should be addressed H. E.', drawing by Osbert Lancaster, in Nancy Mitford, ed., *Noblesse Oblige*, [1956] 2002.

written *Ghastly Good Taste* in 1933, a critique of contemporary architecture in favour of examples pre-dating the Arts and Crafts Movement (Betjeman's father had manufactured Arts and Crafts style fancy goods) (Mandler, 1997: 284). Lancaster's *Pillar to Post* ([1938] 1956) enjoyed an expanded second edition, and *Homes Sweet Homes* (1939), a history of interior design styles, was regularly reprinted.

Noblesse Oblige achieved intertextual influence in the UK. *Punch* magazine devoted an issue to the book – 'Snoblesse Oblige' – with a coat of arms on the cover and a book review section entirely composed of books by peers of the realm reviewed by other peers of the realm (Lynes, [1956] 1991: 38). Social monitor Debrett's reprised *Noblesse Oblige* with *U & Non-U Revisited* and used a similar conceit: the genealogical connections between each of the contributors are detailed in an appendix of family tree diagrams, prepared by Sir Iain Montcreiffe of that Ilk (Ross *et al.*, 1978: 28). In the same year (1978) Debrett's published Douglas Sutherland's *The English Gentleman*, also with a foreword by Montcreiffe and again illustrated with drawings by Timothy Jaques. These titles are the products of a small, dense network, but *Noblesse Oblige* was popular beyond the elite, and was bought by the very people it satirised.

Figure 3.2 Illustration facing John Betjeman's poem 'How to Get On in Society', drawing by Osbert Lancaster, in Nancy Mitford, ed., *Noblesse Oblige*, 2002 (1956).

Another writer whose work exemplifies a shift from traditional to charismatic legitimisation as a result of the decline of the aristocracy is the thirteenth Duke of Bedford. He grew up in relative poverty as a result of his father, Spinach Howland's, eccentricity. Following the Coldstream Guards during the Second World War, the Duke wrote for Lord Beaverbrook's *Sunday Express*. After his first wife had died, Bedford moved to South Africa as an apricot farmer, with his second wife Lydia. Aged 36, he returned to Woburn on his father's death (possibly suicide) to inherit his title, death duties of £4.5 million and a dilapidated Woburn Abbey. The Bedfords had not complied with inheritance tax laws requiring that an heir be assigned at least two years prior to death, so the deaths of the eleventh and twelfth Dukes in 1940 and 1953 respectively resulted in huge debts.

The thirteenth Duke defied his trustees by ignoring the National Trust's Country House Scheme for rescuing at-risk properties, because he felt that the National Trust reduced stately homes to dead museums. He renovated Woburn Abbey himself (Bedford and Mikes, 1965: 34–35; Bedford, 1971: 12). Between 1950 and 1965, 600 historic houses were opened to visitors. The thirteenth Duke was at the vanguard of this trend, along with the sixth Marquess of Bath,

Figure 3.3 'It is a tremendous pleasure sharing one's treasures with others', John, Duke of Bedford, *A Silver-Plated Spoon*, 1959.

who inherited debts and a diminished Longleat in 1946, and Lord Montague of Beaulieu, who inherited in 1951 (Bedford, 1959: 190–197, 202, 215). Woburn opened in 1955, attracting 180,000 visitors (Figure 3.3). The £300,000 per annum running costs were offset by profits; the turnover of the souvenir shop alone was more than half that amount. The Duke competed with Longleat's lions and Beaulieu's motor museum by offering a safari park and a funfair run by the Chipperfield family, thereby redefining the figure of the aristocratic heir as circus impresario. Bedford felt that his peers considered his showmanship to be vulgar and he, in turn, satirised the desultory manner in which fellow aristocrats engaged with the public: 'As long as you perfunctorily permit them to look at some old cobwebs and ramshackle furniture in uncleaned rooms, and with a great deal of condescension, you are not doing anything substantially wrong' (Bedford and Mikes, 1965: 36). Bedford was radical in admitting that he 'enjoy[ed] being a showman and [tried] to be a successful one' (ibid. 87).

The thirteenth Duke readily commoditised his life. He appeared on television, allowed a nudist camp in his grounds, hired himself out as a dinner companion and raffled the services of his butler, James Boyd, as a prize in an American competition: 'The American press turned the whole thing into a circus. The winner's house was invaded by so many camera-men and newspaper reporters [...] that he was unable to carry out his normal duties at all' (Bedford, 1959: 220–221). Bedford's books catered to public interest in his family on both sides of the Atlantic. His autobiography, *A Silver-Plated Spoon* (1959) revealed relative poverty underlying superficial grandeur at Woburn. In the year following its publication, visitors to Woburn reached 431,000 (Cannadine, 1990: 647). It was followed by *The Duke of Bedford's Book of Snobs* (1965), an edited volume of the diaries and letters of his grandmother, Mary, Duchess of Bedford (1968), and *How to Run a Stately Home* (1971).

The Duke of Bedford's Book of Snobs, written 'in collaboration with George Mikes', is a satirical guide to being 'a successful snob' and climbing 'the social ladder' (1965: 8). It was published by Peter Owen, who had set up his own publishing house in 1951 using an RAF paper quota, having served in the Second World War. In the 1960s, Owen successfully published books by celebrity authors, including Yoko Ono, Tennessee Williams, Tariq Ali and Anais Nin, many of which were designed by Keith Cunningham, with covers of economical and arresting graphic strength (Walsh, 2001: 9; Dempsey, 2001), including that for *Bedford's Book of Snobs*. Bedford proposes that only appearances matter, because 'appearance is reality' (Bedford and Mikes, 1965: 21). The difficulty of being a snob is attributed to:

> Marksism. Not Marxism, which has caused but few considerable changes in our ways of thinking and life [...] I have the Marks family – the active and influential half of Marks & Spencer, and first of all the late Lord Marks (formerly Sir, formerly Mr. Simon Marks) – in mind.
>
> (Bedford and Mikes, 1965: 8)

The raw material of one's contempt

Figure 3.4 'The Raw Material of One's Contempt', by Nicolas Bentley, in John, Duke of Bedford *The Duke of Bedford's Book of Snobs*, London: Peter Owen, 1965.

Bedford's advice that suits 'must be made to measure. Ready-made suits will not help you in the snobocratic world' (ibid. 66) is mirrored in Nicolas Bentley's illustration 'The raw material of one's contempt', featuring a man smoking a pipe, wearing a flat cap, shirt and tie, with pens in his top pocket and a suitcase (Figure 3.4).

In his twelve drawings for *Snobs*, Nicolas Bentley (1907–1978) manipulates social hierarchy through techniques such as bathos, scale and the reversal of conventional hierarchy. Bentley's servants are typically more correct than the snobs they serve. 'On House-Parties' advises guests to avoid general embarrassment by never asking hired help taxing questions to which they may not know the answers (ibid. 109). This empathy is reflected in Nicolas Bentley's didactic drawing 'Do not make a joke of the hired help', which juxtaposes laughing guests with the stoic misery of a long-suffering serving man who is unable to defend himself (Figure 3.5). Elsewhere, a doorman turns away an arriving matron in fur and evening dress telling her 'A tiara is never worn in a hotel', and a discussion of fish knives as *nouveau riche* (they

Do not make
a joke of the
hired help

Figure 3.5 'Do not make a joke of the hired help', by Nicolas Bentley, in John, Duke of
Bedford *The Duke of Bedford's Book of Snobs*, London: Peter Owen, 1965.

were a Victorian introduction) is illustrated with a reappropriation of Macbeth's dagger speech, in which a man in shrinks away from an airborne fish knife, observed by a dismayed servant. Bentley's line drawings emphasise character and interaction and often depend on captioning for their humour. Malcolm Muggeridge, editor of *Punch* from 1953 to 1957, noted that social historians would 'find Bentley's drawings invaluable' (1995).

Trained at Evelyn Waugh's alma mater, Heatherley's School of Art in Chelsea, Bentley forged a reputation for economical satirical wit both as an advice writer and regular illustrator of advice. Son of the novelist and *Daily Telegraph* journalist E. C. Bentley and godson of the writer G. K. Chesterton, Bentley considered illustration as a sideline to his writing. He illustrated sixty books, some self-authored (*The Week-End Wants of a Guest, The Week-End Worries of a Hostess*) or written by his father and others, ranging from Jerrard Tickell's *Gentlewomen Aim to Please*, a collection of excerpts edited from Victorian etiquette books (all 1938) to a 1972 edition of T. S. Eliot's *Old Possum's Book of Practical Cats*. During the Second World War, Bentley deputy-directed the Home Intelligence Unit and edited Ministry of Information publications. Afterwards, he was briefly a clown, and then joined Shell's advertising department, where he worked with Rex Whistler, Peter Quennell, Edward Ardizzone and Sir John Betjemen. He later worked as a cartoonist for the *Daily Mail* and *Private Eye*, wrote thrillers, directed a publishing house set up by André Deutsch and was an editor at Nelsons (Muggeridge, 1995; Bentley, 1960).

André Deutsch published Bedford's later book *How to Run a Stately Home* (1971). Bedford and Mikes adopt the literary form of a 'How-to' book for what is effectively autobiography: 'If you are about to open your stately home to the public you would be mad not to read it first. The rest of us can settle for the entertainment offered by the Duke's tips and revelations'. The book describes how Lydia, Duchess of Bedford, had redecorated Woburn, replacing 'all the heavy Victorian and Edwardian pieces' with 'French and Georgian' ones: 'The heavy, dead atmosphere I recalled from my first visits in the thirties had completely gone. It was as if someone had waved a magic wand' (Bedford, 1971: 204). When they opened their doors to visitors, historic houses functioned, like domestic advice literature, to shape taste. Bedford recalls a visitor to Woburn responding to the question of what she liked most about a particular room:

> "The lino. I like it very much indeed. It's exactly what I want for my kitchen." I was pleased. A Stately Home may not be an Ideal Home but it is comforting to learn that at least some people regard the exhibits as they do those in an Ideal Home Exhibition [...] The Ming dynasty is all right, but what they really want to know is what soap you use and where you bought your curtains and vacuum cleaner.
>
> (Bedford, 1971: 49, 50)

Are only interested in the commonplace things

Figure 3.6 'Are only interested in the commonplace things', by ffolkes, in John, Duke of Bedford *How to Run a Stately Home*, 1971.

This sentiment is reflected in a cartoon by ffolkes in which visitors ignore the family portraits displayed in pride of place on the staircase in favour of the contents of the under-stairs cupboard (Figure 3.6).

Social historian Peter Mandler has argued that a culture of visiting country houses, which emerged in a limited way in the eighteenth century and expanded with a nineteenth-century taste for historicism, collapsed into 'near total indifference' in the 1920s and 1930s as part of a rejection of aristocratic leadership and the trappings of elite privilege (1997: 254). Only once the aristocracy 'had been stripped of its political power and a great deal of its economic might' did the interwar and post-war public begin to value country houses, and their owners began to exploit them (ibid. 4–5). Evelyn Waugh's novels, including *Decline and Fall* (1928) and *Brideshead Revisited* (1945), exemplify this shift, as does Noel Coward's parody of Felicia Hemans' ([1827] 2000) poem: 'The stately homes of England we proudly represent / We only keep them up for Americans to rent' in his *Operette* (1938). *Country Life* magazine's illustrated series 'Country Homes and Gardens Old and New', which ran from the magazine's inception in 1897 to the end of the twentieth century, was instrumental in creating a viewing public for country homes, and – through its dependency on advertising from estate agents Knight Frank and Rutley – a buying public, too (Mandler, 1997: 148).

In 1974, the Duke of Bedford contributed to *The Destruction of the Country House*, a catalogue prepared by Roy Strong to accompany his campaigning Victoria and Albert Museum exhibition, which featured a litany of destroyed houses played on a sound loop (Strong *et al.*, 1974). In the peak year, 1955, a house was 'lost' every five days, but Giles Worsley, ex-editor of *Country Life*, has drawn on his magazine's 'Country Homes and Gardens Old and New' series to provide a more qualified survey of the losses of the 1950s and 1960s, noting that attrition rates then were average for the century, with accidental fires and economical asset management as contributing factors (Worsley, 2002). Roy Strong's sensibility, both elegiac and alarmist, continues in the work of English Heritage and also the National Trust, which is increasingly conserving non-elite buildings, such as back-to-back housing in Birmingham. This trend is echoed in television projects such as Endemol's *Restoration* (2003–2009) and various spin-offs, in which viewers voted to support one of a range of heritage projects, including a public swimming baths in Manchester in 2003 and a grammar school near Birmingham in 2004. National Trust visitor figures have risen from '3 million in 1970, to 6 million in 1980', and 10–11 million during the 1990s (Lloyd, 1999) to 17.7 million in 2010/11 (Trustees of the National Trust, 2011).

The thirteenth Duke of Bedford survived the economic conditions underlying the decline of the aristocracy and secured private ownership of his estate by combining traditional legitimisation with charismatic legitimisation. He made entertainment out of the material and personal culture of aristocracy, reinventing himself as an entertainer and opening his home to a paying public. His etiquette book, *The Duke of Bedford's Book of Snobs*, communicated an ideology of aristocratic dominance with flashes of radicalism and complacent humour. His homemaking book, *How to Run a Stately Home*, eschewed practical guidance and humorously reasserted the right of the landed gentry to their estates: 'People often ask me [...]: do I know that being a Duke is an anachronism? Yes, I know that [...] I shall never be found in the forefront of any revolutionary movement dedicated to the abolition of the peerage' (Bedford and Mikes, 1965: 26).

Bedford's books form part of a group of humorous etiquette books preoccupied with class, examples of which appeared during the period of Conservative government from 1979 to 1997, including *Viviana Ventura's Guide to Social Climbing* (1983) and Simon Brett's *Bad Form or How Not to Get Invited Back* (1984). Ultimately, Bedford's role as aristocratic, and charismatic, mass entertainer was based on his commitment to the status quo. In 1974, at the age of 57, the thirteenth Duke delegated the upkeep of Woburn to his son Robin, the Marquess of Tavistock, and emigrated again, this time with his third wife. He died in Mexico in October 2002 aged 85

(BBC News, 2002; Bedford, 1959: [1974] 1975). The fourteenth Duke continued his father's role as a charismatic, aristocratic entertainer by participating with his wife and family in the production of a BBC 2 documentary, *Country House* (Tiger Aspect, 1999–2002). He died the following year and Tiger Aspect ceased filming at Woburn.

Modernism and social theories of class and consumption

We have seen the impact of a lessening of aristocratic authority – in response to social and economic changes – on the voice of domestic advice literature, as traditional legitimisation ceded to a humorous, satirical form of charismatic legitimisation. Now we turn to an associated shift in taste in material goods, from traditional legitimisation expressed in the materials and aesthetics of luxury, to acceptance of modernism in design, legitimised, more or less rationally, for its qualities of hygiene, ease and affordability. Modernism may have been promoted as classless, but in fact it functioned to overturn aristocratic domestic practices and the expression of such values as luxury, status, comfort and hospitality and may therefore be viewed as a class token which ushered in a new set of class values. A comparison of the work of two social theorists throws light on the impact of modernism in the social home.

In *The Presentation of Self in Everyday Life* (1959), US sociologist Erving Goffman drew on his fieldwork in Scotland to develop a dramaturgical metaphor in which spaces and behaviours are divided into front and backstage regions, so that people can maintain conspicuous consumption appropriate to status and setting and remove other aspects of life from scrutiny, thereby avoiding embarrassment. In this, it bears comparison with Elias's 1936 analysis of court society. For Goffman, the social front comprises the 'setting', 'involving furniture, decor, physical layout, and other background items which supply the scenery and stage props for the spate of human action played out before, within, or upon it' and the 'personal front' composed of 'appearance', gesture, clothing, insignia and 'manner' ([1959] 1990: 32), while the backstage is where illusions are devised and stored and 'costumes and other types of personal front are adjusted and maintained' ([1959] 1990: 125). Following Veblen, Goffman noted that people might be used as props, such as footmen, wives displaying a husband's wealth, and executives whose work depends upon the fact that they *look* like executives (ibid. 55, 107; Chartier, 1988: 76). For Goffman, material objects are only interesting as 'sign equipment' for performances ([1959] 1990: 53, 63, 236–239; 1971: 327–328; Collins, 1988: 51). Sign equipment is usually generalised and signifies differently according to setting – for example, a suit that may be worn to work and also for socialising – but sometimes it is specific to one task, such as a wedding dress ([1959] 1990: 39). Goffman recognised the most important pieces of sign equipment as those associated with social class, such as status symbols or expressions of material wealth, but for him, 'a status, a position, a social place is not a material thing to be possessed and then displayed, it is a pattern of appropriate conduct, coherent, embellished, and well-articulated' (ibid. 81).

For Goffman, 'decorous behaviour' means 'showing respect for the region and setting', the audience, and class context (ibid. 111). He argued that people gear their behaviour towards perceived ideals of behaviour, accepting that 'One of the richest sources of data on the presentation of idealized performances is the literature on social mobility' (ibid. 45). Yet he also distinguished between the symbolic value ascribed to 'an act performed unthinkingly under the invisible guide of familiarity and habit, and the same act, or an imitation of it, performed with conscious attention to detail and self-conscious attention to effect'. He concluded that the 'style and manners of one class are [...] psychologically ill-suited to those whose life experiences took place in another class' (ibid. 300). In this statement, there is little place for social mobility. Goffman's 1959 performance metaphor is helpful for understanding social interaction in the home and, by extension, the representations found in domestic advice literature, but – like Elias's 1936 analysis of court society – it is best suited to a pre-war and interwar situation of clearly demarcated upstairs–downstairs divisions in which labour is hidden from guests and performed by staff backstage, rather than a postwar modernist domesticity of flexible layouts accessible to a newly enlarged middle class of smaller means.

Based on research conducted in France in 1963 and 1967–1968, Pierre Bourdieu's 1979 book *Distinction* ([1979] 1986) effectively collapses Goffman's 1959 notion of front and backstage regions. Bourdieu moves the focus from conspicuous consumption to inconspicuous consumption and the aestheticication of everyday life (ibid. 100). Rather than representing a difference between France and the UK and USA, Bourdieu's analysis is applicable in all of those regions and better reflects domestic advice of the second half of the twentieth century than Goffman's nevertheless useful model. Bourdieu articulates a shift which underpins acceptance of modernism in the home, in which utility becomes a taste choice and where even the backstage is open for entertaining and the expression of hospitality and status.

Bourdieu proposed that goods are converted into signs (for example, of distinction or vulgarity) which are 'perceived relationally': 'A class is defined as much by its [...] consumption – which need not be conspicuous in order to be symbolic' as its 'position in the relations of production (even if it is true that the latter governs the former)' (ibid. 483). Communication through commodities is subtly powerful: 'Symbolic capital functions to mask the economic domination of the dominant class' (Bourdieu, [1972] 1977: 197; Calhoun *et al.*, 1993: 5). Or, as neo-Marxist Frederic Jameson has put it: 'For a society that wants to forget about class [...] reification [...] is very functional indeed' (1991: 315). Bourdieu extended the notion of the 'habitus' (inherited assumptions) proposed by Elias, arguing that taste is determined by habitus, which contributes to the generative reproduction of social classes. People endowed with cultural capital view almost every action of daily life as relevant to the judgement of an individual's position within a class 'fraction' ([1979] 1986: 13). This 'aesthetic disposition' depends on a bourgeois situation characterised by a lack of 'economic necessity' and 'practical urgencies' (ibid. 54). Bourdieu has described this function in experiential terms:

> If a group's whole lifestyle can be read off from the style it adopts in furnishing or clothing, this is not only because these properties are the objectification of the economic and cultural necessity which determined their selection, but also because the social relations objectified in familiar objects, in their luxury or poverty, their 'distinction' or 'vulgarity', their 'beauty' or 'ugliness', impress themselves through bodily experiences which may be as profoundly unconscious as the quiet caress of beige carpets or the thin clamminess of tattered, garish linoleum, the harsh smell of bleach or perfumes as imperceptible as a negative scent. Every interior expresses, in its own language, the present and even past state of its occupants, bespeaking the elegant self-assurance of inherited wealth, the flashy arrogance of the nouveaux riches, the discreet shabbiness of the poor and the gilded shabbiness of 'poor relations' striving to live beyond their means.
>
> (Bourdieu, [1979] 1986: 77)

Bourdieu replaces Thorstein Veblen's influential concept of 'conspicuous consumption' with a corporeal understanding of inconspicuous consumption. Veblen's *The Theory of the Leisure Class* ([1899] 1970) was criticised by Elias as subjectively bourgeois ([1969] 1983: 67), while more recently Chris Rojek (2000) has critiqued Veblen's notion of a passive working class as being unsuited to the twentieth century. Bourdieu saw trends in, for example, modernist utility not solely as the product of economic or practical necessity but rather as exemplifying the need for distinction. Appreciation of the beauty of utility, which Bourdieu associated with refined and privileged taste, has enabled home entertaining to take place in regions previously designated as backstage, such as the kitchen. Modernism had been promoted by designers and domestic advisors decades earlier, although it had then only been adopted by an elite group of early adopters. However, during the period of Bourdieu's fieldwork, modernist design continued to be recommended by domestic advisors in the form of flexible dining rooms and living room layouts and kitchens designed for social interaction. These spaces brought about an associated reordering of public parts of the home, as suitable for extra-familial entertaining and private regions.

Bourdieu supports his qualitative statements with quantitative data in *Distinction*, yet his descriptions are static in that they do not account for the fact that beige carpets, elegance and 'shabbiness' meant different things in 1970 than they do today, and those meanings will change again in future. He asserts that there is:

> nothing more alien to working-class women than the typically bourgeois idea of making each object in the home the occasion for an aesthetic choice, of extending the intention of harmony or beauty even into the bathroom or kitchen, places strictly defined by their function, or of involving specifically aesthetic criteria in the choice of a saucepan or cupboard.
>
> (Bourdieu, [1979] 1986: 379)

The reach of lifestyle media in Western society today is such that even those living on the smallest of means are aware of the possibility of expressing taste through everyday domestic objects. Goffman and Bourdieu each provide a static analysis which does not account for shifts in taste, and they are each ultimately pessimistic about the efficacy of taste specialists and didactic discourses such as domestic advice literature, insisting that 'the ordinary choices of everyday existence, such as furniture, clothing or cooking' are derived from 'profoundly unconscious' 'bodily experiences', and reveal:

> deep-rooted and long-standing dispositions because, lying outside the scope of the educational system, they have to be confronted, as it were, by naked taste, without any explicit prescription or proscription, other than from semi-legitimate legitimising agencies such as women's weeklies or 'ideal home' magazines.
>
> (Bourdieu, [1979] 1986: 77)

The 'manner of acquisition' of taste is key here: established members of the middle class would not typically have used advice literature, gathering social knowledge through experiential, familial channels instead. The resultant 'ease' could never be matched by formal book learning, which produced only pedantry:

> The language of rules and models, which seems tolerable when applied to 'alien' practices, ceases to convince as soon as one considers the practical mastery of the symbolism of social interaction – tact, dexterity, or savoir-faire – presupposed by the most everyday games of sociability
>
> (Bourdieu, [1972] 1977: 10)

Here Bourdieu echoes the suspicions of a dominant class about attempts by other to emulate them, but when viewed from the perspective of a working-class or middle-class subject, with an emphasis on correctness rather than ease, advice literature can be seen as an effective tool of self-transformation.

Bourdieu's association of taste and class fractions is too schematic and static to accommodate the increasingly fluid social mobility and more fragmented and rapid fashion markets of the late twentieth century.

Designers, and the domestic advisors who have mediated their work to a consuming public, identified a market composed of a newly enlarged middle class and working-class aspirants in advance of the sociologists who sought to explain social structure. They have been attentive to social changes and have promoted material solutions centred on modernist design presented as desirable in terms of economy and accessibility, flexibility and informality, practicality and utility and also elegance and style. Domestic advice writers have been in the vanguard of encouraging consumers to accept new conceptions of hospitality, comfort and status display necessitated by the introduction of modern design into the home.

Introducing modern design: 'enforced familiarity with this rugged décor'

Domestic advice writers working before the mid-1930s typically adapted aristocratic taste and manners for a broader public, with the exception of the rationalist strain of scientism seen in books influenced by home economics. However, domestic advice books bear evidence of a shift in the 1930s, as a newly enlarged middle class which lacked the resources to entertain on an upper-class scale required more dedicated advice. Hospitality, as represented in domestic advice literature, requires social (behavioural) and material expressions of one's own status and of respect for guests through displays of luxury and, even, excess. The problem of how to express hospitality using a *simple* and *economical* aesthetic taxed authors of etiquette, home-making and home decoration guides alike. Modernist design constituted a challenge to existing models of domesticity, and home entertaining especially. Faced with the simultaneous challenges of catering to a newly enlarged middle class and incorporating modernist design, domestic advice writers on both sides of the Atlantic followed designers in making the latter the answer to the former, and were thus in the vanguard of attempts to reconcile the newly enlarged middle class public to modernist design. In Britain, modernist design communicated an ideology of progress in tune with post-war social reform. Like modernist designers and architects, populist domestic design writers disseminated progressive modernist strategies for living, even while they necessarily catered to the conservatism of the genre and of their audience.

Modernism as it developed in continental Europe during the first two decades of the twentieth century was largely ignored or rejected in Britain by all but a minority, until after the Second World War, even though it was influenced by the British Arts and Crafts Movement's preference for honesty in the use of materials, simplicity and utility. Paul Greenhalgh has interpreted a renewed interest in antiques from 'around

1890' as a response to a declining empire (1995: 114–115) and by 1915, a 'craft ethic' exemplified by the work of the Design and Industries Association and the Omega workshops provided solace for a perceived influx of foreign influences. For Greenhalgh, British modernism was a 'structured compromise' based on 'the bringing together of progressive form with regressive content' in an 'ideological climate which rendered any other approach to modernism economically, politically, and even socially unacceptable' (ibid. 136). Martin Wiener finds another British compromise in 'a "gentrified" bourgeois culture' and 'the rooting of pseudo-aristocratic attitudes and values in upper-middle-class educated opinion', which 'shaped an unfavourable context for economic endeavour' and created a 'culture of containment': 'A variety of modern British practices that has served to humanize urban industrial society – new towns and green belts, the love of gardening, even a wariness of most modern architecture – owes a debt to this social compromise' (1981: 7–10). The failure of housing developments, such as the 1935 Lescaze houses at Churston in Devon, showed that the British middle class still upheld a cottage ideal in preference to modernism. In opening the Small House Exhibition at the RIBA in 1938, Ellen Wilkinson MP complained that 'our only general feeling is that if ever we are going to be bombed, I hope that the enemy will bomb the right things' (Jeremiah, 2000: 86–88).

Domestic advisors worked to reconcile the general public to modernism on both sides of the Atlantic. Christopher Morley notes that, in a broadcast for NBC's General Electric Hour in 1932, Norman Bel Geddes:

> reminds us of the basic truth that efficiency of design always brings beauty and simplicity with it. That is the same truth that Emily Post has always emphasized in her very civilized talks and articles – that the best taste and the best manners are of simplicity adapted to a purpose.
>
> (Morley, 1932)

The channels of influence worked both ways. Sarah Leavitt has noted the influence of Le Corbusier, a Swiss architect working in France, in US domestic advice books. Anna Hong Rutt's *Home Furnishing* of 1935 describes the home as the 'machine in which we live', and in the *Better Homes Manual* of 1931, *Good Furnishing and Decorating* magazine contributor C. R. Richards writes: 'Le Corbusier says [...] that the rational perfection and precise determination of machine products made solely for functional ends creates in them a quality which gives them a style. I doubt that this is the final word' (1931: 447). Leavitt suggests that American domestic advisors promoted modernism – interpreted, chiefly, as the removal of bric-a-brac – even though they were aware that many readers had found Victorian design 'emotionally and aesthetically satisfying' and 'though women certainly read their advice, they ignored it much of the time and continued to decorate their houses with bows and figurines' (2002: 104, 121).

The softening of modern design's functionalism for wider tastes via a 'structured compromise' is a familiar theme in the history of the twentieth-century domestic interior (Sparke, 1995). Less explored, however, is the consistency of linguistic and visual strategies used by domestic advisors to persuade readers of the attractions of modernist design for the home: modern or contemporary design is economical, practical, easy to maintain and informal. Derek Patmore's *Modern Furnishing and Decoration* (1934) exemplifies several of these strategies. First, modernist design was presented as something easily placed alongside earlier styles of furniture. The furniture industry had a vested interest in promoting the mixing of styles of different periods in order to maintain demand for existing models as well as to stimulate demand for new ones. Patmore's book includes a plate 'Modernity in a period panelled room' in which Edward McKnight Kauffer's decorative panel 'Heraldry' and a modern rug inhabit an 'otherwise period scheme' (1934: plate XV). Second, modernist design was imbued with connotations of luxury, style and glamour akin to the 'moderne' style of 1930s Hollywood films. Patmore includes the 1934 'Room from the House of Tomorrow', with a lacquered ceiling, a pink leather three-piece suite and a glass wall, in which luxurious materials render spare forms acceptable.

Third, modernist design has been anthropomorphised through association with a range of desirable personal qualities, thereby appealing to readers keen to attract such characteristics for themselves. In 'The Contemporary Style in Silver', Mappin & Webb tableware is praised for its 'graceful simplicity'. 'Dignity in the Entrance Hall', showing a metal balustrade in a virtually empty stone-flagged hall, exemplifies the association of understatement in design and good manners (Patmore, 1934: plate XIX). Recalling C. R. Mackintosh's designs of 1902–1903 and Syrie Maugham's off-white interiors of the late 1920s and early 1930s, an all-white room designed by Arundell Clarke of London is relieved of its 'severity' through the placement of 'coloured rugs and flowers' (Patmore, 1934: plate III). This tendency persists: Bourdieu notes respondents describing their ideal homes as 'harmonious' and 'imaginative' (Bourdieu [1979] 1986: 248).

Fourth, Patmore eulogises the 'Oriental' practice of 'elimination' in decoration to produce flexible, economical and ostensibly practical designs. Flexibility was emphasised in the promotion of modernist design, perhaps to offset consumer anxiety about investing in novel styles rather than familiar reproductions. The heart of the home, the hearth, is literally sidelined as readers are invited to 'note the ingenious manner in which the copper Sun-ray electric fire has been built into one side of the settee' (Patmore, 1934: plate XVI). Anthony Bertram, too, promoted modernism for its flexibility, practicality and homeliness. Describing parlours – used sparingly for the most formal occasions – as 'those dreary dead rooms reserved for company', Bertram argues:

Surely it is better to have a large friendly family room in daily use, with a dining table at one end and easy chairs and so on at the other. The space can be even further freed by having a dining table that folds away, of which there are now several designs available.

(Bertram, 1938: 73)

The living room could be used for everyday family life, for entertaining, and – in due course – for the new, shared, family experience of watching television.

Margaret Merivale's *Furnishing the Small Home* of 1938 begins – like the example from Betty Crocker already discussed – with a letter to the reader:

Dear Virginia, You once complained to me that you had been unable to find a book which would help you when you were furnishing your small home. You said they were all too highbrow and technical; that they showed too ambitious ideas and were intended for people with more money to spend than you had; and that you were more or less bewildered by the expert jargon with which most of them were filled. Most of these criticisms are, I hope, overcome in this book of mine [which is] intended for you and all those who, like you, have gazed into the windows of furnishing stores and found it a problem to select all the things which will go towards making a home.

(Merivale, [1938] 1944: 5)

Merivale's solution to her reader, Virginia's, complaint is fashionable, modernist design. She presents the war as beneficial for introducing new design possibilities in, for example, plastics.

In just the same way that you would not think for one moment of wearing a hat bought fifty years ago, you must not collect Victorian atrocities if you are furnishing a modern home. [...] I want you to see what is of our own times in furniture and accessories, and to consider their merits in the light of to-day's requirements. Gone are all the scrolls and carvings of years ago, and many of the nooks and crannies which required finger-nail dusting.

(Merivale [1938] 1944: 5)

The 1944 edition has the following postscript: 'My letter to you was written in the spacious days of peace, and now we are at war your choice is temporarily much more limited' (Merivale, [1938] 1944: 15). In *Homes Sweet Homes* (1939), Osbert Lancaster ends his satiric history of decorative styles with the 'Even More Functional':

When Monsieur Le Corbusier first propounded his theory of the house as *une machine à habiter* it may be doubted whether he foresaw the exact form in which it would be translated into fact. That other well-known architectural authority, Herr Hitler, must claim the credit for recent compliance on the part of the insular British with the extreme dictates of the continental functionalists. [In the bomb shelter] exclusive reliance is placed on the inherent qualities of corrugated iron and unbleached canvas. Whether or not enforced familiarity with this rugged décor over a prolonged period will in fact have any very marked effect on the average person's taste in interior decoration one cannot at the moment pretend to say.

(Lancaster, 1939: 78)

Figure 3.7 Utility B2 metal bedstead, introduced May 1945.

Figure 3.8 Oak occasional table model no. 2060, Cotswold Range, Utility Furniture.

The Second World War Utility Furniture Scheme placed modernist design in the home as a matter of patriotic necessity. It paired economical use of materials with simple forms which followed function, to use Louis Sullivan's famous edict. Its structured compromise ranged from Utility bedsteads made of metal tubing (Figure 3.7) showing the influence of continental modernist design (specifically Marcel Breuer's Wassily chair of 1925–1926), to the Arts and Crafts influenced 'Cotswold' range (Figure 3.8), named after a region of middle England noted for the 'chocolate box' beauty that was fought for in the two World Wars (Andrews, 2012: 86) and in which William Morris had been a notable resident, at Kelmscott Manor.

Modernism and UK post-war design reform: 'discriminate among simple things'

In post-war Britain, professional debates about new and appropriate building styles and retailers' initiatives to mediate design principles to customers, such as the Good Furniture Group, were accompanied by government-generated efforts to educate public taste (MacCarthy, 1972: 110). Set up in 1944 by the Board of Trade to improve British design for industry, the Council of Industrial Design (CoID) directed many of its efforts at consumers, such as the *Britain Can Make It* exhibition of 1946 (Bullivant, 1986) and the Festival of Britain of 1951. Judy Attfield has suggested that the 'astringent avant-garde "modern" style of the interwar period' was, by the 1950s, 'regarded as elitist and out of date'. It had been succeeded by the populist 'contemporary' style, known as 'Festival' style during and after the 1951 Festival of Britain (Attfield, 1997: 269; Oram, 2004). CoID produced domestic advice books, including Patricia Owen's *Furnishing to Fit the Family* of 1946 and the didactic series 'The Things We See' (1946–1950), suggested by CoID to the publishers Penguin. The third title in the series, Gordon Russell's *Furniture* (1947), offers a chronological history which includes Russell's own work alongside that of Marcel Breuer and, in a section entitled 'What of the Future?', the work of Luciano Ercolani, Fritz Hansen and Charles Eames, among others. Alvar Aalto is praised, as is, of course, 'Utility Furniture: A Social Experiment'. Other books in the series are similarly defined by media, such as *Houses* (Brett, 1947) and *Pottery and Glass* (Hollowood, 1947), but the first title, Alan Jarvis's *The Things We See: Indoors and Out* (1946), concerns aesthetics in the broadest sense.

In *The Things We See: Indoors and Out*, Jarvis compares photographs of a tree and an electricity pylon to show that 'man can create beauty'. Jarvis contributes to two discursive strands in the literature of design. First, a tradition of teaching consumers to distinguish between good and bad, which extends back to nineteenth-century design reform as exemplified by Pugin's *True Principles* (1841) and Henry Cole's chamber of horrors at the

South Kensington Museum. Second, in isolating for scrutiny examples of engineering and scientific instruments as aesthetically pleasing, Jarvis follows John Cotton Dana's design promotion at the Newark Museum (Maffei, 2000; Shales, 2010) and Philip Johnson's work at New York's Museum of Modern Art (Museum of Modern Art, [1934] 1994).

Jarvis (1946: 6–7) juxtaposes images of cakes and bread to illustrate the superiority of 'a mature taste in either food or furnishings [which] would be made sick by too much sweetness. The other mark of a mature taste is the capacity to discriminate among simple things'. A spread entitled 'Non-Design' lambasts 'artistically dishonest' 'pseudo-design' and the 'copying of old forms to suit new functions', showing as examples a candle bracket adapted for electricity, an ancient chair in rustless metal, a 'useless' plastic model ship and teapots shaped like a cottage and a car (ibid. 60–61). The caption to a pair of photographs showing a woman wearing make-up and two painted ewers reads: 'By vulgarity we mean just this kind of coarseness of body, cheapness of ornament, and insensitive application of make-up. The parallel in the case of pottery is exact, in its florid shape and crude cosmetic decoration' (ibid. 47) (Figure 3.9). The term 'vulgarity' links this value judgement with the language of etiquette and manners and an insistence on good taste, yet a twenty-first-century reader might see this gendered and objectified critique as equally crass. Gender also figures in Bernard Hollowood's *Pottery*

Vulgarity

WE CANNOT RESIST wanting to go beyond the example of ornament inappropriately applied and to give an example of a crude shape poorly decorated. Following our principle that words alone may confuse, the example is reinforced with a visual contrast which defines the meaning of vulgarity. By vulgarity in people we mean just this kind of coarseness of body, cheapness of ornament, and insensitive application of make-up (4). The parallel in the case of the pottery is exact, in its florid shape and crude cosmetic decoration (5).

Figure 3.9 'Vulgarity', in Alan Jarvis, *The Things We See No. 1 Indoors and Out*, 1946.

and Glass; Hollowood praises both hand-made and machine-made pieces but criticises the '"Paintresses" as they are called [who] repeat themselves so often that their work becomes mechanically accurate' (1947: 34). Hollowood's castigation implies a fear that uneducated masses of new consumers might degrade the designed environment with their popular culture preferences. CoID's dogmatic, top-down approach to good and bad design dismissed the variations in modernist design, including jazz modern, or *moderne*, which had counterparts in the USA, such as Hollywood style (Hine, 1986).

Much mid-twentieth-century government-generated design advice was written by one social group for another, with a concomitant gulf between the ideals presented and what was available to the majority of readers. Financially and culturally confident educated middle-class consumers of the 1930s were early adopters of both modern design (Davies, 1998) and electrical appliances (Bowden and Offner, 1996); other consumers followed suit only later. Jonathan Woodham has suggested that post-war design reformers embodied an elite and 'relatively narrow social outlook' (1996a: 55; 1996b; also Atha, 2012; Hiscock, 2000) and that attempts at design reform were perhaps misguided in view of popular antipathy towards '"the steel stuff"' presented as well-designed furniture in the *Britain Can Make It* display of 1946 (1996a: 59–60). But, in 1953, future Design Council head Paul Reilly published an article in the *Ideal Home* annual in which he asserted that contemporary design was 'a classless style'; 'people of all classes', from bus drivers to bank clerks, were buying it. The title of his article – 'Don't be Afraid of Contemporary Design' – suggests that the *Ideal Home* annual readership, at least, might have been hesitant (Reilly, 1953: 130). Even the Design Centre Awards, launched in 1957 to highlight to consumers the best of contemporary design, have been described retrospectively by design historian David Jeremiah as telling 'the public what it should like' (Jeremiah, 2000: 167).

Government-funded attempts to educate public taste were connected to the extensive investment in public housing following the devastation of Britain's built environment during the Second World War (Sillitoe, [1971] 1973: 50–51). Massive growth of council-owned housing and private development created four million new homes in the interwar period, and home ownership increased from 10 per cent in 1914, to nearly 20 per cent in 1939, to almost 50 per cent in 1966 (Benson, 1989: 73; Halsey, 1972: 308). Debates about modernist solutions for post-war housing were disseminated to a general readership in a spate of books. The 'Minimum House' was one solution among many proposed for the public housing projects that increasingly occupied a relatively young architectural establishment in the post-Second World War period (Marwick, 1991: 51).

Houses: Permanence and Prefabrication (Anthony, 1945) recommends prefabricated housing with compact bathroom and kitchen units, and depicts, by way of inspiration, an image of an American trailer park. This publication was attributed to 'Hugh Anthony', which is probably a pseudonym combining the names of its two authors, Hugh Casson (later Director of Architecture for the Festival of Britain, a significant intervention in persuading the public of the benefits of modernist design) and Anthony Chitty (who had worked with Berthold Lubetkin's Tecton Group). 'Hugh Anthony' is also the credited author of *Homes by the Million: An Account of the Housing Achievements in the U.S.A. 1940–1945* (Anthony, 1946), while in the USA, George Nelson and Henry Wright acknowledged the futuristic nature of their recommendations in titling their 1945 book *Tomorrow's House: A Complete Guide for the Home Builder*.

In contrast to the radical ideas of a new generation of architects on both sides of the Atlantic, in the UK the House-Building Industries' Standing Committee publication *Demonstration Permanent Houses 1946* aimed to ensure the future of the house-building industry and promote work for builders (Figure 3.10). Howard Robertson's *Reconstruction and the Home* of 1947, based on a series of articles from the design journal *Art and Industry*, was intended as a digest of 'the most important of those official manuals which are themselves summaries of views assembled from many sources and collected by experts in Committee' but with greater treatment of interior fixtures, fittings and decoration rather than a focus on exterior architecture. Robertson's book resembles CoID publications in its didacticism and lists of manufacturers and suppliers but he establishes an intimate connection between author and reader.

Planners and architects debating new ideas in housing development encountered resistance from those who felt that the practical needs of families were being ignored. For example, communal laundry facilities for flat dwellers, an innovation in the late 1940s, created difficulties for families with children because laundry could not be combined with supervision of children

Figure 3.10 Cover, *Demonstration Permanent Houses 1946*, 1946.

in the home. A successful example of planning was the Lansbury development for the Festival of Britain, which had variously shaped and sized dwellings to suit a range of families (Young, 1954, in Jeremiah, 2000: 178), but Sheffield City Council's planners of Park Hill (1957–1961) ignored antipathy towards flats so that 'socialist principles destroyed the cultures of the people they were representing' (Jeremiah, 2000: 178). The 1957 study *Family and Kinship in East London* showed planners dismantling working-class communities by moving them from cities to suburbs, where amenities and opportunities for interaction were few (Young and Willmott, [1957] 1992). The family portrayed in these cases is silent and designed *for*, rather than participating in what would today be called co-design.

Compiled by Millicent Frances Pleydell-Bouverie from surveys and consultations with women's organisations, the *Daily Mail Book of Britain's Postwar Homes* of 1945 saw professional and non-professional women writing to advise and educate other women. Organisations consulted included the Electrical Association for Women, the National Council of Women, the National Federation of Women's Institutes, the National Union of Townswomen's Guilds, the Society of Women Housing Managers, the Standing Joint Committee of Labour Women, the Women's Advisory Housing Council, the Women's Gas Council and the Women's Group on Public Welfare. The modernist attributes of simplicity and labour-saving efficiency are emphasised, but the women consulted rejected flats or communal housing in favour of the privacy afforded by houses or bungalows. They disliked ribbon developments and preferred housing varied in elevation and 'grouped to form aesthetically pleasing views both to and from the dwellings'. Homes should be 'soundly built' (implying a rejection of prefabrication) with a garden and a mixture of open fires and gas/electric heating. Fold-out plans suggest that a high level of engagement was expected of the reader. Pleydell-Bouverie exemplifies the contribution made by women's groups working together to achieve critical mass based on quotidian expertise in public debates about the home.

Popular modernism: the Woman's Own *Book of Modern Homemaking*

In the period following the Second World War, once the lingering privations of the war and post-war periods had diminished, increased affluence enhanced the ability of working- and middle-class consumers to express status using material culture in the UK and the USA alike (Chaney, 1996: 17). This built on the enhanced access to mass produced consumer goods provided by department stores and mail order, advertising and marketing, increased credit, and improved logistics for international trade and national distribution during the first half of the twentieth century. Modern design was consistently promoted in domestic advice literature for the new middle class, such as Francis W. Yerbury's *Modern Homes Illustrated*, and Margaret M. Justin and Lucile Osborn Rust's *Today's*

Home Living, a US home economics textbook, both published in 1947. As well as being economical in terms of money and space, the formal simplicity and innovative use materials such as plastics and metals meant that modernist design could be recommended for saving time spent cleaning, too. In the UK, in addition to a growth in home ownership, the Beveridge Report of 1942 and the subsequent creation of a welfare state based on free healthcare and national insurance also improved material conditions for working-class people. Poverty levels fell from the 1930s to the 1960s, and during the 1950s 'The personal consumption of manual workers increased by around 25 per cent', mostly in domestic goods (Bourke, 1994: 213, 96). *The Economist* complained of these changes as disadvantaging the middle class: 'At least ten per cent of the national consuming power has been forcefully transferred from the middle classes and the rich to the wage-earners' (ibid. 1994: 23).

By 1967, while groups such as Archigram (1963–1975) (Cook, 1999) in the UK and Archizoom (1966–1974) in Italy articulated radical alternatives to dominant modernist design philosophies, the *Woman's Own Book of Modern Homemaking* (WOBMH) (Figure 3.11) followed Patmore in the

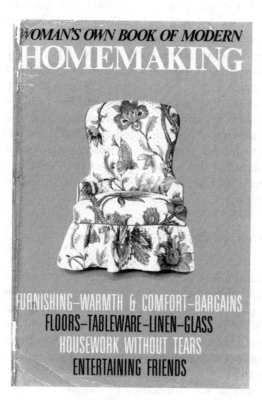

Figure 3.11 Cover featuring chair courtesy of Peter Jones, *Woman's Own Book of Modern Homemaking*, 1967.

UK and designers Charles and Ray Eames in the USA (Kirkham, 1998) in demonstrating that modern design could easily be combined with other styles of furniture and décor:

> Having an Edwardian suite in a Victorian house doesn't prevent you putting Scandinavian modern in the same room – and having comfort with perfect harmony. As every decorator has proved, the beauty of modern furniture is the way it mixes so happily with antiques, Victorian, even reproduction.
>
> (*Woman's Own*, 1967: 17)

WOBMH echoes Patmore in imbuing modern design with qualities such as 'harmony' and in advocating modifications to the conventions of home-making in favour of modern practicality, relaxedness and thrift:

> Thousands of families in this country buy furniture they don't need because convention says they must have a three-piece suite, a matching bedroom suite, and a dining set complete with sideboard. In most cases they would be much more comfortable without them.
>
> (*Woman's Own*, 1967: 12)

WOBMH's rejection of the three-piece suite of furniture was informed not only by decades-old modernist design philosophy, but also by the economic conditions of its readership. Around this time, *WOBMH* readers may have purchased fashionable domestic design for the first time, having previously used inherited goods or done without. *WOBMH* showed women who were, potentially, members of the newly enlarged middle class how to consume appropriately, blending economy and practicality with contemporary fashionability and informality. *Woman's Own* readers were not in the vanguard of taste, and were more likely to be residents of the urban planning initiatives criticised by Jeremiah than the readers of design writing by Patmore, Bertram or Russell. The idea of spending beyond one's means to create a pristine and matching leisure environment in the home was deemed outmoded and associated with stuffy formality. In this, *WOBMH* echoes designers Mary and Russel Wright's seminal domestic advice book, *Guide to Easier Living* ([1950] 1954). *WOBMH* proposed that instead of emulating her grandmothers, the reader should note what the 'young moderns' were buying for their homes: 'Go first to the Design Centre or to one of the specialist cutlery shops now in most large towns, where they show the best ranges, both British and foreign' (*Woman's Own*, 1967: 79).

The continuity of domestic advice between 1934 (Patmore), 1950 (Wright and Wright) and 1967 (*Woman's Own*) demonstrates that domestic advice writers perceived a need to continue promoting modernism, as different audiences required the same message to be delivered in different ways at different times in different places. While Patmore was a professional interior decorator and a leading decorating writer, servicing upper-class and wealthy clients with the latest in fashionable design, and Oxford-educated Renaissance man Anthony Bertram was part of the design establishment as a broadcaster on design for the BBC, the staff at *Woman's Own* wrote for a mass readership of working-class and lower-middle-class women who did their own decorating. The *WOBMH* is therefore more akin to the numerous titles produced by the Good Housekeeping Institute, such as *The Book of Good Housekeeping* (1944, with second and third editions in 1945 and 1946), *Running a Home is Fun* (Edwardes and Smedley [1970] 1975), *Doing Up Your Home* (Green, 1973) and *Good Housekeeping Kitchens* (Austen and Davies, 1976), where economical practicality is the guiding principle, than the professional focus of *The Studio*, the trend-setting *Vogue* or the organ of a privileged lifestyle, *Harper's and Queen*.

Domestic advice literature complemented governmental design reform discourse, delivered through the CoID and, later, the Design Council, in disseminating modernist design to a wide popular readership. The unofficial tandem of domestic advice and government agency advice is shown in the promotion of the Hille Series 1 wall storage system, featured in *WOBMH* (Figure 3.12) and in CoID's book *Storage* by Geoffrey Salmon, also published in 1967 (Figure 3.13). Salmon's book was part of CoID's 'Design Centre Publication' series, with other titles exploring kitchens (Prizeman, [1966] 1970), tableware (Good, 1969), design for children (Rayner, 1967), gardens (Shepheard, 1969), home entertainment technologies (Sharpe, 1968), workrooms (Matthews, 1969), flooring (Phillips, 1969) and lighting (Phillips, 1970). The two images

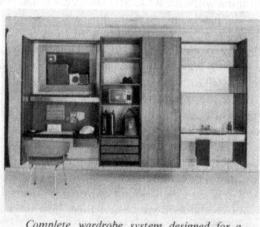

Complete wardrobe system designed for a man—or a business-like woman—includes hanging space, washing facilities, desk top and space for books, television and hand luggage. Hille Storage Wall System

Figure 3.12 Hille Storage Wall System, *Woman's Own Book of Modern Homemaking*, 1967.

Wall storage system. Units are slung between upright side panels which are fixed to the wall at top and bottom. Note inclusion of a vanitory unit. Design Centre Award 1965. Hille. Model: Series 1

Storage units fixed to the wall individually. Beaver & Tapley Ltd. Model: Tapley SL

Figure 3.13 Hille Series 1 wall storage system, Geoffrey Salmon, *Storage: A Design Centre Publication*, 1967.

are almost identical, right down to the position of the towel hanging on the rail. Differences include the space above the desk being filled with wall-hung art in *WOBMH* and by shelves with a portrait bust and modern glass vessels in *Storage*. Different objects occupy the two desks, and the shelving in *WOBMH* contains a hat, a television and suitcases, whereas in Salmon it contains box files and hanging files. Toiletries sit by the sink in the *WOBMH* picture, but are absent from the Salmon version. Hille's Polypropylene chair, designed by Robin Day (1962), completes the Salmon furnishing, whereas *WOBMH* shows a different model. The Salmon caption reads 'Wall storage system. Units are slung between upright side panels which are fixed to the wall at top and bottom. Note inclusion of a vanitory unit. Design Centre Award, 1965. Hille. Model: Series 1' (Salmon, 1967: 42). The *WOBMH* caption reads 'Complete wardrobe system design for a man – or a business like woman – includes hanging space, washing facilities, desk top and space for books, television and hand luggage. Hille Storage Wall System' (*Woman's Own*, 1967: 24). The two books describe the wall storage system for two distinct audiences, with Salmon explaining how it is constructed and that it won a Design Centre Award in 1965 and *WOBMH* speculating on the person who might occupy the space and the ways it might be used. These treatments exemplify gender stereotypes: the Design Centre publication emphasises production and status, while *WOBMH*'s focus is on personal consumption.

In discussing how magazine sources encouraged US consumers of the 1950s to find a place in their home for a television, Lynn Spigel notes that 'media discourses did not so much reflect social reality; instead, they preceded it' (1990: 76). Similarly, domestic advice literature in the UK and the USA alike helped new middle-class readers to accept modern design as aesthetically appropriate for an activity – home entertaining – which had required hosts to bring out their finest wares in an expression of their status and respect for their guests. *WOBMH* counselled that 'modern' design: 'is NOT a passing fashion, nor a designer's gimmick, and like television and electric appliances, it is here to stay' (*Woman's Own*, 1967: 79):

Few things we use about the house have changed more than table ware
[...] go to buy some new ones and you find yourself in the middle of a
small domestic revolution. The cutlery and china which young people
buy today doesn't even *pretend* to look like the stuff their parents use.
The linen has almost vanished. From the material and design to the
method of selling, everything is different. And in most cases very much
better.

(*Woman's Own*, 1967: 78)

Such recommendations of contemporary design as attractive and practical
aimed to counter resistance to relinquishing traditional manifestations of
luxury.

The novelty of modern design resided in new applications of materials
not previously associated with the domestic table. For flatware and tableware, WOBMH accepts that:

Traditional shapes and canteens are still available and you can, if you
like, buy table 'silver' that is an exact copy of your grandmother's, even
to rat-tail spoons and real ivory-handled knives. But more likely you
will look at stainless steel in six- and seven-piece place settings, not just
because this is newer, but because it is *sensible* ... and specifically
designed for eating a meal!

(*Woman's Own*, 1967: 78)

A David Mellor stainless steel tea and coffee service is recommended for
'the uncluttered modern table' (*Woman's Own*, 1967: 80) (Figure 3.14).
Stainless steel is recommended as a modern material which is economical
because (unlike ceramic) it does not break, labour saving because it does
not need polishing (unlike the more elite material, silver), stylish because it
appears in beautiful shapes and is 'designed by silversmiths' and contemporary because it carries 'no fancy work, no needless decoration'. The
writer also points out that stainless steel has been used for tableware since
the 1950s, perhaps to counter thrifty readers' concerns about investing in
anything *too* fashionable.

WOBMH goes on to recommend a 'Dinner service by Spode in the Sussex
shape and Dauphine pattern. By clever designing, 39 pieces do the work of
62 usual in a tea set, coffee set and dinner set' (*Woman's Own*, 1967: 81). In
suggesting a reduced number of tableware pieces, WOBMH follows the
approach embodied in Russel Wright's ceramic tableware, designed in mix
and match colourways with oven-to-table durability, such as his 'Casual' line.
Mary and Russel Wright's *Guide to Easier Living* includes a chart showing
how 82 items in a conventional setting can be replaced with 36 pieces from
Wright's 'Cafeteria' setting (Wright and Wright, [1950] 1954: 35). This
approach to domesticity requires that readers relinquish conventions of hospitality and accept utility as an acceptable aesthetic for the home:

Stainless steel tea or coffee service designed
by David Mellor for the uncluttered modern
table

Figure 3.14 'David Mellor for the uncluttered modern table', *Woman's Own Book*
of Modern Homemaking, 1967.

So cheek by jowl with the traditional fine tableware made for export, we have a vast new range of pottery designed for young moderns who drink coffee instead of tea, who breakfast and sometimes have dinner parties in the kitchen, and don't want flowers on anything. Most of it is made in the same potteries as famous china, but it has been specially created for present-day living and it is doing its job well.

(*Woman's Own*, 1967: 81)

Those in doubt are assured that 'an entirely plain white plate is likely to be more perfect than one covered with decoration'. Clearly, this sort of design would appeal to 'young moderns', but for those who are not young, the advice offers a new paradigm of status. The emphasis on generational difference suggests that this advice was aimed at experienced householders refurbishing their homes as well as those establishing households for the first time. In offering practical economical alternatives to the traditional material culture of home entertaining, modernist domestic advice texts such as *WOBMH* recommended a reconfiguration of domestic space to suit a new pragmatic aesthetic, consistent with a contraction in the scale of expenditure of time, money and resources on recommended home entertaining, as the next chapter shows.

Mediating modified modernisms in design from 1970

Since the launch of Habitat in the UK in 1964, which followed Design Research, a US retailing initiative that educated its customers as well as catering to them (Thompson and Lange, 2010), designer, retailer and restaurateur Terence Conran has played a significant role in disseminating modernist and contemporary design for the UK market. Conran did this partly through publishing; his name has been applied to a long list of domestic advice books, principally on home decoration, in connection with Conran Octopus, the publishing company he set up with publisher Paul Hamlyn. Conran's *The House Book* appeared in 1974, and was revised as *Terence Conran's New House Book* (1985) and *The Ultimate House Book* (Conran and Wilhide, 2003). Other titles include a series of books called 'The Habitat Home Decorator', which resembled the Council of Industrial Design series previously discussed in format and focus; an example was *Better Lighting* (Myerson, 1985). Through his shops and his books and through initiatives such as the Design Museum and its predecessor, the Boilerhouse at the Victoria and Albert Museum, Conran's name has become synonymous with design in Britain and these channels mediate his design philosophy, informed by modernism and Arts and Crafts ideas about truth to materials and simplicity.

However, Conran's aesthetic was one of many which were influential in Britain during the 1970s and 1980s: retailer Laura Ashley's historicist style of mixed patterns, swags and florals contrasts with Habitat's relatively modernist designs. Bernard and Laura Ashley began textile printing in 1953 and opened a shop in 1968, from which an international chain developed (Dickson and Colvin, 1982: flyleaf). Ashley lent her name and her style to a number of books, including *The Laura Ashley Book of Home Decorating* 'designed to help bridge the gap between the shop shelf, laden with an enormous choice of items for the home decorator, and the bare rooms or old decor of your home' (Dickson *et al.*: 1985: 6). *Laura Ashley Decorates a London House* (Clifford, 1985) charts a project to restore a Victorian house in period style using patterns copied by Laura Ashley Limited from museum originals. Like the modernist tendencies with which it contrasts so sharply, Laura Ashley's aesthetic owes a debt to the Arts and Crafts Movement, but in this case it is the Movement's tendency to romanticise a rural, historical ideal which is foremost. This rose-tinted nostalgia is also seen in the marketing of *The Country Diary of an Edwardian Lady* (Holden, 1977) and the tie-in *The Country Diary Book of Decorating: English Country Style* (Sykes, 1990), which also functioned as a counterpoint to the general trend of gradual acceptance of modern design in the British home during the twentieth century.

The UK and the USA both took a turn to the right politically during the 1980s, with Margaret Thatcher, UK prime minister from 1979 until 1990, in a 'special relationship' with Ronald Reagan, US president from 1981 until 1989. For those who could afford it, Thatcherism in politics translated into domestic life in terms of an emphasis on home ownership and conspicuous consumption for the mass middle class. Since her debut with *English Style* (1967), interior designer and journalist Mary Gilliatt has written more than 40 books. *The Decorating Book* (1981) which has sold over three million copies, came complete with a 'design kit' including graph paper, cut-out furniture and swatches, with which readers could plan interior design schemes for their homes. Gilliatt's *Mix and Match Decorating Book* (1984a) is a source book with spiral-bound swatches to enable the reader to identify her or his preferences from a large number of combinations. The formats of these books bring the reader nearer to the work of the professional interior designer. Catering directly to a market of new and prospective homeowners, Gilliatt's *Setting Up Home* (1985), published by Orbis for retailer Marks and Spencer, reassures the reader that 'Property is a good investment' and 'By the judicious planning of moves up the property ladder, the initial stake can be upgraded into a substantial sum' (ibid. 9, 10). On decorating, and with a view to resale, Gilliatt advises: 'If you're limited by funds or opportunity, "keep it simple" is a good rule' (ibid. 9) and 'Plain painted walls and a stripped and varnished floor focus attention on well-styled furniture' (ibid. 10) and, in a nod to contemporary taste, she advises that 'Clean, simple lines of built-in furniture and cool neutral colours are given warmth and impact with clever use of primary colour: a warm yellow floor and touches of dramatic red' (ibid. 19). Embracing the 1980s hi-tech trend, albeit with a Shaker precedent, Gilliatt advises that folding wire chairs can be hung on the wall when not needed.

Inflation of the property market and its inevitable subsequent decline provided the economic base which catalysed the growth of the property television genre in the UK from the mid-1990s. A subset of reality television, property shows tracked people buying, refurbishing or selling homes. A range of aesthetic preferences is displayed in these shows from the maximalism of the themed, amateur decoration of *Changing Rooms* (UK, 1996–2004, with US, Australian and New Zealand franchises; Philips, 2005) to the formalist, sometimes minimalist, tendencies of *Grand Designs* (Talkback Thames, 1999 to present). Contemporary viewers of *Grand Designs*, which mediates a largely modernist design philosophy of reduction and truth to materials, might be surprised by an early work from the *Grand Designs* presenter, *Kevin McCloud's Decorating Book* (1990). Here, McCloud promotes the use of 'inexpensive materials' and 'an unsurpassed array of rich and sophisticated effects' in 'a sure guide to highly effective styling' (ibid. flyleaf). Decorating techniques explained in the book include the anti-modernist 'Aging & antiquing' and 'Faux effects'. McCloud's book illustrates a range of styles from 'Classical Town Styles', 'Medieval Styles' and 'Twenties

Onwards', with the latter demonstrating a sense of the continuance of the modernist project up to the time of writing in 1990 in a more informed version of the *Changing Rooms* approach. *Changing Rooms* exists in opposition to the integrity, simplicity and elimination of modernism. An accompanying book (Barker, 1997) features sixteen room options ranging from an 'Arts & Crafts dining room' and a 'Mexican kitchen' to bedroom choices such as 'Feng Shui', 'Gothic' and 'Bloomsbury'. *Changing Rooms* fans had to wait until Barker's *Finishing Touches: Styling Secrets to Transform Your Home* (2000) to be told 'Pare down what is in your home so that you only have what you love and use – not so much minimalism as purism' (ibid. 14), in an echo of designer William Morris's dictum 'Have nothing in your houses which you do not know to be useful or believe to be beautiful' (Morris, 1880; Naylor, 1988: 210), and 'Less is more in today's decorating' (ibid. 15), echoing architect Ludwig Mies van der Rohe's motto. *Changing Rooms'* recipe of domestic design advice for the lowest common denominator has been internationally successful.

Martha Stewart, the doyenne of US domestic advice, has developed a consistent visual language which extends from the custom-designed font, typography and page layouts of *Martha Stewart Living* magazine, through the products sold under the Stewart name, from crafting and household goods to carpets, paints and kitchen cabinets, and the home designs shown in Martha Stewart Living Omnimedia (MSLO) domestic advice channels. Martha's style, as it is mediated to us in a range of outputs and contexts, combines colonial historicism with modernist reduction. It has, therefore, an aspirational class base in which the traditional legitimisation of heritage combined with the charismatic legitimisation of Martha's persona and sig-nature style, for mass consumption by the US buying public, broadly defined. The historicism comes in myriad forms, from the cornice applied to cupboard tops to the faux bois effect applied to walls, ceramics and cup-cakes. A consistent palette of soft pastels and neutrals includes a blue inspired by the eggs of Stewart's Auracana chickens and Bedford gray, named after her farm in Bedford, New York. These exemplify the process of weaving a biographical narrative around design choices (Conway, 1997: 54). Stewart, too, provides a structured compromise in which elimination and decoration are balanced, albeit unevenly in favour of the latter. Competitor in the domestic advice media industry Time Inc.'s Real Simple is also diversified over a magazine, television, internet and product lines and, as its name makes clear, it too promotes reduction and simplicity for its economy, practicality, hygiene and style. The reader posited by Real Simple's books, including *The Organized Home* (Cronstrom, 2004) and *Solutions* (Hinnant, 2005), has less time to engage in decorating projects than the MSLO reader and values simplicity for its time-saving properties.

At the turn of the millennium, simplicity was reinterpreted, in the UK and the USA alike, in quasi-spiritual applications of 'Zen' aesthetics and in feng shui. In *The Healing Home* (1998), Suzy Chiazzari uses colour, light, smell, water and air, among other properties, in an approach to home decorating that is intended to be uplifting, physically, emotionally or spiritually. Jane Alexander's *The Illustrated Spirit of the Home: How to Make your Home a Sanctuary* (1999) has a chapter on feng shui and sections on paganism and Hestia, goddess of hearth and home. These books promote a narrative about the home as a sanctuary and place for pampering which, as Alexander recognises, exists in opposition to the domestic impact of information technologies. Internet communication has complicated the privacy of the home, and opened it up as a conduit to the world. Even the twentieth-century association of the home with leisure has persisted in the face not only of the invisible labour of domesticity, but also of the increased practice of working from home or 'telecommuting'. Eliminating visual and material clutter from the home, to create calm, minimal interiors, is one legacy of modernism in design. Domestic advice books present decluttering as the answer to the frantic pace of contemporary life and to the problematic build-up of possessions in Western consumer society (Cwerner and Metcalfe, 2003). Decluttering series *The Life Laundry* (Talkback Productions, 2002–2004) spawned two books (Walter and Franks, 2002; Walter, 2003). The linear laboratory style kitchens currently for sale in most mass-market DIY chain stores, including Home Depot in the USA and the UK's Homebase, exemplify modernism for the masses. Modernist design began as an avant-garde approach to life in a new century, but throughout the twentieth century it had been modified and mediated in ways which have allowed it – however reductively interpreted – to reach its fullest market penetration across the social classes in the twenty-first century.

The problem with the solution: discourse of democracy or dominance?

I have examined what domestic advice literature tells us about historical narratives of class in the twentieth century, tracing the conjunction of a lessening of aristocratic authority with the gradual acceptance of modernism in the home. Rather than simply adapting aristocratic taste to the modest abode, domestic advice writers have addressed the needs and desires of smaller householders using the modernist design principles of economy, practicality, hygiene, flexibility, modularity, simplicity and contemporaneity. Even as an ideal discourse, advice literature arguably reflects public taste, and its chronologies, more accurately than the campaigning rhetoric of reformers and designers, because it has a commercial imperative to tailor its recommendations to readers' needs and desires. Domestic advice literature exists as a populist on-demand discourse for a mass, aspirational, market. By consulting ephemeral sources prepared for a mass readership, not associated with the avant-garde, the 'early adopter' or the professional designer, an alternative chronology of the promotion of modernism emerges. While mid-century readers may have been familiar with pro-modernist rhetoric from a range of design reform organisations in the first half of the twentieth century, advice literature guided them in the domestic application of modernist design much later than top-down design reform activity would suggest. Patmore in 1934, Mary and Russel Wright in 1950, *Woman's Own* in 1967, Conran in 1974 and Barker in 2000 advised readers of the benefits of modernism in similar ways. Domestic advisors were instrumental in delivering modernist visions of egalitarian domesticity to a broad readership spanning the classes. This chapter has demonstrated that an analysis of domestic advice literature can offer a corrective to chronologies both of taste, as it has been articulated in design history, and of class change, as it has been theorised in sociology.

However, the role of domestic advice as a discourse of democracy needs qualification. In discussing the food writing of Jane Grigson and Elizabeth David as exemplary of the 'conservative modernity' proposed by Alison Light as characteristic of women's fiction of the interwar period, Steve Jones and Ben Taylor paraphrase Alan Warde thus: 'Novelty threatens us with disruption, but promises excitement, while tradition offers authenticity, but threatens us with monotony' (Jones and Taylor, 2001: 179, cite Warde, 1997: 57–77; Light, 1991). The same double bind is at the heart of the domestic advice genre. On the one hand, it promises solutions to contemporary problems; on the other hand, those solutions are imbued with a retrogressive concern for an authority dependent upon conventions and traditions, both of domestic practices and of the genre. The status of domestic advice literature as a hegemonic discourse is apparent in two ways. First, even as aristocratic advisors used humour and cartoons to palliate the embarrassment associated with their class-based authority in a shift from traditional legitimisation to charismatic legitimisation, they continued as successful advice writers for a newly enlarged middle-class readership who, in consuming these books and visiting stately homes, bought into a hegemony which subjugated them. Second, while domestic advice books encouraged the expression of identity through the consumption of fashionable home decoration, the modernist solutions they presented functioned to reify a newly enlarged middle class formation.

4 *Easier Living? Lady Behave!*
Gender and domestic advice literature

The problem: from *Leisure Class* to 'Mrs. Three-in-One'

In the period after the Second World War, the ideals of homemaking and home entertaining offered by domestic advice writers owed less of a debt to upper-class patterns of practice, and traditional legitimisation, and instead presented entertaining on a reduced scale intended for the growing middle classes: a more rational approach. Simultaneously, the economic changes of the period allowed greater employment opportunities to women. While working-class women had *always* worked, a new job market offered them alternatives to domestic service, which transformed not only their lives, but also the lives of those they had served. It has been argued that domestic service was never as prevalent as 'the literary evidence' suggests, but that 'people of limited means – that is, most people – employed household help in emergencies' (Strasser, [1982] 2000: 164–165). However, it is clear that even women in a position to afford full-time live-in domestic assistance sometimes experienced difficulty finding staff. Those members of the middle classes who needed to revise their domestic practices as a result of losing staff *and* a new group of socially mobile readers who sought to participate in the newly enlarged middle class were both the subjects of this shift from service to self-service (Lees-Maffei, 2001, 2007).

Domestic advice writers tackled these issues. Women accustomed to staff assistance received advice on managing alone, while women new to running a middle-class household were also addressed. Before the Second World War, domestic advisors assumed that readers employed staff, while by the 1970s no such assumption could be made. Managing a home unassisted, especially when entertaining guests – in the role American etiquette expert Emily Post termed 'Mrs. Three-in-One' (hostess, cook and waitress at once) – formed an enduring topic for British and North American domestic advice writers between 1920 and 1970. As more women performed paid employment in the public sphere, so their domestic roles were emphasised in public discourse (Crompton and Sanderson, 1990: 48). Just as readers could learn how to become middle class from domestic advice, so 'a major function of advice books has been to invent, prescribe and normalize gendered behaviours' (Tonkovich, 1995: 14). Women, their work, domesticity and the sources through which domestic knowledge has been communicated had all been marginalised in the historical record until feminist scholarship and recent work in social and cultural history and cultural studies began to reassess their significance. The following analysis of domestic advice literature shows how changes in the roles of women within society and the family impacted upon advice about the design and layout of the home. I contribute a critique of how domestic advice literature sought to provide solutions to the servant problem, meaning the contraction of the domestic service industry in the twentieth century, in the years following the Second World War, during a shift from traditional and rational legitimisation to charismatic legitimisation.

Before the fall: the interwar hostess as conspicuous consumer

Before 1945, domestic advice books depict the ideal hostess as a conspicuous consumer of her husband's wealth and status, and of the great number of goods and services that formed her home, including the labour of her staff, in the manner of Veblen's *Theory of the Leisure Class* ([1899] 1970: 229, 49). Domestic advice books at this time relied on traditional legitimisation, even as their authors presented the advice contained in the books as up-to-date. The hostess was characteristically disengaged, as here in *The A.B.C. of Etiquette by a Society Lady* (1923), published a year before the *Theory of the Leisure Class* first appeared in Britain:

> When receiving callers, it is necessary that the lady should rise or lay aside the employment in which she may be engaged, particularly if it consists of light or ornamental needle-work, and politeness requires that any occupation which completely engrosses the attention, be abandoned.
>
> (A Society Lady, 1923: 14)

The hostess's occupation, needlework, is dispensable. Notwithstanding her role in what has since been termed 'emotional labour' (Hochschild, 1983; James, 1989), here the success of the hostess depends on her attentiveness to others and the suppression of her own reactions:

> The duties of hostess at dinner are not onerous; but they demand tact and self-possession in no small degree. She does not often carve. She has few active duties to perform; but she must neglect nothing, put all her guests at their ease, and pay every possible attention to the requirements of each and all around her. No accident should ruffle her temper. No disappointment ought embarrass her. She ought to see her old china broken without a sigh, and her best glass shattered with a smile.
>
> (A Society Lady, 1923: 38)

Virtually her sole active role is in the procession to the dining room, a performance as much about manifesting status hierarchies among the diners as getting from one room to another. The parlour has been described as the hostess's 'cultural podium', in contrast to private regions of the home (Hepworth, 1999). For guests, too, impassivity was a virtue; *The A.B.C. of Etiquette* offers remarkably similar advice to guests as it does to hostesses and hosts: 'Should you break or upset anything, do not apologise for it. Show your regret by your facial expression. It is not considered well-bred to put it into words' (A Society Lady, 1923: 36). Veblen also extends his account of impassivity to include guests as well as hostesses: 'He consumes vicariously for his host at the same time that he is a witness to the consumption of that excess of good things which his host is unable to dispose of singlehanded, and he is also made witness to his host's facility in etiquette' (Veblen, [1899] 1970: 65, 68). Guests and hostess united in consumption of the host's wealth and all relied for their impassivity on the labour of domestic staff. Veblen noted that at the highest levels of the leisure class, the male head of the household, too, engaged in conspicuous consumption, rather than production. Early twentieth-century domestic advice depicts a host with very little to do, except perhaps carve meat. Sixty years after Veblen explained the sociological importance of a leisured appearance, Goffman's account of hostesses engaged in 'secret consumption' and backstage labour vividly conjures the numerous hidden acts of social labour that the pre-war hostess was required to perform in constructing an illusion of ease ([1959] 1990: 39).

Just as hostesses were involved in impassive and self-effacing concern for their guests, so the hospitality shown in interwar advice literature was extremely labour-intensive. Dinner parties would have begun with drinks in the drawing room, followed by a formal procession to the dining room for a meal of five or more courses, after which the women withdrew, leaving the men to their own amusements for a while, before rejoining them. Lavish entertaining is described by US advice writer Emily Post in her *Etiquette*, first published in 1922 (as *Etiquette in Society, in Business, in Politics and at Home*) and repeatedly thereafter with successive US and London editions. One photograph showing 'The perfect example of a formal dinner in a great house' (Figure 4.1) is described as involving 'no effort on the part of the hostess of a great house beyond deciding upon the date and the principal guests who are to form the nucleus of the party (Post, 1922: caption to plate between pp. 236 and 237). Post overstates the lack of involvement of the assisted hostess, perhaps to underline the grandeur of society entertaining. The hostess assisted by staff would have been held responsible for every decision about dishes served and equipment used, and judged accordingly by her guests.

During the interwar period, domestic advice writers continued to assume that the householders they wrote for would have permanent staff or would employ casual staff when entertaining at home. Servants were depicted in

THE PERFECT EXAMPLE OF A FORMAL DINNER TABLE IN A GREAT HOUSE

Figure 4.1 'The perfect example of a formal dinner table in a great house', Emily Post, *Etiquette in Society, in Business, in Politics and at Home*, [1922] 1940.

domestic advice books so that readers would know how their staff should appear and be treated. Following the Second World War, this assumption became untenable, and domestic writers addressed both staffed and unstaffed circumstances and, increasingly, solely the latter. *The Housewife's Book*, published for a mainstream, rather than privileged, readership, catered for both staffed and unstaffed households (*Daily Express*, 1937). A section on work plans begins with 'Are Plans of Work Helpful?' before providing a 'Plan of work for mistress and one helper', with variations for 'Housewife' and 'Helper' respectively, and a 'Plan of work for a small servantless house (3 or 4 in family)'. Previous analysis of these plans has omitted the plan for the 'helper' and the additional monthly plan of seasonal work in the home (Jeremiah, 2000: 104–105).

Displaying the influence of scientific management and the New Housekeeping, the schedules are followed with the chapter 'Saving Labour', on appliances from vacuum cleaners to grapefruit scissors. This chapter is illustrated with a cautionary photograph of a woman on her knees scrubbing a floor, captioned: 'The backaching method of work should be avoided'. However, the book's cover (Figure 4.2) features a woman identically positioned and smiling, replacing the notion that appliances are labour saving with the idea that housework should be enjoyed. *The Housewife's Book* is therefore ambiguous in its treatment of the housewife as both assisted and unassisted, physically exhausted and smiling. Just as homemaking practices were subjected to scientific management, so the task of introducing new electric appliances for the home fell to domestic advice writers. Appliances have been presented as electric servants, saving labour for working women homemakers, both in contemporary accounts and advertisements and in retrospective accounts of their development, such as the Electricity Council's *Willing Servants* of 1981 (Byers, [1981] 1988). However, the ambiguity seen

Figure 4.2 Cover, *The Housewife's Book*, 1937.

in *The Housewife's Book* accords with Ruth Schwartz Cowan's 1983 critique of the labour-saving effects of electric appliances:

> housework was to be thought of no longer as a chore but, rather, as an expression of the housewife's personality and her affection for her family [...] The servantless household may have been an economic necessity for some people in the 1920s and the 1930s; but, for the first time, that necessity was widely regarded, at least in the public press, as a potential virtue.
> (Cowan [1983] 1989: 177)

The unassisted hostess engaged a new set of ideals as economic and practical conditions led to novel ideological representations. The issue of the servantless household was to exercise the minds of domestic advice writers for the next half century, until unstaffed lifestyles became the norm for the middle class.

'Mrs. Three-in-One', the 'servantless household' and 'party flurry'

The lavish hospitality presented in Post's 1922 *Etiquette* depended on a staffed household, but even for less formal dinners – 'Dinner-Giving with

Limited Equipment' – Post assumes staff will be on hand, including cook, waitress and chambermaid, and the figures depicted staff performing domestic duties. However, Post's fifth edition *Etiquette* of 1937 contained a new chapter, 'When Mrs. Three-in-One Gives a Party', 'addressed especially to the thousands of housekeepers who constantly ask about the various problems of running a house without the assistance of a servant' (Post, 1937: 817). These readers are, in addition, directed to the chapters 'Simple Party Giving' and 'Modern Dinner Giving'. 'Mrs. Three-in-One' – 'cook, waitress, and at the same time a tranquil and apparently unoccupied hostess' – was developed in response to readers' questions and personal observation. Post's pre-eminence means that she has been credited with popularising this emergent character (Cowan [1983] 1989: 180) but she articulated a compelling problem for domestic advice writers. The multiple tasks by which Mrs. Three-in-One was defined had always been the lot of working-class women, but her appearance in domestic advice literature signified a wider social shift towards unstaffed households for middle-class readers. Post may have neglected this constituency in her 1922 text because it was thought not to read, or buy, etiquette books, or because it was deemed too small a market. Or, perhaps the neglect was an oversight derived from her stated motivation for producing the book, which was to preserve the old social order. This move to address middle-class householders with advice centred upon smaller scale and more economical entertaining represents a shift from traditional to rational legitimisation.

The use of characters named after their behaviour was a signature technique of Post's writing, and has been used to situate her work within a tradition of morality writing that began with John Bunyan (1622–1688), author of *The Pilgrim's Progress*, an allegorical account of Christianity published in two parts in 1678 and 1684 (Robinson and Strong, 1970: 173). This technique is part of the dramatisation of writing for homemakers recommended by experts on the subject (Richardson and Callahan, [1962] 1970: 12). However, Unlike Mrs. Stranger, Mrs. Kindhart and Mrs. Oldname, and other aptly named characters in *Etiquette*, only Mrs. Three-in-One received the distinction of an entry in the index of *Etiquette*, along with Mrs. Grundy, an intertextual archetypal prim chaperone not of Post's coinage (Webster and Hopkins, 1930; Markun, 1930; Fryer, 1963). Like Mrs. Grundy, Post gave Mrs. Three-in-One life as an intertextual cultural trope by featuring her in more than one of her books. She appears not only in her eponymous chapter in *Etiquette*, but also at a dessert bridge party in the preceding chapter and in *The Personality of a House*, published in four editions from 1930 to 1948, for both staffed and unstaffed householders (Post [1930] 1948: 397). In the latter, Post suggests that outlines of utensils are drawn on walls (Figure 4.3):

> Not only are the 'indicators' convenient for Mary Three-in-One herself, but necessary guides for willing guests who in their efforts to help their

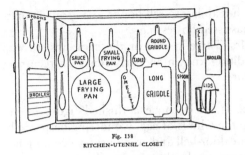

Fig. 138
KITCHEN-UTENSIL CLOSET

Figure 4.3 'Kitchen-Utensil Closet', drawing by Stephen J. Voorhies, in Emily Post, *The Personality of a House*, [1930] 1948.

hostess would otherwise put the kitchen so out-of-order she has to search next day for every item that was used and put it in its proper place.

(Post, [1930] 1948: 485)

Mrs. Three-in-One receives help from guests, not staff. The same technique is recommended for 'her husband John's special tools' (Post, [1930] 1948: 485).

Post's recognition of unstaffed households is further shown in the 1940 edition of *Etiquette*, which has the chapter 'Modern Dinner Giving', and three related chapters, 'Simple Party Giving', 'When Mrs. Three-in-One Gives a Party' and 'New Aspects of Hospitality', all of which address the practicalities of informal entertaining raised by readers. These additional chapters remain intact for the 1960 edition, with the exception that the latter two are renamed 'Cook, Waitress, and Charming Hostess!' and 'Hospitable Hosts' respectively. By 2004, the whole of part five, 'Dining and Entertaining', is written for the reader without domestic staff, and readers wishing to host a very formal dinner are advised to hire staff for the event. In the same edition, a chapter devoted to 'People Who Work in Your Home' discusses babysitters, live-in nannies and gardeners, health-care workers and secretaries.

A British example is Anne Edwards and Drusilla Beyfus's *Lady Behave: A Guide to Modern Manners*, published and revised successively between 1956 and 1969. The authors distinguish between the formal hostess with staff – 'Her job is to sit there keeping calm from the start, having a cocktail with her guests instead of flapping in and out of the kitchen' – and the cook-hostess, who is 'cook, the waitress and the washer-up' as well as host-ess ([1956] 1957: 4, 3). The authors give the cook-hostess precedence: she appears in the first sections, the 'Cook-Hostess Dinner Party' and 'How to be a guest at the Cook-Hostess Party', of the first chapter, 'Dinner Parties'. They applaud her efforts, saying that 'she can be found giving some of the best dinner parties', such as that detailed in the section 'Grand Cook-Hostess Dinner Party – Going to it and giving it' (ibid. 17). Here, and albeit under a modified name, Mrs. Three-in-One is promoted to the opening chapter of an advice manual, as a result of her ability to sell books to a growing market of readers anxious about unassisted hostessing.

The difficulty of acting as Mrs. Three-in-One or the cook-hostess was manifested in the confused condition known as 'party flurry', a recurring theme in domestic advice literature:

> When the guests arrive she is likely to be a flushed figure in the kitchen furiously beating up the whites of egg, wondering desperately how to manage answering the door-bell and graciously welcoming her guests and showing them where to take their coats off, when her mind is riveted on a sauce that will curdle in two seconds. The anxiety which furrows her pretty brow is whether she should stay with the guests and have another Martini or pull herself away from the party and baste the meat.
>
> (Edwards and Beyfus, [1956] 1957: 3)

Edwards and Beyfus advise that 'The star dish can be any one of the courses, but there should only be one to flurry over' (ibid. 5). The hostess's labour must be invisible in order to avoid her embarrassment and that of her guests, at being waited on by a peer, rather than a subordinate. The pretence of ease, the opposite of party flurry, conceals labour thereby rendering it acceptable. As Sarah Maclean cautions in *The Pan Book of Etiquette and Good Manners* of 1962: 'Nothing damps the party spirit more than the sight of the hostess nervously gulping down her soup so that she can rush out to the kitchen and stir the sauce' (Maclean, 1962: 140). Figure 4.4 is a humorous depiction of party flurry by illustrator Belinda Lyon for Pamela Lyons' *Today's Etiquette* of 1967, in which a hostess has dropped her tray in surprise, having noticed animals appearing at her kitchen window to eat her buffet. Given the shift from Post's Mrs. Three-in-One, who is 'cook, waitress and [...] hostess', to Edwards and Beyfus's 'cook-hostess', which implies that the role of waitress has been dropped, it is significant that the hostess lets go of the tray, symbol of her waitress role.

So the two major potential vices of the post-war hostess existed in opposition to one another: a hostess must not enjoy her party too much because the virtuous hostess is impassive in the entertainment of others, but nor must she be seen not enjoying it, in order to avoid her guests' embarrassment. Emotions have been neglected as a catalyst for social changes and for designed solutions alike, and this case study suggests one response. The pivotal question for advice writers to address was how the lone hostess or host could bridge the discrete spaces of frontstage and backstage to easily perform the role of cook and waitress, labours previously carried out by dedicated staff, at the same time as the competing role of hostess. A number of material solutions for the simultaneous performance of these competing social roles were offered, which relied in various degrees on rational and charismatic legitimisation.

Figure 4.4 Illustration by Belinda Lyon for Pamela Lyons, *Today's Etiquette*, 1967.

The solution: from service to self-service

Early efforts at rationalising the burden of the homemaker without staff began with the increasing specialisation of kitchen design. The development of gas-powered lighting and cooking enabled the separation of food preparation from living quarters, and the subsequent replacement of the 'living kitchen', celebrated by architect and author Hermann Muthesius among others, with the 'cooking kitchen' (Bullock, 1988: 181). In her *Household Engineering* of 1919 (first published in Britain in 1923), efficiency advocate Christine Frederick proposed reducing the amount of movement and labour performed in the kitchen by making the room itself smaller: 'We see then that a kitchen, or a place merely for food preparation, can be much smaller than was formerly the case when it was used as a combined sitting room, laundry and general workshop' ([1923] 1919: 19). Frederick's early foray into this territory stems from the relative rarity of live-in domestic servants in the USA during the early twentieth century. Her solutions for 'the servantless household' include a 'Revolving Partition', which enabled a 'table to be set in the Kitchen and moved into [the] living room' (ibid. 376–377, caption to plate). Some of Frederick's solutions may seem far-fetched in retrospect, but they epitomise the way in which domestic advice discourses have engaged rational legitimisation.

Influenced by Frederick, Grete Lihotsky designed what has commonly been regarded as the first fitted kitchen for Frankfurt am Main city architect Ernst May in 1926 (Heßler, 2009). This compact space ensured that all equipment and supplies were readily at hand (Henderson, 1996). However efficient, simple, and even elegant, the Frankfurt Kitchen was deemed to be by reformers, it was a backstage kitchen, a laboratory rather than a social space. The New Housekeeping and labour saving appliances attempted to solve the problem of the unstaffed household. However, as both focused on the backstage regions of the home, neither helped Mrs. Three-in-One in entertaining unassisted in the front and backstage regions of the home simultaneously (Goffman [1959] 1990: 110, 114). Notwithstanding the difficulties of unassisted homemaking on a daily basis, it was during situations of home entertaining that the unstaffed condition of a household became most problematic, as an additional set of tasks related to hospitality and appearances compounded the practical challenges. Distinct from the solutions informed by Frederick's rationalisation, therefore, were a range of solutions dependent instead upon the informalisation of domestic practices. These brought the kitchen into the frontstage through designs such as modernist open plan, kitchen-diners and practices including al fresco dining. These solutions emphasised the modernist tenets of practicality and simplicity, as well as their opposites, comfort and decoration. All the solutions discussed revolve around either bridging or collapsing hitherto distinct domestic regions.

The difficulty of entertaining unassisted proved to be a continuing theme for domestic advice writers. In 1965, almost forty years after Lihotsky's fitted kitchen, the reissued *Esquire Party Book* oscillated between addressing the host with staff, either employed specifically for the party or generally, and the unaided host (Merril, 1995; Douglas, 1991).

> If the host must be the bottle-washer and the butler as well as the chef, moan not! Small loss of dignity – for he somehow contrives that the service be gracious, if informal. He substitutes gadgets and appliances and new equipment for extra hands. He organizes menus that demand less service, *if* more advance preparation. He manipulates courses and guests and eating places so that everyone is spared the awkwardness of inept service or plate-clearing.
>
> (Editors of *Esquire* Magazine [1935] 1965: 127)

Part of a smaller body of literature addressed not to the hostess, but rather to the host (discussed further later in this chapter), the *Esquire Party Book* attempts to rouse enthusiasm for unassisted entertaining, in the face of assumed anxiety on the part of readers of both genders. A widespread solution to party flurry was to reduce the number and type of dishes offered. Multi-course place settings, often depicted as overwhelming for guests and hosts alike, were replaced by a new standard of three dishes for the home cook – starter, main course and pudding – which required simpler settings:

> Times have changed since Mrs Beeton's day when five courses – soup, fish, entrée, roast meat and a choice of sweets – was the accepted number

at any small dinner party. Even at banquets now more than four courses is unusual, and three – something to start with, a meat or fish dish and a sweet – is the usual number at private dinner parties, including those given by people with money and servants.

(Maclean, 1962: 140)

Sarah Maclean's *The Pan Book of Etiquette and Good Manners* exemplifies a general trend towards the informalisation of home entertaining regardless of economic and staffing constraints. What we accept today as sensible may have seemed to fall short of proper hospitality for hostesses of the interwar and post-war periods. Entertaining had traditionally involved sharing with guests the quality *and quantity* of one's pantry through serving complex, time-consuming dishes which – while not necessarily the product of the hostesses own hand – pointed to the expense, in terms of both ingredients and time, which she was willing, and able, to expend on her guests.

The pre-eminent trend in food preparation during the twentieth century, in the USA and the UK alike, was towards convenience foods and eating out, both of which have been associated with women's increasing participation in paid work outside the home (Figure 4.5). Domestic food was significantly altered by a number of developments in the first half of the twentieth century: increased production capacity, the availability of dietary supplements and vitamins, the consolidation of supply into multiple retailers and the importance of refrigeration technology for the types of foods sold, their distribution and domestic storage. Additional advances in branding, marketing and packaging of foods were aided by emergent materials and techniques, such as cellophane and canning, and by the development of television advertising from 1955 onwards. In spite of advancements in nutritional science, malnutrition persisted in both interwar and post-war Britain (Oddy, 2003). Public health scholar John Coveney has noted:

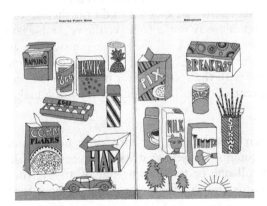

Figure 4.5 Illustration by Seymour Chwast, *Esquire Party Book*, [1935] 1965.

'During the 1950s and 1960s "convenience" foods were increasingly promoted as cooking in the "modern" way' (2000: 133).

Counter-trends, however, included the simple, authentic dishes epitomised in Elizabeth David's influential *A Book of Mediterranean Food* of 1950 (Jones and Taylor, 2001: 172) and the traditionalism of French cordon bleu cookery. Constance Spry, a designer in flowers, and Rosemary Hume ran a cordon bleu cookery school in Britain and published accompanying books on cookery and home entertaining (Spry and Hume, 1956, 1961), just as Julia Child popularised methods she had learned at Le Cordon Bleu in Paris for a US audience in *Mastering the Art of French Cooking*, co-authored with Simone Beck and Louisette Bertholle (Beck, Bertholle and Child, 1961). The year after David's *Mediterranean Food* appeared, the Festival of Britain introduced its visitors to the milk bar and the *Good Food Guide* was launched. Coffee bars and supermarkets proliferated, with the latter moving the balance of power away from manufacture to retailing. The demographic shift towards smaller households and, in Britain, the development of commercial food provision in motorway service stations from 1959 fuelled the spread of the ready meal in advance of the acceptance of microwave technology in the 1980s.

Post-war guests modified their expectations to suit reduced incomes and a lack of assistance. The increasing informalisation of home entertaining, influenced by the North American trends so stylishly depicted in the Wrights' *Guide to Easier Living* (1950), is also found in British sources. *Today's Etiquette* (Lyons, 1967) satirises the hostess's role at a buffet in an image which shows labels being used to mediate between the food and the guests (the fruit bowl, for example, is labelled 'Vitamin C'). In 1956, Edith Barber advised a modest involvement by guests: 'often appetizers served in the living-room will take the place of the first course at the table. The guests may help to pass the appetizers' ([1953] 1956: 32). In the same year, Edwards and Beyfus were similarly cautious in their recommendation of what guests might be expected to do for themselves: 'Most people without help find one way out is to leave the vegetables on the table for guests to help themselves and tell them to begin right away. Gravy and sauce are left on the table too' ([1956] 1957: 7). By helping with the serving, guests helped with the social role of hosting, as all present occupied equal and cooperative roles. The *Esquire Party Book* makes this clear:

> If one of your guests is shy or a stranger, or both, draft her as your assistant [...] The same technique sometimes works wonders in breaking up cliques. You can call one or two people out of an overtime conversation to select records and to pass the hot tidbits (either food *or* gossip).
>
> (Editors of *Esquire* [1935] 1965: 3)

This recommendation exemplifies American informality, epitomised in this advice for teenage American schoolchildren from 1961: 'If you want to have a kitchen party, at which everyone helps to prepare refreshments, you will not need to plan any other activity, since the preparation of the food itself is the activity' (Barclay and Champion, 1961: 170). However, British advisor Sarah Maclean warned ominously that that assistance from guests could be more hindrance than help (1962: 148).

Space constraints offered another reason for recommending a buffet. In 1967, the *Woman's Own Book of Modern Homemaking* (WOBMH) explained that buffet parties 'are great space-savers, so you can accommodate more guests at weddings, birthday parties, luncheon or evening parties'. Variations such as 'Wine and cheese parties' 'require a minimum of prepara-tion, provide plenty of variety and result in surprisingly little washing-up' while 'Tea parties' are recommended because the cost is relatively low and the food can be prepared in advance and served either at table or, more informally, handed round by the hostess, from a large side-table. A final rea-son for entertaining informally, this time on the patio or 'concreted area in the garden', is that it 'will save wear and tear on your carpets' (*Woman's Own*, 1967: 324–237). The increasing popularity of al fresco dining in Britain at this time displays both the growing continental influence in British eat-ing, spearheaded by Elizabeth David, and the American influence. Fashionable garden design, including the adoption of the paved area, or 'patio', for outdoor eating (Taylor, [2006] 2008) recalled the patio's Spanish etymological roots (*OED Online*, 2012). The patio became a popular in the USA as a way of extending compact post-war homes and as a site for barbecuing. US retailer Sears promoted dedicated patio furniture lines alongside its barbecues, while Knoll sold garden furniture by Richard Schultz (Miller, 2010).

Bridging the regions: oven-to-tableware

The party flurry associated with Mrs. Three-in-One centred upon her need to occupy two regions, front and backstage, dining room and kitchen, simultaneously:

> Dinner parties should be planned so that the hostess is detained in the kitchen as little as possible. Nothing is more embarrassing to guests than a flurried hostess darting into the dining room between long absences at the cooking stove.
>
> (*Woman's Own*, 1967: 332)

As well as making the meals themselves easier to prepare and serve, the ideal hostess, who performed the conflicting roles of both entertaining guests and cooking, was directed to use a range of objects to bridge the frontstage and backstage. Simple, sturdy designs for oven-to-tableware eased the burden of

Figure 4.6 'Pyrosil Ware Consort Skillets in plain white. Can be used on top of a cooker. Detachable handles' in Elizabeth Good, *Tableware*, 1969.

the unassisted hostess by saving time spent plating food into presentable dishes. Elizabeth Good's Council of Industrial Design book *Tableware* features a 'Shopping Guide for Oven-to-Tableware' comparing ten materials. Good recommends 'Hamilton' stoneware, designed by Tarquin Cole and John Minshaw and recipient of a Design Centre Award in 1966 for the Govancroft Potteries (1969: 23), and Pyrosil, 'a glass-ceramic body originally developed for the nose cones of rockets' which offers the advantage of being 'strong with high thermal shock resistance' and no disadvantages (ibid. 14–15) (Figure 4.6). For serving cold foods, Tupperware's 'Party Susan' was a variation on the 'lazy Susan', a turntable which facilitates self-service. Party Susan provided six separate compartments, a protective lid and a handle which allowed it to be carried between kitchen and buffet location and was easily turned to ease self-service (its replacement, the 'Serving Center' set has divided compartments but no handle).

Oven-to-tableware and dedicated buffet serving ware were simple bridging devices. More complex solutions included a range of gadgets and appliances designed to ease the burden of post-war hostesses and hosts. The assumption that gadgets replaced domestic staff does not hold true for Britain during the period prior to 1939, when staff were not in short supply, appliances were bought for use by servants, and only those wealthy enough to have servants could afford the appliances (Forty, 1986). However, during the war 'the selling point of household commodities becomes time saved to be used for war work' (Leman, 1980: 74). For the post-war period in the USA, Lynn Spigel makes the point that 'living without an array of machines meant that you were anachronistic, unable to keep up with the more progressive Joneses' (1990: 81). Labour-saving devices aimed at the US post-war housewife had the effect of driving up standards of cleanliness and hygiene rather than saving time

(Cowan, [1983] 1989). Where such devices are no longer marketed as labour-saving, they are instead associated with 'leisure, pleasure and higher standards of consumption' (Putnam, 1993: 157).

Electric plate-warmers and hot plates that enabled pre-preparation importantly freed the cook-hostess from having to coordinate the simultaneous readiness of meal components and assisted serving by allowing food to be left out for guests to help themselves:

> With smaller houses, better planning of kitchens in relation to eating-serving, and the growing tendency to eat at least some meals in the kitchen, keeping food hot is no longer the problem it was when protocol and several flights of stairs separated kitchen from dining room. Nevertheless there are occasions when equipment for keeping dishes hot can be useful: for invalids where food may be prepared in advance and left by a bedside; for parties to save constant trips to and from the table; for eating out of doors; for keeping coffee and other drinks hot.
>
> (Good, 1969: 53)

Again, Good makes a clear connection between the use of spaces within homes and the devices made to bridge them, arguing that a role remains for the plate warmer. Good's reference to 'smaller houses' points to the democratising function of domestic design in the post-war period. *WOBMH* displays a modern plate warmer, in tubular metal on a table set with lace place mats, showing that utilitarian forms associated with modernist design were combined with the more traditional decorative details (Figure 4.7). The caption to the figure directly below draws attention to the 'translucent

Electric plate-warmer for the sideboard by English Electric with translucent china in plain white

Figure 4.7 'Electric plate-warmer for the sideboard by English Electric with translucent china in plain white', *Woman's Own Book of Modern Homemaking*, 1967.

china in plain white' uniting utility and elegance, typifying the presentation of modernist design in domestic advice literature as rational, efficient and easily combined with markers of hospitality and comfort to produce a feminised modernity (Sparke, 1995; Kirkham, 1998).

But while the plate warmer merely preserves what has been achieved in the kitchen, the use of portable cooking equipment at the table turns the dining area into a temporary kitchen and allows entertaining to occur away from the kitchen and the dining room, as recommended by the *Esquire Party Book*:

> The whole family of electric appliances serves beautifully outside, too, if they can but reach an outlet. An electric griddle, its temperature set at 200, accommodates several small saucepans or casseroles. Electric skillets, fryer cookers, and roasters may all be used for accessory cookers, as well as warmers. And if outlets are limited, candle warmers keep dishes up to heat, when they've come directly from the oven in a heavy bake-serve pan.
>
> (Editors of *Esquire*, ([1935] 1965): 155)

Fondue is another example of cooking at the table, again influenced directly by the fashion for continental European modes of entertaining which gathered momentum in the post-war period, with the difference that guests were given the ingredients to prepare their own food. For *WOBMH*:

> Cooking at the table – by electric skillet, rotisserie or a thermostatically controlled cook-and-serve unit – is certainly one way of keeping the hostess in the conversation when tricky things like pancakes or soufflés are on the menu. But when the cooking involves fat or strong flavours such as onion and the dining room has no extractor fan, it can create its own problems with the decorations.
>
> (*Woman's Own*, 1967: 85)

WOBMH advised that such appliances must be used regularly, not just when guests are present, in order to repay their purchase price. Domestic advice writers show electric plate warmers and associated cooking devices literally bridging the gap between frontstage and backstage for the purposes of self-service by providing a microcosmic kitchen in the dining room.

The hostess trolley functions as a bridging device to varying degrees: while a simple trolley eases the transition from kitchen to dining room, a more complex model can function almost as a portable kitchen, for example in the garden, as here in the *Esquire Party Book*:

> Serving carts, with big wheels for navigating rough bricks and slates, are at least as useful as six more hands, both for serving and for cleaning up. If the cart's top has a built-in heating surface, so much the better, for keeping hot things hot is at least as much of a problem outdoors as it is indoors.
>
> (Editors of *Esquire*, ([1935] 1965): 154–155)

Figure 4.8 'Possible design for a service trolley...', illustration by K. Baker, in Geoffrey Salmon, *Storage: A Design Centre Publication*, 1967.

The hostess trolley was endorsed by the Council of Industrial Design in Geoffrey Salmon's 1967 book, which depicts a 'possible' trolley with closed storage for keeping plates and food hot (Figure 4.8), and in a later contribution to the same Design Centre series, when Good warns that 'Electrically-heated trolleys are undoubtedly practical, carrying as they do the complete meal and equipment, but unfortunately most of them are hideous and more evocative of the operating theatre than the dining room' (1969: 53). In contrast, the trolley Good depicts is 'laid for a buffet supper' (ibid. 52): while this trolley saves steps, it is nevertheless meticulously set, thereby reducing its labour-saving value. Similarly, the *Esquire Party Book* advises that whatever modifications are made to the conventional dinner party, the traditional values of hospitality be maintained.

> Whether 'dinner' means pot-luck with pot roast at the picnic table – or filet en brioche on the Spode – the fact that it is dinner guarantees certain niceties. Different niceties, we'll grant you, than they were a generation ago, but niceties withal! It may no longer be served in a dining-room, but the sun-room or loggia or garden that substitutes will be alive with flowers and paintings and music to dramatize the meal. It seldom steps out onto white damask anymore, but the heavy place-mats or colored

cloths that appear instead are no less handsome for all their modern practicality.

(Editors of *Esquire*, ([1935] 1965): 127)

In this paean to informalisation, the modernity promoted is democratic but not at odds with the display of decorative home comforts in the form of flowers, paintings and coloured cloths or place mats.

Collapsing the regions: from hatches to kitchen-diners

We have seen a number of solutions to Mrs. Three-in-One's dilemma focused on *bridging* discrete spaces in the home; another group of solutions revolved around *collapsing* distinct regions. The impassive ornamentalism of the hostess and the emphasis in domestic advice literature on her self-effacement and attentiveness to the needs of guests are connected to a much wider association of woman and home, articulated in the increasingly challenged trope of 'separate spheres' (Kerber, 1988; McGaw, 1989; Rupp, 2003). In this model, women are relegated to the domestic sphere to the extent they become inseparable from it. The separate macro spheres of home as feminised and outside world as masculinised were mirrored in Victorian conceptions of the home through clearly demarcated domestic regions, later termed 'front regions' and 'backstage' by Goffman ([1959] 1990). The social regions were displayed to guests while the backstage parts were inhabited by staff or family. The New Housekeeping continued this separation with a small, efficient backstage kitchen, separate from the social areas of the home. The space-saving fitted kitchens of interwar and post-war homes were welcomed as improvements on the previous conditions of many householders. However, while their size and arrangement made these fitted kitchens exemplary of Taylorist ideas about efficiency, by maintaining the separation between frontstage and backstage, they maintained the burden on Mrs. Three-in-One.

The service hatch, a horizontal relative of the 'dumb waiter', was a transitional solution to the problems of self-service. Sitting between the backstage kitchen and the social parts of the home, it rendered the boundary more porous. A notable precursor is found in the dining room of Thomas Jefferson's house at Monticello, in Virginia, USA, where a rotating door panel with shelves on one side allowed for the delivery and removal of food dishes. This hatch is one of several gadgets in Jefferson's dining room, including interlocking dining tables, dumb waiters for lifting wine up from the cellar, and tables with shelves positioned next to diners so they could help themselves to food during the course of a meal (Fowler, 2005). However, rather than facilitating unassisted hosting, the serving innovations at Monticello functioned to keep slaves and diners apart. The hatch was originally developed for use by servants in the 1920s and popularised by Frederick's *Household Engineering*, landmark text of the New Housekeeping.

Punch magazine satirised hatches in a 1926 cartoon of a maid climbing through a hatch, with the caption 'Do I have to come through this hole every time?' The maid's naive question is used to pillory the Efficiency Movement (Ward and Ward, 1978: 43). By the 1950s, the hatch was a feature of new homes and a commonplace improvement in old ones. Writing in 1962, E. S. Turner associated the hatch wholly with servants:

> In outer suburbia, where hundreds of thousands of bungalows and small houses were going up, builders incorporated 'service hatches' between kitchen and dining-room – just in case the householder was fortunate enough to find a maid. They continued to do so long after it was obvious that no maid could be found. A distinguished architect has described the survival of the serving hatch as a notable example of snobbishness. 'It is an arrangement that overlooks the fact that everyone knows there are no maids in the kitchen, and that men have at last been allowed into the kitchen to do the washing-up.'
> (Turner, 1962: 284, cites E. Lyons, *Daily Telegraph*,
> September 12, 1961)

Turner ignores the use of the hatch by the newly unassisted hostess, even though by 1962 she was a familiar character in domestic advice literature and magazines. Social historian Christina Hardyment suggests two benefits of the hatch, in addition to its capacity for 'saving steps': first, it obscured labour or its material evidence in the kitchen from guests, and second, it 'catered to the growing feeling that it was somehow not quite right for mum to be shut away in the kitchen' (1995: 57). Although developed for use by servants, the hatch was a useful transitional design solution for the unassisted hostess. It responded to the same conditions that catalysed the kitchen-diner and open-plan living solutions that followed.

Hatches did not immediately disappear through disuse, as E. S. Turner supposed, or misuse, as *Punch* joked; rather they were incorporated into more ambitious architectural solutions. Howard Robertson's *Reconstruction and the Home* of 1947 shows 'a pre-war Continental house' with a hatch built in to a storage unit dividing kitchen and dining room, called a 'buffet-dresser fitting' (1947: 31–32). Readers are told that 'on the dining room side the sliding doors are of glass in metal frames'; the opaque doors on the kitchen side remain unexplained as ways of maintaining the invisibility of domestic labour. This design saves labour by allowing equipment to be stored from the kitchen side following washing, and used directly from the dining side. British kitchen design was influenced by Lihotsky's German example and by US influences simultaneously (Holder, 2009). In 1950, Mary and Russel Wright's *Guide to Easier Living* presented similar solutions, allowing greater interplay between food preparation and dining areas. An image from the Walker Art Center's *Idea House II* – built in 1947 in Minneapolis, Minnesota, USA – shows a peninsular breakfast bar, which

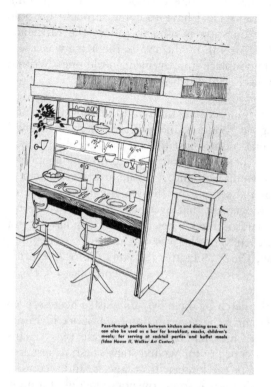

Pass-through partition between kitchen and dining area. This can also be used as a bar for breakfast, snacks, children's meals; for serving at cocktail parties and buffet meals (Idea House II, Walker Art Center).

Figure 4.9 'Room divider/peninsular unit from the Walker Art Center's Idea House II – built in Minneapolis, Minnesota, USA', Mary Wright and Russel Wright, *Guide to Easier Living*, [1950] 1954.

allows serving directly from the kitchen and easy return of crockery. However, it was probably intended only for family dining, as the seating is linear rather than in a conversational arrangement (Figure 4.9). In 1955, Eric Bird and Kenneth Holmes showcased a 'Dining-Kitchen', designed by Frederick Gibberd, in their book *Decorating for the Amateur*. Here, a peninsular unit acts both as a display case and as a way of maintaining a discrete dining area separate from the kitchen:

> The two halves of this dining-kitchen are separated by a cupboard fitting which has doors on both faces and which houses glass, china and cutlery. The pictures and decorative curtain show that meals in the kitchen need not involve absence of comfort and elegance.
>
> (Bird and Holmes, 1955: 86–87)

The emphasis here on display, 'comfort and elegance' suggests that the dining-kitchen could be used for entertaining. The peninsular unit contains closed cupboards in the lower half, a counter accessible from both sides, like a hatch, and glazed display and storage shelves in the upper portion, with a kitchen behind. This is a transitional example, in which a storage unit functions as a partial screen between preparation and eating areas.

The interwar and post-war advice sources that featured an efficient backstage kitchen often also showed an L-shaped living room to zone dining and living areas; for example, Post's *The Personality of a House*. But again, however flexible and suited to a newly enlarged middle-class market the living-dining room might have been, it did little to assist Mrs. Three-in-One. Her workload had been exacerbated by the maintenance of distinct regions of the home for food preparation and food service. During the mid-twentieth century, these distinct regions blurred so that public and private parts of the home combined into multi-functional and flexible spaces. A final solution to the hostess's physical difficulties with self-service is that the guests should go to her:

> Architects and builders, with housewives jogging their elbows, are now providing more space for kitchens, usually double the area they thought adequate in the 1930s. They are bringing them out of the back regions into the main part of the house, giving them a chance of sunshine and a good view from the sink. Walls between kitchen and dining room are coming down and being replaced by counters and cupboard units. Sometimes the kitchen is moved into the area once occupied by the traditional 'front room', or it is linked with the open plan living-room so that whatever she is doing about the dinner, the hostess is never shut out from the conversation or the television news.
>
> (*Woman's Own*, 1967: 59)

By the late 1970s, the prevalence of the kitchen-diner constituted a radical deconstruction of the Victorian ideal home, with its separate rooms for discrete functions. Domestic advisors went further, however.

Domestic advice literature of the late 1960s depicts the kitchen as a site for entertaining guests, in a logical progression from the hatch, and the hybrid kitchen and eating spaces which followed. So the party moved to the hostess-cook for her convenience, rather than vice versa as had previously been the case. This reversal illustrates the importance placed in home entertaining on maintaining the hostess's composure. Peninsular tables and units are both part of the kitchen itself and function as dividing forms, intersecting the domestic space. They are often shown set with formal place settings for dining: 'There's no better space and time-saver than the island unit' (*Woman's Own*, 1967: plate 11 between pp. 128–129). Just as the distinct roles of cook and hostess had been combined into one, so the stringent demarcations of the home into 'front regions' and 'backstage' became blurred in a material manifestation of the informalisation of domestic entertaining. Social problems are met with material solutions, each successively designed to deconstruct the division between front regions and backstage. Joyce Lowrie is not alone in recommending that the hall be used as 'a tiny, formal dining room for grown-ups' (1965: 18). Following Joe Colombo's limited edition Mini-kitchen for Boffi of 1963 (*Domus*, September 1964: 418; Ambasz, 1972: 123), John Prizeman's 'Sketch for Add-on Cooking Post' (Leslie, 2000: 92, plate 47) and Ilana Henderson's ingenious revolving kitchen (Good, 1969: 57) (Figure 4.10) negate the existence of the kitchen as a discrete space and redefine it as an object for use in any room. Henderson's revolving kitchen was developed with Bird's Eye, manufacturer of convenience foods. Good shows it along with more traditional furniture, such as the kitchen dresser, in a blend of old and new typical of the domestic advice genre. In an era in which broader influences of food preparation and consumption from the Mediterranean allowed a redefinition of home cooking as creative, Post's 'Mrs. Three-in-One' and Edwards and Beyfus's 'cook-hostess' increasingly left behind the more subordinate role of waitress. As Constance Spry and Rosemary Hume put it: 'The contemporary cook-hostess has the best of it, for she sees her efforts appreciated and hears the dishes discussed, which is a pleasant innovation' (Spry and Hulme,

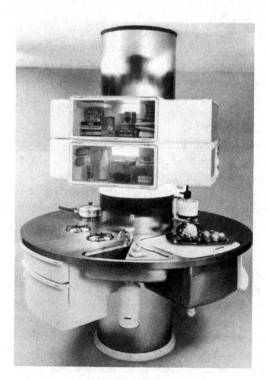

Figure 4.10 Ilana Henderson's revolving kitchen, in Elizabeth Good, *Tableware: A Design Centre Publication*, 1969.

1956: 56). However, just as her waitressing duties were eased by the solutions offered, the collapse of frontstage and backstage produced a situation of greater visibility and continuous performance for the cook-hostess, thereby increasing her social labour.

The problem with the solution: *More Work for Mother*

How successful were these more or less rational, and modernist, attempts to ease women's domestic roles? June Freeman has noted the 'emergence in the early years of the twentieth century of a revisionist ideology that shifted the emphasis away from getting women out of the home to easing the work of women within it' (2004: 34). In the case of 'labour-saving' appliances, Cowan ([1983] 1989) has argued that ensuing higher standards of cleanliness militated against the reduction of domestic work. And in reviewing ideas on kitchen design, Bullock has critiqued architects' new housing strategies as the imposition of a middle-class ideal on largely working-class communities (1988: 188), although their adoption was relatively limited until after the Second World War (Loehlin, 1999: 31). Traditional ideas about gender continued to exert a decisive influence on the divisions of domestic labour, as Jean-Claude Kaufmann has shown ([1992] 1998). While Joanna Bourke has argued that domestic education was a route through which women 'actively sought to redefine their status as women within the household' in a 'risk-averse' form of resistance to male dominance in the home (1994: 68–69, 80), Susan E. Reid (2005) has pointed out that advice published in Soviet Russia in the post-war period concerning the ways in which a woman might make the double burden of work and home easier, functioned to strengthen the idea that such a double burden was hers. Domestic education has been critiqued as a method of restricting, particularly working-class, women and girls to domestic roles (Attar, 1990; Davin, 1979; Dyhouse, 1981; Purvis, 1985; Turnbull, 1987). This analysis of British and American domestic advice literature demonstrates that the solutions it offered warrant a similarly sceptical view, as its portrayals of family roles functioned to naturalise inequality.

Ebullient bachelors: domestic advice literature for men

Writing about the importance of planning and managing housework, Catharine Beecher and Harriet Beecher Stowe recommend to the reader the 'apportioning of regular employment to [...] *all* her family'. Yet, the advice that follows is exclusively concerned with assistance from children and nothing more is said about husbands ([1869] 1991: 228). Nearly a hundred years later, Mary and Russel Wright state: 'it is important to have everyone share in the work to some extent' and they provide a schedule for housework to be shared by wife and husband ([1950] 1954: 135, 140). However, this is exceptional. In the 1970s, Loehlin has argued: 'Many [women] preferred to work part-time, since their increased work outside the home was not matched by their husbands' increased work inside the home' (1999: 176). Here, prescription is consistent with practice, as representations of men are comparatively absent from domestic advice literature, akin to the 'invisible men' in studies of representations of fathers (Nelson, 1995; LaRossa, 1997, 2004). Just as Veblen's ornamental hostess denoted her husband's wealth, so the leisure of the post-war host relied on and therefore communicated his wife's domestic skills in coping unassisted. Because domestic advice literature portrays men's domestic engagement as leisured, men seeking domestic advice would have consulted books aimed at women. Men's domestic contributions are most prevalent in do-it-yourself magazines marketed to a largely male audience (Gelber, 1999; Goldstein, 1998). This applies to the UK and the USA alike. Bourke has argued that interwar and post-war suburban housing improvements and higher levels of home ownership for working-class families distanced men from their paid work, and offered greater space and motivation for domestic hobbies such as carpentry. Boys received training in manual skills and gardening at school, as a correlative to girls' domestic training (Bourke, 1994: 85). The association of women with domesticity and the concomitant absence of representations of men in domestic discourse attracted a number of critiques. *Playboy* magazine's cookery column challenged a conformist middle-class 'feminized and suburban domestic ideal' (Hollows, 2002: 142), while the magazine presents home decorating as an expression of masculinity (Osgerby, 2001; Wagner, 1996; Snyder, 1998). However, representations of male engagement with domesticity underplay the daily grind of household labour (deemed to be women's work) showing instead the leisured and occasional domestic involvement of men, as in domestic advice books.

Of course, advice books are written for men, including, notably, success manuals (Hilkey, 1997). However, relatively few of these concern domestic advice. And, the relatively few domestic advice books to have addressed domestic matters for a male readership focus on the special case of home entertaining rather than daily homemaking practices. The ebullient *Esquire Party Book* proclaimed the virtues of self-service to lone male hosts as adding positive qualities not available to staffed entertainments:

> Once upon a time when you wanted to give a party, you called Ye Olde Family Retainer and said 'Dinner for 12, please, James.' BUT THAT WAS LIGHT-YEARS AGO. NOW when you want to give a party, it's on *you*. You plan it; you shop for it; you cook it; and nine times out of ten, you serve it. [...] For the joy of today's entertaining at home is the chance it gives YOU to make each party your own – *your* style, which is after all the best style for you. [...] Your welcome is the Prime Meridian – the starting point from which to reckon the success of each party – so try to open the door yourself for each guest.
>
> (Editors of *Esquire*, [1935] 1965: 2)

The repetition of the word 'you' emphasises the pivotal role of the host and the opportunity his party offers for self-expression. The confidently humorous tone of this text belies the concern for which it caters and may reflect its address to bachelors rather than housewives. Hostesses are mentioned occasionally, usually where the menu requires assistance; this dual address is shown in Seymour Chwast's book jacket, with a waiter on the front and a waitress on the reverse.

Desmond Briggs's *Entertaining Single-Handed* (1968), also directed at male readers, similarly employs a bullish voice distinct from that of many domestic advice books and emphasises self-expression in home entertaining.

> you must compose your menu with the care of an impressionist, so that nothing clashes, everything blends yet contrasts with piquancy. Equally you should dip your culinary brush into a palette made up of the delicious, the strange, the provoking, the fresh and the humble.
>
> (Briggs, 1968: 66)

Here, the act of home entertaining is aggrandised by comparison with the expertise of a fine artist. The cover features an image of a cook hiding behind the kitchen door while serving crowding guests from a saucepan. Even this depiction of party flurry can be interpreted as a complement to the cooking. The absence of male characters, and their leisured disengagement where they do appear, results in a grossly unequal distribution of labour in domestic advice literature:

> If there is no reliable man around the house or children of a sensible age, detail someone to help with the serving. Decide who is to do what. Men usually fix the drinks and do the carving, while the hostess serves up the food and clears it away.
>
> (Edwards and Beyfus, [1956] 1957: 6)

By women, for women?

We saw in Chapter 1 how women's authorship of domestic advice increased from 1880 onwards and that this has been associated with female empowerment (Arditi, 1996: 417; Curtin, 1985: 419). Much domestic advice literature to have addressed the unassisted hostess was produced *by* women, *for* women, and contains a great deal of positive supportive advice. Yet, domestic advisors can nevertheless be seen functioning conservatively by attributing to women the greater part of domestic labour, thereby perpetuating the home as a space of leisure for men.

In 1962, Sarah Maclean's *The Pan Book of Etiquette and Good Manners* counselled: 'if you find yourself enjoying your own party, it's ten to one your guests aren't' (1962: 151). Maclean refers to the amount of work undertaken by the hostess to secure the pleasure of others, but in so doing she also perpetuates the impassivity of the hostess of 1923. That Maclean's book is aimed at a female readership is denoted not only by the choice of author – a journalist for *Woman* magazine – but also by its cover design, which shows a pensive female protagonist wondering about etiquette questions such as 'what is ... the right food and drink to serve?' (Figure 4.11). In 1986, Lady Elizabeth Anson argued, persuasively, that 'there is surely very little point in giving a party unless you, as the host or hostess, can enjoy it too', although her concern for her readers' pleasure is tied to her promotion of her party planning company, thereby returning the hostess to a consumer of the labour of others (Anson, 1986: 17).

These examples – of a heavy domestic workload (whether or not in addition to work outside the home), of women not enjoying themselves 'too much' and of the representation of women as consumers rather than producers – demonstrate how domestic advice literature, as a discourse by women for women, has missed the opportunity of more radical solutions and has reproduced patriarchal conditions. Advice discourses can offer alternatives to the prevailing patriarchal ideology, such as that promoted by radicalised middle-class housewives in the USA (Murray, 2003; Hartmann, 1998). In terms of published advice, rather than activism, however, those

Figure 4.11 Back cover, Sarah Maclean, *The Pan Book of Etiquette and Good Manners*, 1962.

that appear radical or subversive can be shown, under analysis, to be less progressive. I have shown how domestic advice arouses anxiety in order to market solutions. The sources I have examined in this chapter suggest that this motivation might be at the heart of domestic advice literature delivered in the ostensibly definitive book format. As well as providing solutions that advisors thought women needed, such sources also accorded with broader social norms and pressures.

In 1962, Helen Gurley Brown's *Sex and the Single Girl* was first published in the USA, with a British edition the following year. While Brown's subjects are conventional – advice about men is combined with guidance on decorating and entertaining – her address to a single girl was radical at the time, as domestic advice books were associated with being in training for, and setting up, a marital home and were given as wedding gifts. Brown notes that magazines do not help much with the 'special' problems of the 'Single Girl': 'All the recipe pages do is make it pretty clear that if you aren't stuffing a twenty-pound bird with chestnut-and-bacon dressing you are weakening the moral fibre of the nation' and 'The very word "entertaining" sounds kind of snooty and married'. Cook books, too, are implicated. They 'are hardly the ally they should be to a neophyte cook. Instead of taking a girl gently by the hand and making things *simple*, they have a cavalier way of calling for stock ... or leftover chicken' (Brown, [1962] 1963: 148). But, 'reading cookbooks like literature can help make you a good cook, once you get over your initial fright' (ibid. 148). Brown's observation that magazines did not address the needs of single girls was prophetic: by 1965 she was editor of *Cosmopolitan*, remaining in post for 32 years and then monitoring *Cosmopolitan*'s international editions (Brown, 2000).

The single girl Brown depicts is an independent, feisty and pleasure-seeking careerist, quite different to the impassive ornamental hostess in temperament as well as class. Brown's book clearly exemplifies charismatic legitimisation. Her writing echoes the ebullient tone of advice for bachelors:

> Cooking gourmetishly is a particularly impressive skill for a career woman. Everybody expects fluffy dumplings from a wife and mother [...] *Your* head, they figure, is too stuffed with schemes for becoming the first woman Prime Minister or stealing somebody's husband to be able to cope with the recipes. It's fun to hand them a surprise! Put on an organdy apron, retire to the kitchen and come back with impeccable Eggs Benedict. Then listen to the purrs and praise ... very soul satisfying.
>
> (Brown, [1962] 1963: 146–147)

In its joyful emphasis on entertaining as leisure, this passage recalls advice for men, from the *Esquire Party Book* to *Entertaining Single-Handed*. Brown recommends that the single girl should invest some of her earnings in hiring a decorator for her flat, which should be designed to attract men with lots of pictures and travel posters, a small television, books, a simple hi-fi, a well-appointed kitchen, big towels, etc.:

> Brown, perhaps even more than feminist Betty Friedan, whose *Feminine Mystique* followed *Sex and the Single Girl* in 1963, sensed the profound misogyny which was spreading under the suburban 'dream houses' like seepage from a leaky tank. Men resented their domestication, and hated the company of sexless 'Moms.' Brown advised her single girls to avoid the Formica practicality of the suburbs and transform their apartments into lairs of erotic fascination.
>
> (Ehrenreich and English, [1978] 1989: 287)

A market for more or less subversive discourse emerged during the 1970s, from the feminism of *Spare Rib* and *Ms.* magazines, launched in 1972 in the UK and the USA respectively, to the insistence on individualist freedom that characterised *Cosmopolitan* under Brown's editorship. These publications stood in contrast to many more formulaic magazines for women and each, in very different ways, tried to empower readers in terms of class as well as gender (Ouellette, 1999). Both in *Sex and the Single Girl* and in her editorship of *Cosmopolitan*, Brown was influential in offering alternatives to the association of women with domesticity that dominated representations of women in domestic advice. However, Brown's promotion of women as seductresses was hardly progressive in the permissive society and, in retrospect, was a pyrrhic victory.

The domestic advice genre was parodied for failing to offer effective solutions for the unassisted housewife. Parodic domestic advice books at least lightened the readers' lives with laughter, thereby engaging charismatic legitimisation. In the same year that *Sex and the Single Girl* first appeared, Peg Bracken's *The I Hate to Housekeep Book: When and How to Keep House without Losing Your Mind* ([1962] 1963) appeared as a follow-up to *The I Hate to Cook Book* (1960), which sold three million copies before its fiftieth anniversary edition of 2010. The *Appendix to the I Hate to Cook Book* (1966) was published in the UK as *The I Still Hate to Cook Book* ([1967] 1980) and subsequent spin-off titles referenced literary history: *The I Hate to Cook Almanack: A Book of Days* (1976), published in the UK as *The I Hate to Cook Book of the Year: A Book of Days* (1977), and *The Compleat I Hate to Cook Book* (1986). *I Try to Behave Myself: Peg Bracken's Etiquette Book* (1964) appeared in the UK as *Instant Etiquette Book* ([1964] 1969). Bracken's popularity sustained two memoirs, *A Window over the Sink: A Mainly Affectionate Memoir* (1981) and *On Getting Old for the First Time* (1997).

Bracken's irreverence can be viewed as part of the domestic humour genre of the 1950s and 1960s, which included the fictionalised autobiographic short stores of Shirley Jackson, discussed below. Bracken's chapter 'How to Be Happy When Miserable' addresses 'days which lose their momentum before they ever get any, and the only sort of job you are up to is a small one, like twirling your cowlick' ([1962] 1963: 91). The situation Bracken describes was articulated the following year as 'The Problem that Has No Name', in Betty Friedan's *The Feminine Mystique* ([1963] 1982). Bracken's recommendation of 'an automatic dishwasher' (an expensive item in 1963), and of the benefits of paid assistance, suggests that her audience is a middle class one. Dedicated to 'the occasional or random housekeeper', Bracken humorously advised: 'Keep the pots and pans you cook in out of sight, in the cupboards or drawers. The only people who should hang up their copper cooking pots are those who enjoy polishing pot bottoms' ([1962] 1963: 3–4). Bracken advises that cleaning should start in a different room each time, so that 'you will at least peter out in a different place each time' (ibid. 4). Ultimately, however, Bracken's book remains wholly conservative. The title implies a rejection of domesticity, but the book comprises short cuts and thrifty solutions that may allow women to spend less time and money performing domestic labour, but are no more revolutionary than that. Bracken recommends that if readers feel overwhelmed by the number of domestic tasks they must perform in a day, they should start all of them, making it impossible not to finish them all: 'you must forge ahead, that's all' (ibid. 95–96). She even suggests that the homemaker's misery be soothed through further exposure to the work that is making her miserable in the first place:

> On the theory that she couldn't be more miserable anyway, [a friend] devotes a day to doing all the repellent jobs she should have done long ago: cleans the coat cupboard, polishes windowsills, answers old cob-webbed letters, mends her husband's workshop overalls. This seems to clear her decks.
>
> (Bracken, [1962] 1963: 93–94)

Even the suggestions which do not revolve around domestic work are further reinscriptions of conventional feminine roles, such as Bracken's recommendation of 'a really excellent manicure, then get out of your blue jeans and into your high heels' (ibid. 99, 101). Bracken recognises the depression Friedan describes as endemic among women of the period, and yet she urges her readers to get the job done with advice by turns ridiculous and deadly serious, epitomising the contradiction of these progressive texts.

Ostensibly more radical than Bracken's humour is that of US comedienne Phyllis Diller, whose *Housekeeping Hints* appeared in 1966 (Figure 4.12). Dedicating her book to 'all the ladies who would rather skip the housework', Diller claimed that 'When you have mastered this book your house will be a mess, your marriage a flop, your children vagrants, and your friends just a memory – or your money back' (1966: flyleaf). Chapters such as 'The Hostess with the Leastest' include advice such as 'Do not have company when the sunlight is streaming through the windows. Everything shows up. Either entertain at night, or close the drapes and break the cord.'

Figure 4.12 Cover, *Phyllis Diller's Housekeeping Hints* by Phyllis Diller, 1966.

And a list of 'What Amy Vanderbilt Doesn't Tell You' displays the self-referentiality of the domestic advice genre, albeit for comic effect and charismatic legitimisation.

Some feminist scholars have argued that domestic humour can be regarded as a transformative 'discourse of discontent', promoting solidarity among housewives and resistance to sexist role definitions (Moskowitz, 1996). Jessamyn Neuhaus has tested this theory using the case study of Shirley Jackson, author of two collections of fictionalised autobiographical short stories, *Life Among the Savages* (published in the USA in 1952 and in the UK in 1954) and *Raising Demons* (1957). For Neuhaus, Jackson 'was no feminist: she never overtly questioned those norms regarding domestic roles'. Letters to Jackson show that her fans were 'resigned to the inevitability of women's domestic duties and, in that sense, her domestic humour did not push them to question their circumstances. But it also suggested to them a strategy for pursuing a career that blurred home and public by writing about the domestic.' They used her 'housewife humour as a starting point for articulating the importance of pursuing a greater sense of self, or subjectivity' (Neuhaus, 2009: 120).

Betty Friedan censured domestic humour writers for encouraging readers to 'dissipate in laughter their dreams and their sense of desperation' while the authors themselves enjoyed their own extra-domestic professional successes ([1963] 1982: 57). The social reinforcement of the reductive home-centred roles available to women damaged self-esteem and produced unhappiness and frustration, Friedan argued. She criticised domestic discourse for exacerbating the problem that has no name, as home economists suggested more domestic education to better prepare women for their home roles:

> For over fifteen years, the words written for women, and the words women used when they talked to each other, while their husbands sat on the other side of the room and talked shop or politics or septic tanks, were about problems with their children, or how to keep their husbands happy, or improve their children's school, or cook chicken, or make slip-covers.
>
> (Friedan [1963] 1982: 31, 16)

Friedan proposed that 'education, and only education, has saved, and can continue to save, American women from the greater dangers of the feminine mystique'.

Friedan's concluding chapter 'A New Life Plan for Women' stresses the satisfaction to be gained from a professional career, but she cautions that unless domestic arrangements are revised accordingly, women's workloads would be unacceptably increased ([1963] 1982: 311). Friedan's critique therefore extends to modernist domestic designs and practices:

> Take, for instance, the open plan of the contemporary 'ranch' or split-level house, $14,990 to $54,990, which has been built in the millions from Roslyn Heights to the Pacific Palisades. They give the illusion of more space for less money. But the women to whom they are sold almost *have* to live the feminine mystique. There are no true walls or doors; the woman in the beautiful electronic kitchen is never separated from her children. In what is basically one free-flowing room, instead of many rooms separated by walls and stairs, continual messes continually need picking up. A man, of course, leaves the house for most of the day. But the feminine mystique forbids the woman this.
>
> (Friedan, [1963] 1982: 216)

The tyranny of open plan living for women is exemplified in the case of Mies van der Rohe's house for Edith Farnsworth (Friedman, 1996), in which a male architect visited his vision of an open plan house on a female client. Just as the all-purpose kitchen was replaced by the small food preparation kitchens of Frederick's *Household Engineering* and Lihotsky's 'Frankfurt Kitchen', so the open-plan solutions designed to assist the cook-hostess in performing competing roles simultaneously increased women's domestic work by collapsing the front region and backstage, thereby effectively removing the backstage. Daniel Horowitz has argued that Friedan deliberately presented her own life as one which typified the situation she described, and underplayed her own radicalism and professional achievements, in order to placate a right-wing culture of McCarthyism into which her book was launched (1998; Hennessee, 1998). Radical solutions are not easily accepted by a conservative mainstream audience.

Friedan popularised an argument which had been broached before in domestic advice literature. Amabel Williams-Ellis's *The Art of Being a Woman* (1951) contains a chapter which asked 'What's Short in my Diet?' and considered a number of causes women's unhappiness, including 'not a lack of practical adventure but that they feel cut off from the adventure of the mind. They hunger for more learning and study or for more artistic experience' (1951: 124). The book's flyleaf pinpoints the dilemma:

> Home, of course, is deeply important, but will a home in which the wife and mother is a 'Human Sacrifice' really be a happy one? On the other hand, what about the career woman who gives up her emotional life as a bad job?
>
> (Williams-Ellis, 1951: flyleaf)

Novelist and broadcaster Williams-Ellis was the wife of architect Clough Williams-Ellis and she is described in her book's author biography through association with her father (a writer), cousin (writer Lytton Strachey) and brother (writer and politician), which also reassures prospective readers that Williams-Ellis 'has certainly not written a solemn feminist tract' (Williams-Ellis, 1951: flyleaf). She had been literary editor of *The Spectator*, and 'was able to do the double job of home and work and to take a lively interest in the main aspects of the world around her'. The text explores the competing roles performed by women, echoed in the cover illustration by Bradley of an aproned woman reading, surrounded by smaller women shopping, dancing, in a nurse's uniform, in overalls brandishing a spanner, in ceremonial dress, and in trousers and boots, raking the earth (Figure 4.13). It seems that the solution to the problem of women's roles is multiplication not simplification: for Williams-Ellis the fulfilling female life comprises a variety of roles.

Bradley's 1951 image of the multiple women on the cover of *The Art of Being a Woman* compares with Jan Mitchener's 1972 image of ten men performing professional roles that impact, more or less directly, on the home (Figure 4.14). The latter appears in Shirley Conran's *Superwoman* (1975). Using the encyclopaedic format of a two-column list of action points, for quick reference, Conran promotes women's fast competent performance of

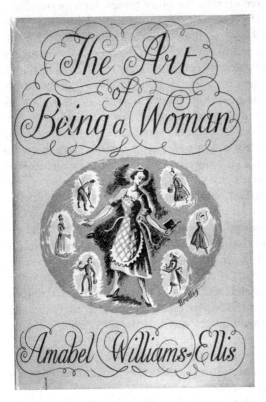

Figure 4.13 Cover, Amabel Williams-Ellis, *The Art of Being a Woman*, 1951.

Figure 4.14 'How to Get Hold of the Men in Your Life', illustration by Jan Mitchener for Shirley Conran, *Superwoman*, [1975] 1977.

household tasks in order to free up time for other things, such as running a business or getting an Open University degree (a message elaborated in the follow-up, *Superwoman 2*, of 1977). Conran's motto 'life is too short to stuff a mushroom' has entered common usage. Yet, given the progressive nature of the informal, youth-oriented lifestyle promoted by Conran's husband, Terence – designer, Soup Kitchen restaurateur and Habitat retail founder – her book is surprisingly conventional. Mitchener's drawing illustrates a page entitled 'How to Get Hold of the Men in Your Life', where the reader is supposed to fill in telephone numbers for the various tradesmen who assist in the smooth running of the home. It shows a policeman, a carpenter, a florist, a butcher, a milkman, a plumber, a window cleaner and a vet, all male, thereby emphasising that men should do these jobs for women. Mitchener and Conran's *Superwoman* is a domestic consumer, not a domestic producer like Bradley and Williams-Ellis's woman. While post-war sociologists and social scientists argued that industrialisation deprived women of their functional role within the household and that a shift in the home from production to consumption ensued, many of the major domestic technologies continue to involve production, such as laundry (Cowan [1983] 1989: 85). Like the open-plan living spaces promoted for the fact that they enabled women to perform several simultaneous tasks, Conran's *Superwoman* promises to advise women in how they can do it all. In this it differs very little from Amabel Williams-Ellis's suggestions of a generation earlier. The period between 1951 and 1972 had been a significant one for the international women's movement and second-wave feminism, yet this is not reflected as much as it might have been in the conservative domestic advice genre.

Brown, Friedan, Bracken and Conran all published best-selling works, which placed women's experiences on the mainstream agenda, using charismatic legitimisation. However, the commercial success of these books resulted partly from the way in which their radicalism, such as it was, was incremental and leavened with conservatism. Brown's emphasis on sexual independence and the role of seductress confines women to the stereotypical role of man's helpmate. Bracken's humour is essentially hollow and functions to reinstate hegemony, like that of Bedford and Mitford (discussed in Chapter 3). Rather than suggesting that partners should shoulder more domestic work, these sources emphasised strategies for women to cope alone. Parodic domestic advice challenges the conventions and authority of the genre: this is a positive thing, as is making women laugh to help them to reconcile themselves to a disproportionate domestic workload. However, it did not do any practical good for women in terms of *reducing* their competing roles. As welcome as it may have been for women, and even men, to read advice with the sweetener of knowing, conspiratorial humour, these books were arguably more cynical than the textual models they intended to parody and subvert. These books subvert the conventions of the advice genre only temporarily, before returning to conventional advice. In so doing they bring more disappointment, at least to a retrospective reader, than those books which have struggled to remain current, such as Post's *Etiquette*. Advice for women which positioned itself as subversive and yet remained ideologically within the mainstream is, perhaps, the most cynical of all. Domestic advice literature, as a discourse by women for women, thus missed the opportunity for a more radical solution to the problem of women's happiness.

Conclusion

This chapter has examined some of the solutions presented by domestic advisors in response to the emergence of a readership who wanted advice on how to entertain without domestic staff, principally the newly unassisted middle-class hostesses, but also women from the materially reduced upper class, and the aspirational working class. Representations of the unassisted hostess in domestic advice literature suggest that far from fitting the production-to-consumption model, the work of the hostess may equally be expressed as the reverse. Domestic advice literature presented the pre-war and interwar hostess as a lady of the leisure class acting in a largely symbolic capacity, consistent with Veblen's model of conspicuous consumption, and underplayed her domestic duties, due to their hidden nature. The new character of Mrs. Three-in-One, and the consequently undeniable engagement of the hostess in active labour, severely hampered the expression of existing virtues.

Domestic advisors of the post-war period offered visual and textual representations which ostensibly solved the problems of the unassisted hostess, while also constructing an ideal in which women competently performed multiple simultaneous roles. Accommodation of the newly unassisted hostess was recommended through modifications to the design and layout of the ideal home, in a series of solutions which engaged rational legitimisation. Modernist design values such as space-saving, flexibility, multi-functionality, informality and practicality were applied in the design of bridging devices and practices. Front and backstage regions were bridged by trolleys, hatches, appliances and oven-to-tableware. Discrete kitchens, sitting rooms and dining rooms – popularised prior to the twentieth century – were collapsed in preference for a return to multipurpose flexible rooms, such as living-dining rooms, and ultimately the open-plan kitchen-dining space and the kitchen dinner party. Open-plan and flexible spaces functioned to reduce Mrs. Three-in-One's work as a waitress, but by opening up the backstage space of the kitchen to the frontstage spaces of reception areas, such solutions increased the labour of the unassisted hostess by exposing her work to the gaze of her guests. It has been argued that domestic advice literature is incapable of changing social relations and is instead doomed to replicate them (Armstrong and Tennenhouse, 1987); so the redesign of the home in response to new social problems can be seen as similarly ineffectual. These material solutions enabled the coterminous performance of competing roles, and therefore the more radical and effective proposition that labour might be distributed more equally within the household was avoided. Advice literature aimed primarily at women, advice for a male readership, and parodic quasi-advice books writ-ten by women, for women, which engaged charismatic legitimisation, all had the opportunity to promote radical solutions to the problem of women's unequal burden in the home, but while domestic advice literature for women simply offers tips for managing unassisted, and domestic advice literature for men typically presents domestic labour as a leisure activity for a bachelor, domestic humour is arguably the most cynical of all, because its authors know that they are tackling an inequitable situation, and their answer is sim-ply to laugh, rather than try to change things.

Open-plan and multi-functional domestic spaces have continued to be popular with domestic advisors and householders so that home entertaining has been subject to the aestheticisation of everyday life discussed in Chapter 3. More recent developments such as the Cittàslow movement founded in 1999 and the Slow Food movement (Pink, 2007), a return to seasonal food, increased awareness of nutrition and health issues, and pressing ecological concerns have combined to make convenience foods and supermarket shop-ping unattractive for some consumers. The practice of cooking from scratch further increases the domestic workload for householders, and particularly women. The battery of devices designed to assist food production in the home increases year on year, as manufacturers and retailers continue to promote bread makers, ice cream machines, waffle makers and yoghurt- and cheese-making equipment, with each implying a further process to be undertaken in the domestic kitchen. These appliances increase the domestic workload, rather than reducing it, in a manner Cowan has noted ([1983] 1989). Concern about the time involved in cooking is exemplified by the popularity of titles such as *How to Cheat at Cooking* (Smith, 1971, 2008), *Martha Stewart's Dinner at Home: 52 Quick Meals to Cook for Family and Friends* (2009) and *Jamie's 15-Minute Meals* (Oliver, 2012). It may be possible to produce a meal quickly using ready-made ingredients, but not all aspects of domesticity can be completed with such ease. Domestic advice literature has not always func-tioned in the best interests of women. Advice books that promised *Easier Living* actually promoted *More Work for Mother* (Wright and Wright, [1950] 1954; Cowan, [1983] 1989).

5 Advice and *The Teenage Consumer* at home

The youth problem: advice and the generations

In the years after the Second World War, recognition of what was termed the 'youth problem' permeated the British media and was a continuing theme in US media sources. The rise of the teenager presented new problems for advisors to address. Chapter 4 showed how domestic advice literature attempted to ease the burden of the unassisted hostess by using social and material strategies that bridged, and then collapsed, the regions of the home; so advice about the cohabitation of teenagers and their parents was also marked by duality. This chapter examines the social and material solutions offered by domestic advice writers to teens and their parents as having been characterised by both flexibility and fixity, and examines how advice writers attempted the tricky task of addressing two generations at once.

The rise of the teenager

What is a teenager? 'Teenage' is used as a popular synonym for 'adolescence'. While the teenage years are strictly defined as those from 13 to 19, the behavioural patterns that characterise the teen years typically extend further to what we might term a 'long teenage', similar in age range to that of 'adolescence' and, even more broadly, 'youth'. G. Stanley Hall's *Adolescence* of 1904 was influential in the identification of the emotional patterns of 'storm and stress' and the recognition of adolescence as a distinct life stage (Hall, 1904; Arnett, 2006). This recognition, and mass culture responses to it, constitute the 'rise' of the teenager. American historian John R. Gillis places the discovery of adolescence between 1870 and 1900, the 'Era of Adolescence' from 1900 to 1960, and 'The End of Adolescence' in the 1960s, as young people became increasingly involved in political unrest and benefitted from social and legal changes which increased their autonomy (Gillis, 1981). The history of the English language, too, points to the increasing prominence of teens in interwar, Second World War and post-war America and Britain. While 'adolescence', 'adolescent' and 'teen' have long etymologies (the latter dates from the seventeenth century), 'teen age' dates from 1921 in the USA and 1948 in the UK, with 'teenager' and 'tween-teens' as neologisms of 1941, 'Tweens, Inc.' as a brand name from 1946 and 'tween' in use from 1964 (*OED Online*, 2012).

In 1942, American sociologist Talcott Parsons coined the term 'youth culture', and the American Youth Commission published its report *Youth and the Future*. 'Youth is a time of frustration', the report admitted. 'Escape from parental control' is listed as one of the distinct 'Needs of Youth':

> Under the impact of modern conditions of living brought about by the automobile, the radio, the motion picture, and other factors, as well as the upward trend in the age of school leaving and of beginning employment, the social organization of life in the adolescent years has changed since the time before the first World War. Those who spent their own adolescent years in the old order have had great difficulty in adjusting to the new situation when confronted with their responsibilities as parents. Fortunately, this particular period of difficulty will soon be past. The 'flaming youth' of the early 1920s have now become themselves the parents of adolescent youth.
>
> (American Youth Commission, 1942: 111, 107, 173)

The Commission was set up in the aftermath of the Depression, to plan for the futures of young people in a period when the 'youth problem' meant, principally, youth unemployment (Bell, 1938). The increasing cultural prominence of teens after 1945 has been attributed to the hastening onset of puberty, the segregation of young people in institutions of formal education and the extension of the period of training and education for young men and, to a lesser extent, women (Moran, 2000: 15). In Britain, Butler's Education Act of 1944 raised the school-leaving age to fifteen (it was raised again to sixteen in 1973), and the 1963 Robbins Committee recommendation of a significant expansion of higher education increased the student population (Cook and Stevenson, 1996: 110; Lord Chancellor's Department, 1967; Sillitoe, [1971] 1973: 99). So the period between childhood and the adoption of the conventional responsibilities of adulthood, such as long-term financial commitments and parenthood, was extended in the post-war period. This period was also significant in the history of youth culture due to demographic and economic factors: there were more teenagers, those teenagers spent more and had more money spent on them. Forty years after the American Youth Commission's report, a social study of young people – this time in Europe – identified youth unemployment as merely symptomatic of the core problem of socialisation (Coleman and Husén, 1985).

Historians have argued that the economic and social context for the teenager's rise was established in the USA and the UK by the 1920s (Fowler, 2008: 1; 1996; Savage, 2007). However, not all members of a society experience the same trends at the same time and family issues, in particular, can take a 'generative' form of influence from one generation to the next. The very unrest which, for Gillis, marked the demise of youth culture in the

1960s also ensured its rise to notoriety in the mainstream media, which reported the teenager as a relatively novel cultural persona over a much longer period. Popular histories have represented the 1960s as a flowering of youth culture – the 'youthquake' – and as a beginning, rather than an end. Indeed, domestic advice writers have continued to respond to the problems of, and problems with, teenagers up to the present day.

The Teenage Consumer

In 1959, Britain's largest advertising agency, the London Press Exchange, published a report by British social scientist and businessman Mark Abrams entitled *The Teenage Consumer*. Abrams has been criticised, retrospectively, for presenting the teenager as new, when youth culture was already well established by this time (Fowler, 1996). Yet, his work anticipated the economic effects of rising birth rates in the 1950s and 1960s, which have been described by demographer David Coleman as 'the most interesting feature of post-war fertility in the developed world' (2000: 40). Abrams predicted that 'between now and 1969 the number of teenagers in Britain will increase by at least 20 per cent' (1959: 17). Post-war employment opportunities for young people exceeded those of their parents. A growing market of teenagers and young people forged identities separate from parents and other authority figures, through the leisure and consumption trends of youth culture, including wearing distinctive styles of clothing, hair and make-up, informal social interaction such as impromptu late-night parties, extensive engagement in public entertainments, especially music-centred events, and the consumption of novel 'lifestyle' goods and services. Abrams explained that teenagers spent their money 'mainly on dressing up in order to impress other teenagers and on goods which form the nexus of teenage gregariousness outside the home' (ibid. 10). Manufacturers, designers, marketing professionals and retailers targeted the disposable income of the newly distinct youth market, just as they targeted the parents of babies and young children (Cross, 1997; Jacobson, 2004). Teen magazines contributed to the defining of the teenager consumer (Massoni, 2006; Savage, 2007: 441–454).

In the USA, by the mid-1960s over half of the population was aged under thirty (Briggs, 1994: 100). In the same year that Abrams' *The Teenage Consumer* appeared in Britain, US magazine *Life* reported on a 'New, $10 Billion Power: The U.S. Teen-Age Consumer':

> To some people the vision of a leggy adolescent happily squealing over the latest fancy present from Daddy is just another example of the way teen-agers are spoiled to death these days. But to a growing number of businessmen the picture spells out the profitable fact that the American teen-agers have emerged as a big-time consumer in the U.S. economy. They are multiplying in numbers. They spend more and have more spent on them. And they have minds of their own about what they want.
>
> (*Life*, 1959)

Teenagers wanted different things and more of them: 'What Depression-bred parents may still think of as luxuries are looked on as necessities by their offspring'. Hence the teen's economic impact: 'If parents have any idea of organized revolt, it is already too late. Teen-age spending is so important that such action would send quivers throughout the entire national economy.' *Life* depicts the extent of teenage consumption, in a series of photographs profiling Californian Suzie Slattery as a typically pampered teenage girl. The demographic growth of teenagers post-war, the increased earning potential of young people and associated uplift in social status, and widespread recognition of teens' distinct needs and behaviours in mainstream media and advice discourses contributed to a belief that young people needed their own spaces for relaxation at home.

If contemporary commentators on youth culture veered between chronicling – and generating – moral panic and celebrating the colourful characters seen in cities and on high streets, so historians have focused on the public, social and commercial effects of youth culture at the expense of its domestic impact (Cohen, 1972; Hall and Jefferson, 1975; Austin and Willard, 1998). This emphasis on public youth cultures has obscured the engagement of girls, who participated in youth culture 'upstairs in their bedrooms' (McRobbie and Garber, 1991; Steele and Brown, 1995; Lincoln, 2004). Yet, social anxieties about youth culture are reflected in representations of the teenager in domestic advice literature, where the home functions as a microcosm, a society in miniature, and the teenager is the singular of youth culture's plural. The relationship between environment and behaviour, and the belief that shaping an individual's space shapes the individual, has preoccupied child experts, designers and architects alike, but they have focused on institutional rather than domestic sites. Children's rooms have not received the same level of academic attention accorded to rooms for adults (Ogata, 2008–2009), and teenage rooms have been similarly neglected. Yet, intergenerational tension has surely been most acutely felt in the home, where young people and parents exist in close proximity (Goldscheider *et al.*, 2001). This tension goes largely unrecorded, though an exception is Adrienne Salinger's photographs of teenagers in their rooms accompanied by statements from the teenagers themselves, often concerning their relationships with parents or other authority figures (Salinger, 1995). The public and institutional emphasis of popular and academic accounts of youth culture alike has meant that historians have consulted cinema, fashion and popular music at the expense of advice literature, which is also complicated by being neither a direct record of practice, nor entirely fictional.

Americanisation and transatlantic influences

In post-war Britain, both youth culture and consumerism were bound up with fears of Americanisation. Historian Ross McKibbin has observed that 'the history of England in this period is also the history of the English idea of America' (1998: 523). Americanisation was assisted by the foreign consumption of Hollywood movies, and youth culture was understood in Britain partly through American films such as *The Wild One*, with Marlon Brando (1953), and *Teenagers from Outer Space* (shown in the UK as *The Gargon Terror*) of 1959, which contrasts positive and negative models of teen behaviour (Baker, 2005; Clapp, 2007; MacKinnon, 2004). Youth culture has been associated with rebellion in both the USA and the UK, and castigated and feared in adult discourses as threatening acceptable standards of social life. Yet in its more radical manifestation as counterculture, youth culture has been a powerful force for social change, championed by 1960s philosopher Herbert Marcuse and demonstrated through the 1968 student riots from Washington DC to Paris (Marcuse, [1964] 1972, 1969).

Notwithstanding the more alarmist reporting of youth culture, historian Arthur Marwick offered the qualification that 'the much publicised activities of tiny minorities have distracted attention from a very genuine liberation of the mass of the people' (1996: 9). As social scientist John Barron Mays noted in 1965:

> Not many young people deviate, perhaps not enough care to question the established order and are constrained to think critically and constructively about what society ought to be like and how individual citizens ought to behave. There is a problem of over-conformity as well as a problem of deviation to contend with: there are social problems which arise from a new kind of social anarchy and nihilism and others which are the product of excessive rigidity.
>
> (Mays, 1965: 53)

The post-war period is often characterised as a time of social upheaval and liberation, but many people's lives changed little and slowly. Domestic advice books assisted the process of social change. Less-formal codes of conduct did not stop people from seeking guidance about how to negotiate teenage social life. Rather, the increasing incidence of advice publishing since 1945 suggests that youth culture, and its apparent permissiveness, stimulated the market for social guidance.

Post-war domestic advice books display an ambiguous attitude, in which even the smallest details of social life could be interpreted as evidence of Americanisation, threatening British conventions of propriety. The word 'Hi' was associated with US informality, so British advice author Pam Lyons insisted in *Today's Etiquette* that 'even in younger circles, "Hi" is definitely "out"!' (1967: 45). In turn, American advice authors were self-conscious about what they regarded as distinctly American habits. Californian teachers Betty Allen and Mitchell Pirie Briggs reflected in *If You Please! A Book of Manners for Young Moderns*: 'It seems to be a part of the American philosophy to welcome variety and change. In dress we are inclined quickly to discard the old and eagerly grasp the new' ([1942] 1950: 34). In *Behave Yourself! Etiquette for American Youth* they imply a distinctly American aesthetic when they assert that 'Good grooming is as much a part of modern life as is streamlining' ([1937] 1945, 1950: 16). Although the preface to the first edition of *If You Please!* (1942) refers to the book as a 'companion volume' to *Behave Yourself!* the two books display extensive textual similarity, with sections rearranged and retitled but otherwise reproduced verbatim. Allen and Briggs also wrote *Mind Your Manners* ([1957], 1964, 1971).

Dick Hebdige reminds us that 'a number of ideologically charged connotational codes could be invoked and set in motion by the mere mention of a word like "America" or "jazz" or "streamlining"' (1981: 53; Maffei, 2003). Hebdige suggests that American culture was viewed negatively in post-war Britain because it was associated with British dependence during the Second World War. Nevertheless, American and British youth cultures enjoyed mutual influence. 'Swinging London' exported fashion and music to the USA, and vice versa, just as a transatlantic domestic dialogue saw texts that originated in the USA published simultaneously or subsequently in Britain, and vice versa. For example, Edith Barber's *Short Cut to Etiquette* was published in New York in 1953 and in Britain in 1956, to follow her *The Short-Cut Cook Book* (1952). Barber (1892–1963), a journalist, is described in American terms in *Short Cut*'s author profile as the '"first lady" in the field of home economics and entertaining [...] always interested in informalizing and simplifying the rules of etiquette'. When examined together, domestic advice books from the UK and the USA show a joint concern for, and dialogue about, the social conduct and domestic practices of young people.

From emulation to distinction

As we saw in Chapter 1, advice for children is not a recent development: parents have long looked to domestic advice writers, among others, for solutions to the problems of intergenerational conflict in the home. An early example is Erasmus of Rotterdam's *De civilitate morum puerilium* (*On Civility in Children*) written for a prince's son in 1530 (Elias [1939] 1994: 43). Schlesinger has suggested that advice for children formed the bedrock of American advice literature, referring to a 1747 book by George Washington derived from English and French texts ([1946] 1968). A shift occurred at the end of the nineteenth century from moral and religious models of social education to scientific approaches (Stearns, 2003; Hulbert, 2003). Elias followed G. Stanley Hall in proposing a model of child development which mirrored the development of society, in which the young adult matures, perceives herself or himself as separate from the outside world and gains self-control. Increasing social interdependence, such as the division of labour and trade links, demanded that individuals internalise control (Elias, [1939] 1994: 518, 257). For Elias, therefore, apparent informalisation was based on increased levels of self-control, in a 'civilizing process'. Advice books mediate ideals about the roles of young people in society, guide the development of self-control and aim to assist with the practical task of achieving domestic harmony (Kitchens, 2007: 462). Therefore, periods of apparent informalisation arguably require more advice, not less. The advice sector of the publishing industry has been expanding up to the present day both in the USA and in the UK, where, between 1975 and 2000, 'the number of advice books for parents published in this country increased fivefold' (Halpern, 2003: 20–22; Hardyment, [1983] 2007).

As children emulate their parents, they reproduce existing social structures (Burkitt, 1991: 198). Bourdieu's notions of habitus and generative structuralism, based on Elias's 'socio-genetic law', have the individual caught 'wittingly or unwittingly, willy nilly' in a cycle of reproducing social meanings: 'Because his actions and works are the product of a *modus operandi* of which he is not the producer and has no conscious mastery' the individual will 'always outrun' 'his conscious intentions' (Bourdieu, [1972] 1977: 79). Based on fieldwork carried out in 1963 and 1967–1968, Bourdieu's generative structuralism nevertheless underplays differences in the ways parents and teenagers behaved during the post-war period.

The earliest examples of advice books for children and post-war manuals alike emphasise observation and learning by doing as the most effective methods. Barber's *Short Cut*, written 'primarily for teen-agers and their mothers', according to the flyleaf, exemplifies this: 'It is a very good custom to allow young children to appear at teenage and other informal parties. They learn social ease that is invaluable in later life and they love to help at a party.' Experiential learning of this kind is internalised and produces easy, natural results: 'If there has been a good training in childhood, good manners become almost automatic.' Observational learning requires that parents set an example: 'which is far more telling than instruction by word of mouth' (Barber, [1953] 1956: 20, 24). Domestic advice writers assume a link between the behaviour of parents and that of their offspring. Pam Lyons asserts: 'It is a fact that well-mannered parents have, in ninety nine out of a hundred cases, well-mannered and well-behaved children' (Lyons, 1967: 9). Her book contains sections called 'Teaching Children the Art of Etiquette' and 'The Parents' Attitude towards their Children's Romances' which imply a parental readership, while sections aimed at teenagers include 'Taking an Interest in a Boyfriend's Hobbies'. Here it is assumed that parents have influenced their children and not the reverse.

The simple idea that children observe and emulate the behaviour of their family elders becomes complicated when different conduct is required of

Figure 5.1 'Don't grab your favorite page and go into seclusion', Betty Allen and
Mitchell Pirie Briggs, *If You Please! A Book of Manners for Young
Moderns*, [1942] 1950, 191.

parents and children. For example, sometimes resources are distributed
equally between family members, while at other times uneven distribution
occurs and the emulation model cannot function. In *Behave Yourself!* Allen
and Briggs criticise a teenager who has chosen to 'go into seclusion' with his
'favorite page' at the meal table. However, 'If father wants to read the paper
in quiet, that is his privilege' ([1937] 1945, 1950: 7). *If You Please!* repro-
duces this point of advice with a photographic illustration (Figure 5.1).
Here, the head of the household is allowed to dispense with instruction by
example. Young people, therefore, need to distinguish between situations
requiring emulation and those requiring deference.

   Post-war youth culture complicated the emulation model in several
ways. First, the manners adopted by adults and young people increasingly
diverged as young people adopted behaviours distinct from those of
their parents. Second, social informalisation increasingly led parents and their
children to behave in similar ways but, ironically, not in ways which could
serve as models for learning, because such behaviour departed from the
conventions parents wished their children to observe. Under these circumstances familial emulation would lead to parental condemnation and a
sense of injustice among the young. Third, at the same time, the young
were increasingly seen to lead the way, culturally and stylistically, as I will
explore later in this chapter. We have seen how domestic advice writers
have always presented their advice as a response to a present moment of
unprecedented informalisation. Just as historian Michael Curtin saw evidence of informalisation in late nineteenth-century etiquette manuals'
relaxation of the chaperone system (1987: 246), so this chapter shows
mid-twentieth-century domestic advice writers managing post-war youth
culture. It has been proposed that the increasing coverage of youth cultures
in public discourse effaced the voices of 'wise elders' such as grandparents

and parents and led to 'dependence on outside help and advice' including advice writers, psychologists and social workers (Lasch, 1977: 172). Lasch refers to Benjamin Spock's extremely successful parenting manual *The Common Sense Book of Baby and Child Care* of 1946, which sold 750,000 copies within a year and subsequently a copy 'was sold for every child born in the United States'. For Lasch the outpouring of published parenting advice has 'undermined parenting'; Peter Stearns admits that it has 'enhanced parental worrying and reduced their confident pleasure' (2003: 227). Advice literature ensures continued sales by both soothing and fuelling readers' concerns.

Domestic advice writers needed to produce books which conveyed parent-approved behavioural conventions to young people in a way that was palatable to both generations. For instance, Barber sympathised both with young readers – 'You have now reached an age where you may occasionally feel inclined to revolt against your parents' authority, which you took for granted all through your childhood' – and with parents: 'With the cigarette habit so common with both men and women, it is difficult for parents who are smokers themselves to take a completely forbidding attitude.' She recognised the convergence of youth and adult behaviours, for example in reminding readers that the phone should not be 'monopolized': 'This is a common practice of teenagers and, unfortunately, of some adults who should know better' (Barber, [1953] 1956: 63, 62, 39). Adults were as susceptible as young people to the introduction of behaviour prompted by conjunction of informalisation, consumerism and new communication technologies (Fischer, 1992; Spigel, 1990: 81). A decade later, Lyons complained that 'In this age of progress, when children are allowed more and more freedom, trying to instil in them a sense of a code of conduct can be extremely difficult'. Teaching teenagers table manners, for example, was 'even more nerve-racking as modern living is swinging away from the "table" for meals and is more in favour of trays round the television' (Lyons, 1967: 16, 14). The emulation model disintegrated not only because parents and children behaved differently, but also because teens and parents shared the same informal behaviours and disregarded convention.

Teens had independent reading practices, as Sherri Cavan observed in her fieldwork at the San Francisco Public Library: 'while mothers mediate between the etiquette books and both young children (ages 4–8) and pre-adolescents (ages 8–12), adolescents (those 13–18) almost always obtain the books themselves' (1970: 557). Accordingly, teenagers were addressed in books of social and consumer guidance, textbooks and via dedicated magazines, both in the UK (Currie, 1999; Tinkler, 1995; Carter, 2005) and in the USA (Zuckerman, 1998; Walker, 2000). Examples of relevant textbooks include Marion S. Barclay and Frances Champion's *Teen Guide to Homemaking*, published in New York and London (1961); Jean Barker's *Your Own Work* (London, 1968) which was part of the 'Modern Living' series (edited by the aptly named Mrs. E. R. House) with volumes on health, safety, friends, food, dress, looks, holidays, motherhood and childcare, nursing and community service; and, from another educational context, the finishing school, Mary Young's *In Search of Charm* (1962). Mary Young was Principal of the Mary Young Model School and Agency, and chief tutor in 'Poise, Dress and Personality' for London County Council. These books demonstrate how adult authors thought teens should be addressed, provide snapshots of the representations of adults and teens in circulation during the post-war period, and characterise the problems they aimed to solve. The American Youth Commission advised that for 'topics which are not suitable for classroom instruction':

> The best solution may simply be the use of good reading materials which are put in the hands of young people without ever being made the subject of recitation, examination, or discussion between teachers and pupils. The unaided printed word is a universal means of communication and instruction.
>
> (American Youth Commission, 1942: 175)

Post-war advice writers in Britain and the USA juggled conventions of behaviour derived from the Victorian period with those newly minted in response to contemporary informalisation. These behavioural poles can be seen in generational and familial terms, as tension between youth and age, teenager and parent. The challenge of the teenager in the home prompted advice writers to recommend solutions centred upon flexibility: social, behavioural solutions using compromise, cooperation and sharing and to material solutions based on the flexible teenage room.

Solutions: flexibility and fixity

Social solutions: 'a compromise may be made'

From 1945 to the present, the most common solution recommended for the peaceful coexistence of teenagers and parents in the home has been flexibility, in the form of cooperation, compromise and sharing. In *Behave Yourself!* (1950) Allen and Briggs attempt to align themselves with a teenage audience by admitting that, yes, 'parents are all a bit conservative'. They advocate empathy: 'If you are worth your salt you will never be ashamed of your parents. Maybe their clothes are a little out-of-date, but it doesn't take much effort to figure out that that is probably why *your* clothes are in the latest style.' They prescribe deference: 'don't forget to let the older members of the family precede you when entering a door. Courtesy requires it.' And they appeal to their teen reader's desire to please: 'Father will be impressed if you can manage occasionally to reach a state of solvency in your personal allowance.' Allen and Briggs suggest that the teen reader should confide in her mother: 'She's your friend, and if you make her your confidante as well, she can be trusted not to tell all she knows.' Above all, they promote inter-generational cooperation: 'Don't invite the gang to dinner without first paving the way by asking your mother's consent. It may be the cook's night off' (Allen and Briggs, [1937] 1945, 1950: 12, 10, 12, 112, 9). This empathic approach is also seen in Dr Dorothy W. Baruch's *How to Live with Your Teenager* (1953), which mediates recent academic findings.

A decade later, in their *Teen Guide to Homemaking*, first published in the USA, Canada and Britain in 1961, Marion S. Barclay and Frances Champion recognise that:

> In any family where adults and children of different ages and disposi-tions are trying to get along together there are almost certain to be times when discord will arise. Teen-agers and parents are likely to disagree at one time or another on such issues as spending money, sharing the work at home, getting in at night, clothes, choice of friends, doing homework, and type of social activities.
>
> (Barclay and Champion, 1961: 363)

With the recognition that teens and parents disagree comes the impli-cation that they will negotiate a solution, rather than the teens simply conforming to their parents' wishes: 'Working out problems in the family has to be the responsibility of everyone, and it certainly requires a united effort.' Echoing Allen and Briggs, Barclay and Champion recommend that to 'promote happy relations with parents' teens should empathise with parents, try to understand their points of view, express affection towards them and pride in them, share household labour, leisure time, decision-making and conversation, and be loyal, honest and courteous (Barclay and Champion, 1961: 363–366).

Intergenerational empathy, cooperation, and compromise were enhanced when teenagers performed adult roles within the household. Barclay and Champion's book recognised that when 'all the adults are employed away from home', teenagers 'must assume many home responsibilities'. They cite questionnaire responses showing that teenagers 'frequently or routinely prepare family meals, take charge of the family laundry, do home cleaning, and often take care of younger brothers or sisters'. Teenagers, therefore, 'have immediate need for' advice. Editor Helen Judy Bond claims in her introduction to the text that: 'There is no person who has had a more sig-nificant influence on the family of today and that of the next generation than the teacher of home economics in the Junior High School' (ibid. ix). As Supervisor of Homemaking Education in Hillsborough County, Florida and State Supervisor of Home Economics, Tallahassee, Florida, respectively, Barclay and Champion sought to meet this need for advice. The *Teen Guide to Homemaking* was designed to support teaching. The book's content addressed personal development, dress and grooming, homemaking, family relations, nutrition and recipes through filmstrips for classroom use; a teacher's edition with a resource guide; running side-bars with numbered lists to aid recall; and lists of further information sources, follow-up activities, and a concluding 'matching quiz' in each chapter.

As with Allen and Briggs's advice of 1950, so the *Teen Guide to Homemaking* represents the teenage party as a situation best approached through compromise. Barclay and Champion recognise the teen preference for informality: 'Teenagers enjoy a party that is gay and casual. Getting together to play records, dance, play games, watch TV, or just talk are the most usual kinds of parties among teenagers' (ibid. 168). But while informality also informs the fabrication of the party environment – 'Party decorations can be as simple or as elaborate as you like [...] It is more usual today among teenagers to have very simple decorations, if any' (ibid. 174) – it does not extend to the guests: 'Regardless of the fact that some teen-agers do "crash" parties, it is not acceptable behavior, and even though your host or hostess may not seem to mind, his or her mother undoubtedly will not like it' (ibid. 172). Here, the sensitivity towards teenagers' needs cedes to a firm address which presents parents' preferences as paramount and, in so doing, echoes advice of a decade earlier.

The emphasis on empathy and cooperation in books aimed at teens is also found in books for parents. Six years after the *Teen Guide to Homemaking* appeared, a British text, Pam Lyons' *Today's Etiquette* (1967), featured the work of illustrator Belinda Lyon, including a depiction of a mother nervously regarding an impromptu influx of her daughter's friends (Figure 5.2). Author Lyons applies popular psychology to the problem of intergenerational understanding: 'There is nothing more soul-destroying for a teenager than to be reprimanded – even worse in company. Teenagers have enough complexes without adding to them unnecessarily.' Allen and Briggs's suggestion that young people confide in their mothers is here matched with Lyons' encouragement to parents to share their teenager's social lives by equating their experiences with those

Figure 5.2 'This does not mean, of course, that a teenager should arrive home every evening with a starving crowd', illustration by Belinda Lyon, in Pam Lyons, *Today's Etiquette*, 1967.

of adults: 'And the interesting point is that youngsters seem to mature so much earlier year by year. Boys and girls have a casualness about them that is both becoming and beguiling and is certainly way in advance of their counterparts [sic] behaviour of even fifty years ago' (Lyons, 1967: 31, 30, 60). Contemporaneous views of adolescent psychology include Fleming (1963) and Miller (1969). Lyons' text is of course less casual than the behaviour it describes. By comparing the behaviour of contemporary 'boys and girls' with that of fifty years before, rather than the usual period deemed to represent a generation, twenty-five years, she avoids committing parents to the realm of history.

In discussing the way teens socialise in the home, Lyons recommends a permissive parental approach to teenagers: 'When the children reach the age of fifteen or sixteen and start their own personal lives they should be allowed a certain amount of freedom [...] if possible, permission should always be asked from the parents first – but permission should always be granted'. Parents are told that 'home can take on a new meaning for teenagers' and are encouraged to adopt a relaxed approach with a threat:

> If a child feels there is always a welcome for his or her friends at home the chances of the child growing away from home are lessened. There is nothing more sad than an old couple left by themselves wondering why their children never come to see them. It is usually because they did not encourage their children to bring their friends home in earlier years.
>
> (Lyons, 1967)

Although she advocates permissiveness, Lyons empathises with the frustration of parents: 'no matter how "with it" and tolerant they are, they have the right to insist on a set of rules – for the sake of the entire family's harmony as well as for the individual' (Lyons, 1967: 30, 31, 62). Lyons negotiates the inter-related effects of youth culture, the permissive society (*Guardian*, 1969) and informalisation by ultimately reinforcing existing social conventions.

Advice written for teens displays the influences of developing sociological and consumerist discourses. For the 1982 edition of the *Teen Guide to Homemaking*, retitled *Teen Guide*, the two original authors were replaced by a team led by Valerie Chamberlain, Professor of Home Economics at Texas Tech University and later Emeritus Professor of Education, Nutrition, and Restaurant-Hotel Management (1971–1985) and Professor of Nutritional Sciences and Home Economics Education at the University of Vermont, Burlington. The *Teen Guide* encouraged critical thinking about, for example, consumption choices, media literacy and how we construct family ideals. The 'Family' section provides a sociological explanation for changes in families. Contemporary children are seen 'more as individuals than as extra workers'. A family is a '*consumer group*'; its '*resources* include material goods like income, land, a house, and personal possessions' [italics in the original]:

> Resources also include the talents and skills of each family member. For example, one person may be good at keeping the family budget. Another may be an excellent gardener or mechanic. A grandparent may be a talented painter, or a teenager may play the guitar for family fun. All are valuable to the family in making life more enjoyable.
>
> (Chamberlain *et al.*, 1982)

Readers are reminded that 'Every parent has a personality [...] they are people just like you. Forgiveness, understanding and love should go both ways, from parent to child and from child to parent' and that cooperation 'promotes a feeling of unity' (Chamberlain *et al.*, 1982: 95, 90, 107, 111). The section goes on to address child development, childcare and 'careers helping families and children', while the following section, 'Home', presents domestic spaces as enriching and flexible resources which accommodate a range of shared and solitary activities. Cooperation is the core message of Lawrence Bauman and Robert Riche's *The Nine Most Troublesome Teenage Problems and How to Solve Them* (1986), in which each chapter addresses a problem as voiced by a parent, such as 'My Kid Won't Take on Responsibility'. Other chapters tackle anger, lies, boredom, school performance, communication, friendship, unsuitable friends and sex. The teenage problems are shown to be parental problems, too, with solutions requiring changes in parents' and teenagers' behaviour alike.

A decade later, Judith Wilson's *Teen Zone* (2007) (Figure 5.3) encourages parents to adopt a relaxed and flexible approach to social interaction in the home:

> If teenagers know you operate an 'open house' policy (within limits!), they are more likely to hang out at home rather than in more unsuitable places. Plus it's fun to spend time watching TV or playing pool with your kids. These are the sociable years before they leave home, so enjoy them while you can!
>
> (Wilson, 2007)

Wilson invokes safety, enjoyment and departure in quick succession, thereby echoing Pam Lyons' 1967 advice to parents, which threatened loneliness. Wilson also recalls Barclay and Champion's discussion of teenagers performing adult roles within the household when she recommends that school-leavers who are still living at home should contribute financially to the household bills or, if they are unable to do so, they should contribute in-kind by decorating, cooking and maintaining the garden (Wilson, 2007: 90, 134).

Figure 5.3 Cover, *Teen Zone: Stylish Living for Teens* by Judith Wilson, 2007.

As we have seen, domestic advice writers typically situate their advice during a time of unprecedented social change. We might assume, therefore, that advice for teens and parents has become increasingly permissive, as behaviour has become increasingly informal. However, advice books from the closing decade of the twentieth century and the first decade of this century display considerable variation. Many authors, especially British ones, admit that drink, drugs, sex and violence are typical aspects of the teenage experience. Teen coach Sarah Newton draws on her experienced as a police officer working with repeat offenders in writing advice for teens. In the same year that Wilson's *Teen Zone* was published, Newton's book, *Help! My Teenager is an Alien* (2007) advocated the use of life coaching principles to modify teens' behaviour. Clearly stated, agreed patterns of behaviour and the setting of boundaries are presented as beneficial for teens and parents alike, while the details of what is allowed and what is proscribed are left for individual families to determine.

Boundaries are also important in a number of campaigning books, which prescribe a considerably purer existence than the majority of literature aimed at teens. *Boundaries with Teens: When to Say Yes, How to Say No* (2006) by Dr John Townsend is a US publication also distributed in the UK. Townsend's chapter on 'Parties' relates a situation in which the author's son asks, in a coded telephone conversation, to be driven home from a party because alcohol was being consumed. Townsend qualifies: 'I don't want to give you the wrong impressions. My kids and I have had many conversations in which they strongly wanted to stay, and I insisted they leave.' For Townsend, parties 'can cause an adolescent to regress', and 'Some parents don't allow their teens to go to parties in general because of the risk that their kids will be exposed to alcohol, drugs and sex.' Townsend recommends that parents should be clear about expectations and consequences, including banning alcohol and drugs, sexual involvement and physical aggression, and insisting on adult supervision. Parents should investigate the hosts and the guest list, offer to help at the party and plan an exit strategy for the teen: 'the more parents who require that teen parties be safe, the more safe parties there will be' (Townsend, 2006: 237–241, 237–238, 238). American and British domestic advice literature, especially that for teens and their parents, exemplifies differing social attitudes to alcohol. Alcohol is seen as instrumental in transforming a domestic space, such as a dining room, into a party venue (for a European comparison, see Demant and Østergaard, 2007: 517–537, 525).

Domestic advice writers have emphasised the communication between the generations and an interpersonal flexibility centred on compromise and cooperation. Adele Faber and Elaine Mazlish's *How to Talk so Teens Will Listen and Listen so Teens Will Talk* (2005) is an adaptation of their book for children ([1980] 2001). It suggests exercises designed to improve parents' and teens' communication skills. The authors draw on their professional experience by framing their advice in the form of a fictionalised workshop series, with dialogue between group leaders and participants, and cartoon illustrations ostensibly reproduced from the information sheets circulated to participants. While the specific case studies – such as strategies for dealing with a teenager's messy bedroom – are instructive, the book's narrative drive derives from the characters improving their communication skills, to deal constructively with a variety of issues. It is through talking to one another effectively that teens and parents are able to achieve harmonious family relations and determine what is needed in terms of flexible domestic design arrangements and the varied affordances of the teenage bedroom, in order to allow each to be content and comfortable within the home. However, while design and other practical solutions may be realised only through effective communication, advisors are clear that they also function as powerful routes to achieving and maintaining harmony.

Material solutions: 'why not share it between you?'

In addition to emphasising flexibility based on the interpersonal practices of cooperation and compromise, post-war advisors promote the benefits of flexible material solutions centred upon dedicated domestic accommodation for teenagers. This advice derives from the recognition of distinct teenage behaviours at the end of the nineteenth century, and a perceived connection between environment and behaviour, as well as shifting notions of privacy more broadly (Goldscheider *et al.*, 2001: 488–489; also Christensen *et al.*, 2000). Readers are told that children's bedrooms become increasingly private spaces for introspection – 'Moping in their bedroom' – and self-discovery as they grow up into teenagers (Clifford-Poston, 2005: 51–57). From the interwar period to the present, advice has abounded on the accommodation of teenagers. Writing in the American *Scribner's* magazine of 1937 about how to cater for children who will be at home during the summer holidays, Katherine Kent suggests 'the basement room – that adult holy of holies – is full of possibilities for the leggy, experimental age. Since it is seldom that both generations use it at the same hours, why not share it between you?' (1937: 90–91). The flexible space shown in the magazine accommodates a wide range of different activities for all members of the family and features a workbench, a mini-piano, a marionette theatre and a milkshake bar.

Satisfactory accommodation for children has been presented as character forming and socially beneficial (Stearns, 1998: 404–405). In *How to Plan Your Bedroom* (1955), Mary L. Brandt notes: 'If your children grow up in tasteful surroundings, they will learn quickly to appreciate color and the part proper furnishings play in making life happy and pleasant. They are much more apt to learn order too, and the necessity for caring for their things' (1955: 88). British author Joyce Lowrie echoes this idea that parents can mould their offspring through moulding their homes in her *Practical Homemaking*:

> For a girl in her teens, a pretty room is the greatest encouragement to take care of her own appearance. If she is given a room in which to store her clothes properly, a large, well-lit mirror and good heating, she is far less likely to fling her clothes on the floor and disregard her personal appearance.
>
> (Lowrie, 1965: 21)

This advice is echoed in magazines for teenage girls where, a more recent study observes, 'advice about organizing and tidying bedrooms' continues the 'parental voice of urging the young to acquire middle-class notions of cleanliness, tidiness, orderliness, and the attendant qualities of responsibility and pride of place necessary for the functioning of an orderly civil society'. Claudia Mitchell and Jacqueline Reid-Walsh argue that magazine representations of teenage girls' rooms demonstrate that 'surface *is* depth, private *is* public' and 'the logic of anyone being able to interpret who the girl is from looking at her room may be seen as a regulatory device' (2002: 137).

Domestic advice writers disagree about the relationship between rooms for children and those for teens. *Design to Fit the Family* of 1965 was aimed at parents 'who want an attractive home that works – a home that will accommodate them (and their savage children), now and in the future'. The authors, British design experts Phoebe de Syllas and Dorothy Meade, recommend that:

> For teenagers the 'nursery' will need a complete overhaul to rid it of any suggestion of the nursery look. If the original tough furniture has survived, and was sensibly chosen in the first place, it can fit just as well for bigger clothes, model kits, record-player, chemistry sets, etc., with a new arrangement and a coat of paint. But they will probably want to plan their own room anyway, and much better that they should.
>
> (De Syllas and Meade, 1965: 54)

In 1984, British interior designer and prolific home decorating author Mary Gilliatt emphasised the ease with which a child's room could be modified to suit teenagers, suggesting that a new set of bedlinen and a rug is sufficient. She does add, however, that 'with any teenager, it is a good idea to install a washbasin in the room, to discourage them from monopolizing the bathroom!' (1984b: 17). The same motivation prompts Wilson's recommendation of dedicated washrooms for teenagers as 'not so much a luxury as a necessity' (2007: 56). Journalist Jane Lott's 1989 book *Children's Rooms* comprises a range of suggested rooms for babies and children of all ages, making clear their common building blocks. She notes of a room for children 'five years and beyond' that 'the basic elements of a sub-teens bedroom are already in place' (1989: 84). Authors agree, however, on the importance of the teen's involvement in the fabrication of her or his room. As seen above, De Syllas and Meade refuse to advise readers on this matter, adamant that the teen's own input is superior. Gilliatt, too, has confidence in teen decorators, giving them credit for their innovative design ideas:

> even if their ideas are bolder, weirder or more adventurous than you bargained for, let them have their head if you can bear it [...] Never mind if they come up with an all-purple room; they're the ones who have to live with it, not you.
>
> (Gilliatt, 1984: 36)

Those domestic advice books which address accommodation for teens in greater detail emphasise the teen's need to entertain others at home. In *Children are People* of 1940, Emily Post is considerably exercised by 'one of the most disturbing problems that modern parents are called upon to face', namely 'When the Boy Friends come to See Susie':

> According to present-day custom, outside of exceptionally big houses, the living room is given to Susie while father and mother spend the evening in their bedroom [...] Sitting in their bedroom evening after evening is not very comfortable; but, what is of far more serious moment, it

is not very good for the family morale. It is not good for Susie's attitude toward her parents. When the parents, in any way whatever, give their children first place and take second themselves, there is an unavoidable belittling of their prestige [...] that turns an act of loving unselfishness into a disturbing suggestion of abdication.

(Post, 1940b: 298)

Post recommends flexible furniture for the dining room, so it can serve as a sitting room for teenagers, thereby reserving the living room for parental use. Post's example specifically concerns interaction between boyfriends and girlfriends, hence the emphasis on downstairs reception rooms. However, advice for accommodation of teenage interaction with friends usually suggests that the teenager's bedroom be furnished to allow entertaining.

The *Teen Guide to Homemaking* delineates the four functions of the teenage room as: sleep and rest; dressing and grooming; studying; and leisure and entertaining (Barclay and Champion, 1961: 204). These competing requirements are easily met in a single room. Flexible furniture is key: shelving should be adaptable to match changing needs, beds should folded up or bunks should be used. The *Woman's Own Book of Modern Homemaking* (*WOBMH*) recommended bunks by Conran Ltd., which 'separated to form two smart teenage sofas' (1967: 33). Barclay and Champion's room for a 'young fisherman' has a desk resting between two storage chests. Other solutions included flexible multi-functional space separators such as screens, alcoves and partition walling, used for zoning various activities. Barclay and Champion show a trellis symbolically dividing study, sleeping and grooming areas in a room shared by teenage girls. Adele Whitely Fletcher's *How to Decorate with Accessories* (1963) depicts a dressing table placed inside a cupboard, so that it can be concealed when, for example, entertaining guests.

Sian Lincoln has examined the use of music by teenagers to zone their bedrooms and 'as a medium through which the boundaries of public and private spaces are necessarily blurred' (2005: 399). Rosie Fisher's *Rooms to Grow Up In* (1984) showcased the painted children's furniture sold by her company, Dragons. Her teenager's room looks like a study with a bed in it (Figure 5.4), while her advice on furnishing a space for teenage entertaining, entitled 'Living with loud music', includes fitting thick carpets and curtains and replacing wardrobe doors with a curtain for sound absorption (Fisher, 1984: 108). Wilson's *Teen Zone* also tackles noise:

Either you're accused of making too much, such as playing music, or everyone else's noise disturbs you when you're studying. Extra insulation between two rooms will be achieved by lining the dividing wall with built-in cupboards (preferably in both rooms). Or cover an entire wall with cork tiles: they are inexpensive, insulate against noise and provide a dramatic area for display.

(Wilson, 2007: 29)

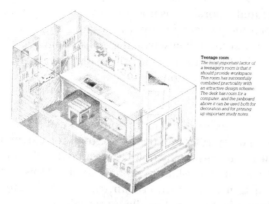

Figure 5.4 'Teenage Room', in Rosie Fisher, *Rooms to Grow Up In*, 1984.

Of course the teen room should be 'a multi-functional room: a place to entertain friends, to study and to sleep. But with clever planning – from a chill-out seating zone to a special area for scented candles and a tranquil view – it can also become a bolthole from the world', 'a positive place to retreat to, rather than as a place to hide away in anger' (Wilson, 2007: 11, 29).

Although 'one child equals one bedroom' is ideal, domestic advisors recognise that siblings sometimes need to share (Mitchell and Reid-Walsh, 2002: 122). Sharing doubles the demands made of the teenage room. Each inhabitant requires space for resting, grooming, studying and entertaining, whether simultaneously or at different times, resulting in a dualistic mirroring trope. For example, in *The Teen Guide to Homemaking*, Barclay and Champion explain that: 'Careful planning and arrangement will provide space for double desks and double chests. Add the colors you both like, and with individual accessories, the room will be attractive and inviting' (1961: caption to a plate between pp. 172–173). Separate desks, built across a fanlight window, with discrete storage and lighting provided for each inhabitant mean that only the space and the aesthetic are shared. The follow-up *Teen Guide* of 1982 depicts 'some ways to let two people express their own personalities and enjoy a feeling of private space' (Chamberlain *et al.*, 1982: 176). In addition to familiar variations on the room divider, the *Teen Guide* also suggests using a platform to differentiate two halves of a shared room. Wilson recommends that either two of everything can be arranged in a room of two halves, or that siblings can share an 'entertaining space, perhaps with a TV and beanbags, a shared wardrobe and a long bench-style desk where you both study' with only the area around each bed reserved as individual space (2007: 76).

'A girl can work magic in her room'

The flexibility required of the teen room, in catering for a range of disparate activities, and accommodating one or two people, is further complicated by its use in expressing gender. Although the *Teen Guide to Homemaking* (1961) was written 'for youth of both sexes', it offers gendered solutions. Writing about domestic advice in the USA, Leavitt (2002: 132) describes this gendering as a twentieth-century phenomenon. In addition to distinction by colour (pink for a girl, blue for a boy), design recommendations for boys have typically employed plain, geometric décor while girls have been presented with decorative finishes and floral motifs. Boys' rooms emphasise education and hobbies. In a room for a young fisherman, previously mentioned, scientific knowledge is suggested through maps, globe, barometer and charts of fish species, which are echoed in the rug pattern. The British *WOBMH* also associates boys with learning and activities and girls with appearance (*Woman's Own*, 1967: 14): 'Think ahead to children who will outgrow a small chest of drawers or a half-length wardrobe, to daughters who will have long evening dresses, sons with shelves of school-books and messy hobbies'. These post-war examples are echoed in recent advice books such as Wilson's *Teen Zone* (2007):

> Teen boys will find it easier to create a distinctive look inspired by a favourite activity, from surfing to music, rather than conventionally picking colours or wallpapers. [...] It is a myth that teenage boys don't care about their bedrooms. But they do have a different take on them to girls. Pattern, luxurious texture and the display of beautiful things don't matter: the presence of the correct 'kit' – be that computers, guitars or a sound system – certainly does. [...] The look and layout concern them, but it's the stuff inside that really matters.
>
> (Wilson, 2007: 36)

Wilson attributes to boys a concern for depth over display, thereby engaging a key binary opposition summarised in John Berger's dictum 'Men act and women appear' (1972: 47). Just as 'gender' refers to a set of learned practices deemed socially appropriate for girls and boys, so the rooms in a home invite gendered norms for their inhabitants.

If the decoration of teen rooms has reflected stereotypically gendered aesthetics, flexibility and multi-functionality have been emphasised for both sexes, and are therefore a function not of gender, but of age. But, while De Syllas and Meade and Gilliatt attribute design skills to young people in general, other advice sources have presented interior design skills as particularly feminine. Barclay and Champion explained how 'a girl can work magic in her room' through designing, decorating and craft projects (1961: caption to a plate between pp. 172–173). Consultation with parents was advised, but independence was encouraged. The *Teen Guide to Homemaking* shows girls designing a room using swatches, model, paint can and tape measure, demonstrating creativity, competence and thrift by fitting a new slipcover to an old chair and decorating a mirror frame; these girls engage with the iconography of femininity by beautify-ing both their spaces and themselves. The teen decorator's model interior anticipates the active learning strategies proposed for engaging adult audiences in home economics instruction, for example in Genevieve Callahan and Lou Richardson's discussion 'Building More Interest in Home Planning' in their book *Home Economics Show-How and Showmanship* (1966: 45–54). Social historian Bill Osgerby has noted how 'young people's sartorial preferences' were linked to a 'decline in cultural values and standards' (1998: 13) and domestic advisors had much to say about dress and personal grooming (Barber, [1953] 1956: 74–75; Allen and Briggs, [1937] 1945, 1950: 19–20). Yet young people's preferences in interior design were accepted and encouraged to the extent that interior design strategies seen in teenage rooms were adopted throughout the home in the second half of the twentieth century.

As well as depicting the teenager as competent in interior design, the *Teen Guide to Homemaking* makes clear her (and his) role as a consumer. Most of the images in the book are credited to commercial sources and therefore function as indirect classroom advertising. The Singer Sewing Machine Company contributed an image in which a girl's dress and a chair's slip cover are appliquéd and embroidered with mermaids, dolphins and rosebuds. The photograph of a girl decorating a mirror frame is cour-tesy of Q-Tips cotton swabs, and indeed she is using that product. An image of a teenage decorator contributed by the Dow Chemical Company bears comparison with a contemporaneous Dow advertisement showing a decorator at work with his ladder, trestle table, brushes and paints, though the setting is commercial. Incorporated in 1897, Dow began by selling bleach, but by 1959 the company was advertising paints among its prod-ucts, for example in *Paint Manufacture* (June 1959), hence another Dow image in the book, showing the transformative effect of paint in a before-and-after image of a girls' bedroom. Making interior design choices would have been, in some senses, empowering for teen readers, as they created an arena in which they could exercise agency and which, arguably, consti-tuted 'the only acceptable avenue for articulation of self and resistance'. Yet, this type of consumer education has been regarded ideologically limit-ing, as it 'links an illusory choice of products (or brands) to individuality', 'determined by an individual's access to money' (Raby, 2002: 444). The use of advertising and marketing materials in schools has attracted par-ticular criticism (Spring, 2003). The *Teen Guide*'s use of advertising imagery was concurrent with a period when British 'New Left' writers lamented youth consumption as a symptom of Americanisation and a portent for the future of British culture (Hoggart, 1958; Bentley, 2005). Christopher Lasch bemoaned the linkage of family values and consumer-ism (1977: 19). In training young people, and especially girls, to become consumers, domestic advice literature echoes wider discourses (Stearns, 1998: 404–405; 2003). Penny Tinkler has shown how the lessons in consumerism and femininity found in magazines for girls and young women groomed readers for patriarchy (1995: 7).

'This is true of older children as well as adults'

Domestic advice literature offered solutions to the problems associated with the behaviour of young people, but young people were increasingly championed as trendsetters in both design and lifestyle. Writing in 1965, John Barron Mays emphasised the role of youth as 'a necessary stage for the perpetuation of the traditional culture and as a lever for forcing changes in the structure of society [...] It bridges the past and the present and, at the same time, helps to mould the future' (1965: 53). In the period following the Second World War, young people rejected traditional ideals of elegance, dignity and luxury in preference for a lack of ornament. Young homemakers used home decorating as a tool of differentiation from parents 'not only through their taste but by the priority they gave it in relation to other aspects of their life' (Attfield, 1999: 81). Yet, the style choices of teens and young people were increasingly favoured by adults, too, as appropriately informal.

The flexibility and multi-functionality of the teenage rooms shown in post-war domestic advice literature epitomised pre-war modernist ideals of domestic design which responded to economic constraints and informalisation (*Woman's Own*, 1967: 78; Lees-Maffei, 2001: 187–206). Flexibility became an increasingly compelling domestic principle during the second half of the twentieth century, reversing the preceding pattern whereby the various parts of the home had become more specialised. In her study of post-war American children's rooms, Ogata notes that 'the juxtaposition of a mother's, or maid's, work area and children's play area was often couched in the promotional language of "flexibility"' (2008–2009: 131). In *Practical Homemaking* (1965), Joyce Lowrie recommended a variety of flexible solutions. Open plan could be modified in order to meet the increasing privacy needs of the family:

> Sliding panels between the living-room and entrance hall open up some, or all, of the spaces to each other in summer and for entertaining, or close them off when privacy is required. We all need privacy. This is true of older children as well as adults.
>
> (Lowrie, 1965)

Lowrie advises that 'all bedrooms double as work-rooms or sitting-rooms', a dining room could 'double as a study, an extra sitting room or even a guest room', and a hall can accommodate a housekeeping desk if not a study (1965: 13, 14, 17, 18). She contrasts a fireplace showing the influence of 1930s *moderne* design in a belated adaptation of Art Deco step form with another converted into storage and display space, following the installation of central

Chimneybreast before and after conversion.

Figure 5.5 'Chimneybreast before and after conversion', in Joyce Lowrie, *Practical Homemaking*, 1965.

heating (Figure 5.5). As this example shows, a modernist emphasis on function and an aesthetic appreciation of utility, flexibility, multi-functionality and disregard for convention characteristic of advice for teen rooms was increasingly applied to adult spaces within the home in the post-war period.

The influence of teenage rooms on the wider home reaches an apogee in the development of a flexible multi-purpose parents' room. Hilary Gelson's *Children about the House* of 1976 is refreshingly dedicated to creating a safe and stimulating environment for children of all ages throughout the house, rather than in their own rooms. However:

> All parents need their own escape routes from family – either in the form of a bedroom, home-office, sitting room or study, depending on the size and scope of the house. Children need not be excluded from such areas altogether, but they should clearly understand that entry is by invitation only and that a closed door indicates a parental bid for peace and quiet.
>
> (Gelson, 1976: 44)

Gelson advises that the parents' bedroom, 'likely to be the only possible refuge in a small home', can be refitted as a 'dual-purpose bedroom/sitting area'. Various space-saving solutions include dispensing 'with a conventional bed altogether, preferring a folding bed/storage unit'. Gelson's 1976 text was prescient. Recently in the US, the 'owner's retreat' (a politically correct synonym for the master bedroom) has increasingly been marketed by homebuilders and estate agents as the parents' sanctuary from the rest of the family, often with a sitting area and study in addition to en suite sleeping quarters (Vollmer *et al.*, 2005: 7). Here the usual pattern, of the teenager being confined to a microcosmic home-within-the-home and making as few demands as possible on the home's shared resources, is reversed and parents are confined to one multi-functional room. Writing in 2003, Eugenia

Santiesteban, in her US publication *Living with Kids,* regards bedrooms as sanctuaries for adults, children and teenagers alike but, crucially, 'children should be welcome in any room, including the parents' bedroom' (2003: 10, 98). In Wilson's *Teen Zone* (2007), teens are welcome throughout the home as well as being granted aspirational architect-designed spaces for work, rest and socialising, attractively photographed by Winfried Heinze. In addition to 'Boudoirs for Girls' and 'Crash Pads for Boys', separate chapters treat 'Washrooms', 'Game Dens and Media Zones' and 'Sociable Spaces'. Rather than fitting competing accommodation needs into one room, Wilson's teenager enjoys a suite of rooms. Here we see another reversal in which the entire home is the teen space, as is the dedicated suite of teen rooms, while the parents' space is open to teen ingress.

These are exceptions, however: domestic advisors have typically promoted accommodation that allows teenagers privacy and autonomy within the confines of a single room. Advice to teens emphasises using as little time and space as possible in shared rooms (living room, bathroom and kitchen) and tidying away any evidence of having been there after use ('Good Manners Around the House', Barclay and Champion, 1961: 358; also, Munroe and Madigan, 1999). The teen room is a microcosmic home within the family home. It is a material manifestation of the intermediate space between childhood and adulthood, family home and outside world, parental care and self-sufficiency. Whether for younger children or teens, 'the bedroom space [...] offers the greatest possibility for children-in-control' (Mitchell and Reid-Walsh, 2002: 114). Young people are seen to respond positively to having a space they control, filled with their own things, featuring a door sign reading 'PARENTS KEEP OUT' or some variation (Munro, 1998: 75). Abbott-Chapman and Robertson (2001: 493) have collected data showing that home is a favourite place for 40.3 per cent of girls and 18.1 per cent of boys. For one young person, the bedroom is 'my own place, peaceful, everything's there. My own things around me. I can play my guitar' and for another 'it is quiet and I can think'. Home is 'a place I know and can trust. I can be myself there'. The teen room as represented in domestic advice literature is a gilded cage, in which every activity is anticipated and accommodated, but which reinforces the idea that the remainder of the home is the preserve of adults. A solution presented as being of benefit to teens can be seen, therefore, to best serve adults.

However, new media have made public our private domestic spaces. Television and the internet bring the world into the home, and enable users to enter the outside world without leaving home. A teenager might physically occupy a safe space at home, in the care of her or his parents, while intellectually occupying an internet 'chat room' that may or may not be safe. Teenagers are not chaperoned through their internet encounters in the way that young people were steered through controlled social situations in the first decades of the twentieth century:

As responsible parents or guardians you would never leave a child alone in a strange area, let them visit a city unsupervised, let them enter adult-only shops or clubs, or meet a total stranger. Unfortunately, every time the child in your care logs on to the web without supervision they face the same potential dangers as they do in all of the situations above.

(Parsons, 2007: 110; UK Council for Child Internet Safety, 2012)

Here the dangers of the web are equated with space. The internet has provided young people with a forum for the expression of their ideas and opinions. Teenage voices are published more copiously online than they ever were in print, whether in forums such as Teenadvice.about.com, which contains advice by adults, for example '10 cool Teenage Room Ideas' (Ashworth, 2012), and teens' views in a Teen Advice Forum (About.com, 2012), or in social networks such as Facebook, where advice is given both informally and intensively. The teen room is no longer wholly *within* the home.

Problems with the solutions

Progressive as the acceptance of flexible youth-oriented domestic styles might appear, when considered alongside the censuring of the social practices of the young in domestic advice, it is also characteristic of a tendency to polarise young people into what Hebdige has termed 'youth-as-trouble' and 'youth-as-fun' (1988: 19). Osgerby has noted that 'Throughout the post-war period a recurring duality saw young people both vilified as the most deplorable evidence of cultural bankruptcy and, almost simultaneously, celebrated as the exciting precursor to a prosperous future.' Although these 'stereotypes' 'often bore tenuous relation to social reality', 'their symbolic power was potent, images of youth serving as a key motif around which dominant interpretations of social change were constructed' (Osgerby, 1998: 14). Gillis has noted the utility of such dualism for those interested in 'improving' youth: 'If the model adolescent stood for everything pure and stable in a period of internal and external tension, the juvenile delinquent embodied everything to be feared and resented, making him an indispensable part of the social world of the child savers' (1981: 170–171). More recently, youth experts Phil Cohen and Pat Ainley have called for the reformulation of 'the "classic" contradiction between the symbolic power of the adolescent body associated with its sexuality, looks and style and the political/economic powerlessness of youth as a socio-legal category' (2000: 90; Espejo, 2003). This reductive binarism or duality underpins post-war advice for and about teenagers. We have seen this in the comparison of experiential familial social education and book learning; the interplay of emulation and distinction; the overarching motifs of flexibility and fixity; the relationship between social and material solutions for the problem of the teenager in the home; the shift from permissiveness to boundaries; the mirroring tropes of the shared room; and in the complex relation between the teen room and the rest of the home. This final part of the chapter examines dualities in the mechanics of giving advice, whether symptomatic of rifts or developed as ways of overcoming them.

The servant of two masters

Evidence of the difficulty of mediating between teens and their parents is shown between the lines of domestic advice. Barber's *Short Cut to Etiquette* ([1953] 1956) follows the pattern of advocating flexibility and compromise when the generations come into conflict in family life. For example, in choosing dresses: 'If you don't care for the white or pastel shades your mother is likely to favour, a compromise may be made and a dark colour chosen.' When teens are hosting parties, Barber suggests that mother could 'preside and hand out plates' and, presumably, supervise the proceedings. However, closer reading reveals ambiguity in terms of the audience addressed. She begins boldly: 'Teenagers, this book has been written especially for you. It gives you the rules of etiquette for occasions that may arise during your adolescence and later on in your adult life. It should answer many of the questions that puzzle and perturb you.' Here, Barber aims to ingratiate herself with her readership by offering tailor-made advice and sympathetic understanding. However, on the next page a different motivation is revealed: 'This book has been designed and written in the hope that it will help you establish a way of life that will be accepted by your parents and friends, by your teachers and later your employer, and by everyone you meet.' So the text intends to shape teens into what adults and other authority figures want them to be. A sleight of hand exemplifies the complexity of advising the post-war teen:

> It would, therefore, be presumptuous and futile to write a book of 'teen-age etiquette' which did not recognise the amazing swiftness of these years. One year you girls are worrying because 'the boys huddle at one end of the room and won't dance with us'. The next moment, it seems, you want to know how to handle boys who cut in too frequently! And almost before anyone can answer that question, you are out in the adult world, following careers, marrying, and starting families of your own!
>
> (Barber, [1953] 1956)

Here, Barber simultaneously caters to teenagers' desire to be viewed as adults and parents' anxiety about the rapidity with which teenagers grow up ([1953] 1956: 13, 21, v–vi).

A clear address to a non-teenage audience is found in Barber's section 'Teenage Customs', the very title of which suggests the third-party perspective of the tourist, anthropologist or parent: 'Raiding of the refrigerator unexpectedly by teenagers can become a serious problem if no limits are established. It is a good idea to have one shelf set aside, if possible, for raiding' (ibid. 25). The sudden, unplanned activity implied by the term 'raiding' is here anticipated and catered for. The person addressed in this passage is in charge of the refrigerator and is therefore likely to be an adult. So Barber positions herself at one moment with the teenager attempting to forge a personal style distinct from those of her or his parents, and at another with the parent who tries to maintain domestic control in the face of unanticipated demands on the household. That the author is a servant of two masters, teen and parent, is also shown through contorted language:

> It is sometimes difficult to persuade young teenage girls that blue jeans are not appropriate for every occasion. The sandals that you love may, however, be worn with simple sports dresses that are always in order in country or city, except for party wear. Shoes should be shined and clean even if they are well worn.
>
> (Barber, [1953] 1956: 11)

Here the opening observation situates teenage girls as the third party; it is followed with a direct address to the girls as 'you' and the quotation closes with the imperative parental voice.

Part of Barber's difficulty in advising young people stems from the way she distinguishes herself from a teenage readership. In the quotation above, she criticises the prevalence of jeans; elsewhere she complains that 'expressions such as "Oh boy!" and "OK" are so over-used that they become monotonous. Teenagers are often offenders in this respect'. A disconnect between author and readership is shown in the placing of Barber's discussion of dating in a section entitled 'Cinema Etiquette': cinema attendance dropped in the decade following Second World War in the UK and the USA as young people rejected such family entertainment in favour of distinctly teenage amusements (ibid. 53; see Docherty *et al.*, 1987: 26–27; Sillitoe, [1971] 1973: 175). Elsewhere the author's guidance falters: 'When sitting at a soda fountain or milk bar, discover, by watching the actions of others, whether or not a tip is customary.' Barber's circumspection here may stem from local variations in practice, or it may relate to the fact that soda fountains and milk bars were the province of the young. Barber's ability to articulate advice is occasionally jeopardised by the sensitivity of the subject: 'Don't take alcohol! There are a number of excellent reasons for observing this rule.' The reasons remain unexplained, but a (knowing, adult) reader might infer them (ibid. 18, 49, 67). Perhaps Barber does not explain further because she does not want to make alcohol seem attractive or to pre-empt parents' decisions about when to raise such issues. Barber's *Short Cut* exemplifies, in several ways, the failure of advice writers to adequately advise young people.

Domestic advice writers also reveal their attitudes towards teenagers through their language choices. Catastrophe and comic desperation are constant tropes, from De Syllas and Meade's now outmoded reference to 'savage children' of 1965, recalling Shirley Jackson's humorous book *Life Among the Savages* (1952), to Sarah Newton's *Help! My Teenager is an Alien* of 2007, which continues the combination of humour, otherness and alienation of the film *Teenagers from Outer Space* of 1959. Melodrama suffuses *Teenagers: The Agony, the Ecstasy, the Answers* (MacFarlane and McPherson, 1999), and the notion of survival is common, from *Coping with Teenagers* (Lawson, 2003) to *Surviving the Terrible Teens: How to Have a Teenager and Stay Sane*, especially Chapter 1, 'Who Is This Creature I Spawned' (Mann *et al.*, 2008). Vet and anatomist David Bainbridge's *Teenagers: A Natural History* adopts a 'zoological approach' (2009: 1, 310). Lindenfield (2001: 27–28), on the other hand, tells parents not to imitate teen talk for fear of making themselves a laughing stock with their children.

Life stories: Today's Etiquette

The linguistic contortions performed by post-war domestic advice writers in attempting to serve two audiences have a broader correlative in the narrative structure of the texts. Commonly, an expansive preamble attractive to young people, acknowledging the new and distinct nature of post-war informality and permissiveness and suggesting the wealth of opportunity available outside the home, expressed in an accessible, friendly and hip authorial voice, is gradually undermined by a familiar narrative structure which progresses inevitably through grooming and courtship towards marriage and the etiquette of weddings, housewarming and entertaining. Pam Lyons' *Today's Etiquette* (1967) exemplifies this pattern as it attempts to negotiate the social conventions of existing etiquette and domestic practices and the increased informality of the permissive society. The title, *Today's Etiquette*, emphasises contemporaneity, and the illustrations are fashionable, but the narrative structure is conventional (Table 5.1). Lyons' introduction on the extensive opportunities available to young women cedes to the conventional life course. The books opens with 'teaching children the art of etiquette' and family etiquette (engagements, births and deaths). Subsequent chapters are 'Boy Meets Girl', 'Boy Dates Girl', Boy Marries Girl', 'Dressing to Please', 'Boy Takes Girl to Dinner', while the later chapters address etiquette for adult life: 'Entertaining and Being Entertained', 'Writing Letters', tipping, 'Hatch and Dispatch' and 'Manners for Meeting and Working with Others'. This temporal progression accompanies a spatial one, in that the entire post-marriage sequence concerns extra-domestic matters – eating out and tipping, entertaining guests from outside the family and performing as guests in the homes of others, communicating with the outside world on the page and extra-familial relationships. This pattern conforms with Miller's narrative frame of beginning, sequence and reversal. The successive phases

Table 5.1 Life course narrative analysis of Pam Lyons, *Today's Etiquette*, 1967

Contents	Page	
Living our lives courteously	8	} Children's manners = lifecycle [time]
Boy meets girl	39	⎱
Boy dates girl	60	⎰ Courtship = lifecycle [time]
Boy marries girl	87	
Dressing to please	118	} Inter-phase preparation
Boy takes girl to dinner	140	⎫
Entertaining and being entertained	160	⎪ Courtship = lifecycle [time]
Writing letters	193	⎬ Married social interaction
To tip or not to tip?	205	⎭ Extra-domestic [space]
Hatch and dispatch	215	} Life course [time]
Manners for meeting and working with others	226	} Extra-domestic [space]
Index	184	

of the life course presented by the narrative structure of *Today's Etiquette* suggest a conservative ideology confirmed through close reading of the chapters.

Lyons incorporates new informalities, such as families no longer sitting together at table for set mealtimes, into her advice, but she also points out the continued relevance of convention. Her discussion of parenting acknowledges post-Spock permissiveness, but traditional approaches are favoured: 'Good manners may be frowned on by progressive people, but whatever their opinions, it must be admitted that manners are an integral part of upbringing if a person is to become an accepted part of the community in later life.' Here, 'progressive people' are asserted linguistically as other – 'their opinions' are not the same as 'our opinions' – so the author and the reader are correspondingly positioned as non-progressive. Rather than prescribing behaviour from the progressive vanguard, and responding to the emergent currents of second-wave feminism, Lyons displays mainstream contemporary prejudices and appears, in retrospect, to promote traditional attitudes about gender roles and upbringing, for example in the assertion that 'small girls love to assume the role of "little mother"' (Lyons, 1967: 9, 11). Far from philosopher John Locke's *tabula rasa*, here domesticity is presented as a genetic predisposition, as sex and gender are conflated. This exemplifies what Adorno has identified as the '*fait accompli* technique', in which matters are presented as having previously been decided, thereby relieving the reader of that responsibility ([1957] 2002). Lyons' narrative structure positions the boy as active and – by omission – presents the girl as passive. Even the final chapter, which is nominally about working relationships and thereby implies coverage of married women working outside the home, actually returns us to a conventional marital order; topics addressed include dealing with domestic staff and tradesmen, a mother's duties

towards her child's school teacher, babysitting, voluntary work and relationships with doctors, lawyers and bank managers, leaving only the last
three and a half pages for 'office manners'.

Text and (visual) subtext

The textual contortions and ambiguity employed by domestic advice
writers concerned to cater simultaneously to two audiences, teen and parent, are matched by a schism between text and image in many of these
sources. This is the case in spite of training, such as *How to Write for
Homemakers*, which emphasised that 'In modern communications, words
and pictures interlock as closely as the two sides of a slide-fastener [zip]'
(Richardson and Callahan [1962] 1970: 3; Callahan and Richardson,
1966: 92 ff.). In promoting domestic ideals, advice writers represent both
positive and negative examples. Indeed, cautionary representations of
young people abound in domestic advice books. Teens are shown displaying
either ineffective or overzealous concern for their personal appearance,
prying into siblings' private correspondence, borrowing without returning, throwing impromptu parties (Figure 5.2), and hogging an unfair
share of family resources, such as food and drink, the most comfortable
armchair, the car, the bathroom, the telephone and newspapers (Figure 5.1).
Allen and Briggs's books typify a tendency in domestic advice literature
to show in the illustrations what is censured by the text. Depictions of
teenagers having fun – listening to loud music, socialising, eating and
drinking – carry captions expressing disapproval and encouraging readers not to identify with the misconduct shown. Depictions of undesirable
teen conduct might function as scenarios of identification for young people, in a manner unplanned by authors and possibly even illustrators, and
might, therefore, form the best depiction of the practices that would have
been promoted by rebellious youth, if only it had been given an authorial
voice in post-war advice books.

While Pam Lyons' text for *Today's Etiquette* is conservative, Belinda
Lyon's illustrations are fashionable and youth-oriented. A discussion of
bridal wear is accompanied by an image of a bride and bridesmaids dressed
in blue jeans and jumpers, thereby encapsulating debates about appropriate
dress, fashionable taste, formality and informality. A dry passage about
clothing suitable for the country is accompanied by a loosely drawn image
of a man on horseback waving to a woman with flowing hair, holding some
flowers (Figure 5.6). The flower child imagery is at odds with the caption
'Clothes that co-ordinate to carry you through both smart and casual occasions are the order of the day' (Lyons, 1967: 12, 134–135). Throughout the
book, Belinda Lyon's imagery centres upon informality and risqué slips of
etiquette. A woman who has either forgotten or discarded her manners
reclines, drinking, on a table thereby causing the other guests obvious
embarrassment. Another woman is shown embracing, and exchanging roses

Figure 5.6 'Clothing suitable for the country', illustration by Belinda Lyon, in Pam
Lyons, *Today's Etiquette*, 1967.

with, a stranger ('... If Mrs. Brown is interested enough to want to know
her companion's name') while two shocked flanking figures represent the
appropriate reaction for readers. Other images present young people as
distinct, socially, from those around them. An apparently noisy party takes
place in front of neighbours who remain uninvited. A young woman is
helped by a man to escape her upstairs room at dusk, unnoticed by her parents
in the room below. The implication of a daughter eloping with her fiancé is
supported by the caption 'Marriage in Scotland is not as legally complicated ...'.
Belinda Lyon's illustrations lighten the conventional text, and thereby ingratiate the author with a teenage readership, through humour, fashionable
imagery and depictions of irreverent teenagers and compromised adults.
The conservative text is upstaged by the fashionable illustrations, which
provide a subversive subplot. Lyon's images of young people flaunting convention invite readers to identify with the wrongdoers rather than the ideal
conduct promoted in the text.

Popular culture has both excoriated and emulated youth culture. The
binaristic, dualistic and paradoxical depictions of youth lamented by
Hebdige and others are easily discerned in domestic advice literature.
However, attempts by adults to accommodate young readers through the
leavening of conventional textual guidance with fashionable and humorous
illustrations of undesirable conduct arguably form the genre's most successful, although inadvert, address to young people. By depicting censured
conduct, Allen and Briggs, Lyon and others, arguably provided young readers with an opportunity for subversive reading and a visual lexicon of

dissent and rebellion in lieu of published teenage views. This is not unique to advice literature; for example, in discussing Colin McInnes's novel *Absolute Beginners*: 'Fiction offers an alternative textual space for the representation of subcultural identity' (Bentley, 2005: 73 discusses Hall, 1959 and McInnes, [1959] 1964). The illustrations in post-war domestic advice aimed at teenagers function in several ways: idealised images reinforce the advice in the texts; cautionary images reinforce the textual advice too; fashionable imagery enfranchises a teen audience for conventional textual guidance, and cautionary images figure teen dissent as a channel for the communication of sub-narratives at odds with the textual conservatism.

For teens, by teens?

If adult domestic advice concerning teenagers is marked by dualisms, what about advice for teens, *by* teens? Very few examples exist in book format, but an exception is Doris Webster and Mary Alden Hopkins' *Mrs. Grundy is Dead: A Code of Etiquette for Young People, Written by Themselves* (1930). Webster and Hopkins collaborated on a number of works of advice and self-help, but the cover for their *Mrs. Grundy is Dead* depicts a 'Book of Etiquette' discarded in a waste paper basket, and the text echoes this message:

> The standard books of etiquette to which young persons are referred have hitherto been written by members of the older generation and frequently prescribe obsolete forms. [...] This book is written by the young people themselves. The social technique described is not necessarily what the late Mrs. Grundy thought proper but what the young people say they are actually doing.
>
> (Webster and Hopkins, 1930: 3)

Schlesinger saw Webster and Hopkins' book as evidence that 'modern ideas of behavior had become legal tender', citing *Manners Make Men: A Practical and Sparkling Manual of Modern Etiquette Written By University Men* (Powers and Putnam, 1939) and *Lady Lore: A Swingtime Handbook for Girls* (Putnam, 1939), both published in the same year, as 'similarly inspired' (Schlesinger, [1946] 1968: 54, 53). Mrs. Grundy was an intertextual cultural character and archetypal prim chaperone who appeared across popular culture, as noted in Chapter 4. To proclaim her death was undoubtedly significant, but it was not original, as it had been conceded during the interwar period. Emily Post, who enjoyed an exemplary debut into society and saw herself as a beneficiary of the system, strongly upheld chaperonage in the first edition of *Etiquette* of 1922, but followed fellow advisor Lillian Eichler and relaxed her position in the revised 1927 edition with a chapter 'The Vanishing Chaperon and Other New Conventions' (Eichler, [1921] 1922; Post, 1922, 1927; Nemy, 1997; Schlesinger, [1946] 1968: 52).

While *Mrs. Grundy is Dead* is valuable for the exceptional way in which it responds to the fact that the 'standard books of etiquette' are written by the older generation, it does not live up to its titular promise of offering 'A Code of Etiquette for Young People, Written by Themselves.' Arditi overstates the case when he describes Webster and Hopkins' book as 'the most "revolutionary" of the new manuals', and 'quite radical: overwhelmed by the absurdity of the available manuals, young people, simply, set out to establish their own etiquette' (1999: 33). The authors sent out a questionnaire to 'a thousand men and women in every walk of society and business life'. Yet, the responses were solicited, selected, summarised and synthesised for publication by the editors. The ways in which young people make decisions about points of etiquette are praised:

> When a young man gives a party in his apartment, does he have to have a chaperon? Smith on the whole thinks yes. Bryn Mawr says yes. A group of daughters at home say yes. On the other hand we have a bunch of noes, some of them from Louisiana, the University of Vermont, the University of Syracuse, a group of society girls, and some young women in New York, although none of these groups is unanimous. [...] In many answers we find the motif that runs straight through the answers to this questionnaire – it depends. "It depends on the man" [...] "It depends on the situation," are frequent answers. Again the girls are evolving their own technique, using their intelligence instead of applying the rules.
>
> (Webster and Hopkins, 1930)

Significantly, the flyleaf asserts that: 'This book is indispensable to every one who wants to be well informed about the latest modern behavior. Incidentally, it offers diverting reading for any one interested in how young people think, act and talk today' (Webster and Hopkins, 1930: 21, 64–65, flyleaf). Here, the book is recommended as a primer for adults wishing to learn about the young, rather than as a guide for young people themselves. So it exemplifies the adult world view which has dominated the genre.

Like Webster and Hopkins, Allen and Briggs emphasised the authorial involvement of teens in their advice books. In the revised 1950 edition of *Behave Yourself!* they 'thank the many young people who have written to us about their social problems, and we can only hope that this latest edition will continue to serve their needs' ([1937] 1945, 1950): v–vi). A revised edition of *If You Please* (also 1950) was dedicated to 'all the boys and girls who have asked for a companion volume to *Behave Yourself!*' The authors express:

> Special appreciation to those young people who were interested enough to write us such friendly letters, telling us some of the things they would like to have included in a new book on etiquette which

had not been covered in our earlier book, *Behave Yourself!* If they read carefully, they will find many of their suggestions incorporated in this edition.

(Allen and Briggs, [1942] 1950: v, vii)

Although these texts purport to be both *for* and *by* young people, the credibility of their claims is weakened by textual similarities between successive editions, and between the two titles, as well as their portrayal of young people as antisocial antagonists.

Founded in 1975, Children's Express was a landmark project launched during a period in which children's and teens' voices were largely excluded from published media. Children's Express newspapers, magazine and syndicated stories for the US national press represented the voices of the young, while adults retained editorial control. The first Children's Express book, *Listen to Us: The Children's Express Report* (Kavanaugh, 1978), is not an advice book, but it is didactic. It contains an edited selection of children's own words on a wide range of social topics, so that adult readers can better understand children's views. Accounts of working on the project by some of the associate and assistant editors testify to the beneficial nature of the extensive consultation process. Children's Express closed in 2001, but continued in modified local form under several different names, including, in the UK, Headliners. By publishing the views of children, *Listen to Us* sought to inform young readers through exposure to accounts of a range of different experiences.

More recently, advice books have displayed a new emphasis on children's and teens' voices. This is especially true of self-help books addressing family and emotional issues, rather than domestic advice literature wholly focused on homemaking, home decoration and etiquette. Personal testimony has an important role within the fostering of emotional intelligence that forms the self-help project. Conversely, domestic advice literature prioritises expertise over personal testimony, and does not feature the voices of homemakers, children and other potential audiences as extensively, if at all.

Teenagers: The Agony, the Ecstasy, the Answers is rich in frank accounts from both parents and teens. Teen voices offer advice to parents: 'Thomas has a last word of advice for parents: Kids grow up. I'm trying to give my parents the message that they've got to trust and respect me and also they've got to have an understanding of me socialising and wanting to be out late.' And teenagers are shown reciprocating the support that their parents offer, for example during parental separation and divorce: 'My oldest son James, who is seventeen, has been a wonderful help. He checks up on me and offers endless support whenever I am feeling down. He rings every day when he's away from home' (MacFarlane and McPherson, 1999: 49, 100, 119). Similarly, *Surviving the Terrible Teens* (Mann *et al.*, 2008) incorporates direct testimony from teenagers and their parents drawn from 170 questionnaires and the views of a 'Parents Panel'. Other self-help books use a greater degree of editorial mediation to represent readers' concerns. *Get Out of My Life – But First Take Me and Alex into Town* provides the 're-created voices of teenagers and their parents' to offer 'a distillation of what really goes on', 'Their accuracy will be for you to judge'. Following an imagined argument between a parent and a teenager, the authors conclude: 'Forty years ago the above conversation would rarely have taken place, but [teenagers today] treat the adults in their lives in a manner that is less automatically obedient, much more fearless, and definitely more outspoken than that of previous generations' (Wolf and Franks, 2002: ix, 1–2). A much earlier example of an author giving advice through imagined teenage characters is Orson Scott Card's Mormon text *Listen Mom and Dad: Young Adults Look Back on their Upbringing* (1977).

While teen voices are not as prevalent in home decorating advice as they are in the self-help genre, their limited engagement can be discerned. Judith Wilson's *Teen Zone* 'is aimed at parents – because they hold the purse strings – but there are special sections written for teens. Get your kids to check out the Why Don't You... panels for quick, creative ideas, plus the Hot Topics boxes to get them thinking about shared issues!' One 'Hot Topics' box, entitled 'Going Green', begins: 'Your parents may not be quite so eco-minded as you are, so you might want to tell them a few key water-saving facts' (Wilson, 2007: 7, 60). This suggests that teens educate and advise their parents on the benefits of installing a shower over a bath, and a water-saving loo. Teens, here, are spoken for and to, rather than being given the opportunity to directly voice their concerns.

The Emily Post Institute provides a notable exception to the exclusion of teenage voices in published advice. Five generations of the Post family have produced books for different market segments. In *Children are People* of 1940, Post tells parents 'How to Understand and Guide Your Children', advising give and take. Here, 'children' includes teenagers and offspring away at college. *Emily Post Talks with Teens about Manners and Etiquette* of 1986 was billed as 'straight talk [...] from the first lady of etiquette', although the 'first lady' referred to is Elizabeth L. Post, who wrote the book with Joan M. Coles. While the book lacks authorial input from teens, evidence of an address *to* teens is shown in the informal voice, the use of illustrations and text boxes to break up the text, and a light hearted succession of imagined interactions, many of them featuring undesirable behaviour, such as this telephone call: 'Receiver: Hello; Caller: Oh @#*! [and hangs up]' (Post and Coles, 1986: 15). In 2007, Emily's great-great-granddaughter Lizzie Post wrote *How Do You Work This Life Thing?* to advise the 'newly independent' – 18–25-year-olds who have left home – on getting along with housemates, among other things (Post, 2007). The book was promoted on YouTube and through Lizzie Post's now defunct blog. Lizzie's sister, Anna, author of *Emily Post's Wedding Parties* (2007), also wrote a blog, 'What Would Emily Post Do?' (2007–2010) and oversaw the Emily Post Institute's podcast series. Emily Post herself has a posthumous Facebook page, which attracts grateful comments from users of her advice. The Emily Post Institute has adopted social networking technologies and interactivity in response to the development of user-generated channels for the communication of peer advice.

Although teen voices remain marginal in mainstream domestic advice book publishing, teenagers have engaged extensively in online social networking (Weber and Mitchell, 2008: 25–48; Buckingham and Willet, 2006; Weber and Dixon, 2007) and some of this peer interaction fits the category of published advice. Infamous examples include the numerous 'pro-ana' websites, which ostensibly provide peer support while actually promoting anorexic disorders, and similar sites exist for self-harm and suicide cults (Jackson, 2008; Ferreday, 2010). But, the majority of young people's online activity is more mundane; informal advice about what to buy, how to use it, how to style oneself and one's surroundings forms part of this everyday discourse. Teen Voices was launched in 1988 specifically to empower girls through media broadcast. Teen Voices Online publishes teen writing as a counterpoint to the commercialism of consumer publishing: 'people choose to see you as they want to, despite what you wear or how you look or how smart you are' (Teen Voices, 2011). While parents, too, are active online and seek advice from web sources (Rashley, 2005: 58–92), teenagers' online participation is distinct because it represents a relatively rare territory of free expression for teens, and as such it can be seen to constitute an extension of the teenage bedroom, with 'the symbolic and practical properties of an individually owned and controlled space' (Hodkinson and Lincoln, 2008: 27). Indeed, in some web-based gaming environments, such as Second Life, teen participants virtually 'decorate' their own spaces, choosing wallpaper and other decorative items, and even Facebook uses the material metaphor of the 'wall' to match the computer's own 'desktop' and 'wallpaper'.

The online participation of young people has raised a new set of problems for address, including anxieties about the kinds of material and people the young have access to, and the extent of their involvement in web-based gaming and social networking: 'For children and parents already absorbed in the fraught emotional conflicts of negotiating boundaries of public and private, dependence and independence, tradition and change, this presents a new burden' (Livingstone, 2009: 179). Livingstone notes that young people are accorded the status of 'youthful experts', yet studies of children's and teens' online participation has centred upon their media consumption and safety, rather than emphasising their roles as cultural producers and peer-to-peer advisors (Seiter, 2005; Comstock and Scharrer, 2007; Denvir *et al.*, 2011; Gould *et al.* 2002). However, to indicate the fluid and active conjunction in the digital sphere of two previously demarcated activities, production and consumption, the coinage 'prosumer' is used (Lister *et al.*, 2003: 390). It is important to remember how far young people have come in broadcasting their voices. Patricia Holland notes that 'of all social groups, children have been the least able to explore their view of themselves in the public domain'. Trapped 'by received definitions, which are underpinned by powerful adult emotions', children who have 'gained greater access to a public voice' 'have been able to make a significant contribution', forcing adults to 'readjust our concept of childhood and its contexts'. So while Livingstone admits that 'despite considerable enthusiasm for going online and becoming "youthful experts", [...] there is only qualified evidence that the internet is bringing about any of the changes anticipated' (2009: 2), Holland reminds us of a core aim in insisting that it is important that 'Children should certainly be heard as much as they are seen' (Holland, 2004: 205–206). The same is surely true of teenagers.

Conclusion

Youth cultures identified at the end of the nineteenth century, and popularised during the early decades of the twentieth century, achieved greater recognition in mainstream cultural discourse in the period following the Second World War II, both in the UK and in the USA. Young people in Britain followed their US counterparts in forging social lives and consumer practices distinct from those of their parents, leading to tension between the generations. Widely debated in the public sphere, the effects of youth culture were particularly felt in the home, where teenagers and parents cohabited. Parents looked to domestic advice writers for guidance on living with their teenage children, and teens also turned to these sources. Domestic advice writers recommended flexibility, both through social, interpersonal solutions based on compromise, cooperation and sharing and through material solutions built around accommodation of the teenager in a dedicated, multi-purpose room. The ideal teen room not only represented the epitome of a modernist domestic aesthetic based on multi-functional flexibility and informality, but also influenced interior design trends throughout the second half of the twentieth century. However, fixity is seen in the increasing emphasis on setting interpersonal *and* physical boundaries for teens, including the four walls which separate the teenager's multi-purpose space from the remaining – and by implication adult – parts of the home.

Domestic advice literature about, and for, teens has failed in several ways. Advice literature exists as a published textual discourse destined always to be less successful than immersive, experiential modes of learning, which were compromised during a period when parents and teens no longer behaved in the same ways, or shared patterns of behaviour deemed (by parents) as inappropriate for young people. Many publishers and advice writers failed to consult or collaborate effectively with the young people to whom they purported to offer advice. The highly ambivalent attitude to youth displayed in domestic advice books exemplifies a widely noted tendency to compartmentalise young people into good and bad; this is likely to have alienated, as much as educated, young people and exacerbated, rather than ameliorated, relations between the generations. Teens have been characterised as the antagonists in books purportedly aimed at them. Rather than fulfilling its transforming potential, recent domestic advice books show the genre to be conservative and nostalgic, with few exceptions. Even advice books specifically for young people have promoted a parental ideal rather than addressing teenagers' needs and aspirations. The voices, needs and desires of teens have been undermined through narrative and linguistic strategies operating in favour of adult hegemony. Teenage peer communication on domestic and social matters existed in spoken rather than published discourse, until the recent expansion of online publishing channels associated with Web 2.0 user-generated internet content.

Conclusion

Domestic advice literature provides a crucial testimony for social changes engaging issues of class, gender and age in the second half of the twentieth century. Social issues, design problems and problems in the giving of domestic advice are inextricably related. Domestic advice literature is an ideal discourse articulated in response to social realities, and it is inherently ideological. It exists to solve problems, but the solutions it provides raise further problems for address, as I have shown. By looking *at*, rather than *through*, domestic advice literature, we can conclude that that while promising self-improvement, and self-help, domestic advice literature has not always functioned in the best interests of its intended readers.

During the post-war period, in the UK and the USA, the competing needs of family members determined by developing class, age and gender roles resulted in a fracturing of domestic advice discourses which represented, visually and textually, fabricated problems and imagined solutions for modern family life. These solutions were based on a complex negotiation of privacy and openness. I have drawn attention to a number of hybrid spaces which evolved as a result of the negotiation of social and material factors in the post-war home. Members of the newly expanded middle classes did not seek to emulate the aristocratic tastemakers whose influence was rapidly declining during in the post-war period; rather, the domestic advice books they consulted recommended patterns of domestic life appropriate to their commitments and income. Within this process of informalisation, modernist design provided a series of domestic solutions centred upon flexibility, enabling multiple uses of the relatively limited number of rooms available in middle-class homes of the mid to late twentieth century.

We have seen Mrs. Three-in-One occupying various bridging spaces, from a combined kitchen-dining room to a dining booth or nook in the kitchen, a breakfast bar in the kitchen or on its border and a hatch between kitchen and dining room. She is shown employing a range of bridging objects, from the infamous hostess trolley to oven-to-tableware, tabletop cooking appliances and warming trays, and engaging in bridging practices, from planning and hosting self-service buffets to the serving of convenience foods. These hybrid or bridging spaces, objects and practices collapsed what Goffman termed front and backstage regions and enabled successful unassisted hostessing by managing transparency and openness.

Similarly, the teenage consumer was seen to need a space that accommodated a range of competing practices, from sleeping, grooming and studying to leisure and entertaining – the difficulty of providing one space that accommodated these competing activities was exacerbated by the necessity of sharing a room with a sibling. In addition, a children's or teenagers' room was seen to have the potential to be improving, if correctly arranged and provided for. All of this was achieved through the use of zoning, partitions, flexibility, storage and – in the case of sharing – mirroring. The teenage bedroom – a microcosmic home within the home – offered a compromised privacy within a more-or-less public home.

Yet, aside from the enabling emphasis of these flexible solutions, they also exemplify, or manifest, conflicts of power within the home. Middle-class householders were encouraged to become expert consumers as an increasing range of household goods was promoted to them through domestic discourses. The kitchen-dining bridges mentioned *were* enabling; they enabled what historian of technology Ruth Schwartz Cowan has termed 'More work for mother'. And, while the teenage bedroom, properly equipped, allowed the teen some privacy in the home, it also removed her or him from the remaining parts of the home, so that teenagers were not heard, or seen, in the adult home. In each of these cases, then, we can see the solutions provided in domestic advice books as hegemonic.

A defining aspect of domestic advice literature since 1945 has been a shift in its modes of authority. The dominance of traditional legitimisation was dismantled in the twentieth century, initially by rational authority and then by an emphasis on the advisor's charisma and personality. Although these three modes of authority coexist, and can be found in action in domestic advice literature across the lifespan of the genre, a pattern emerges which accords with larger social changes in class, gender and age. As the economic and cultural dominance of the aristocracy diminished, so advice for a growing middle class placed less emphasis on traditional legitimisation; advice was couched in humour and referred increasingly to a charismatic mode of legitimisation. Gradual acceptance of modernist approaches to domestic design provided consumers with a material manifestation of the rejection of traditional authority, although the rationality of modernism was softened for mass acceptance. In published advice on homemaking, and food, traditional legitimisation was ousted first by rational legitimisation in the form of home economics and domestic science, as they were filtered from higher and school education to a mass readership through works of domestic advice. However, while rational methods may have fitted the workplace, they did not hold sway for long in the affective space of the home, as the working kitchen returned to a living kitchen. Charismatic authority has increasingly been used to educate and inspire both female and male readers of domestic advice throughout the twentieth and twenty-first centuries. In writing for teenagers and their parents, domestic advisors of the post-war and permissive eras paid lip service to social change while reasserting traditional values. However, traditional legitimisation has been less and less compelling as a mode of authority for young people and their parents, and charismatic legitimisation has taken precedence as the most effective way to deliver advice to the young. There is great scope for increased publication of peer advice for teenagers and online forums form the most promising channel.

The publishing possibilities offered by the internet, and particularly Web 2.0, in which users, or readers, provide content, have the potential to transform the mechanics, location and content of domestic advice literature. Internet users can access a plethora of advice through subject-specific blogs, advice from friends, family, colleagues and a wider contact group via social media posts and amateur films, for example on YouTube. Many bloggers enthuse about, circulate and recirculate images of houses, interiors and objects, often for sheer pleasure rather than with any practical application in mind. Large numbers of Japanese housewives photograph the beautiful meals they prepare each day and publish them online as inspiration for others, while professional content providers such as Martha Stewart's Omnimedia team encourage readers and viewers to send in their own photographs of completed craft projects and evaluations of the advice offered. The hierarchy of authority which gives voice to the advisor and silences the advisee – the person consuming the advice – is critically dismantled when readers are able to appraise advice in comments that are published beside the advice that engendered them and are available to subsequent readers.

In the online environment, the problem is not finding advice, but rather judging its value based on the advisor's expertise. Anyone with access to a smart phone or a computer (whether at home, at a library or in an internet cafe) has the potential to become a producer, as well as a consumer, of domestic advice and this peer-to-peer exchange replaces expertise with accessibility and eliminates an advice literature hidebound by its insistence on traditional legitimisation. Nevertheless, online readers will continue to seek authoritative advice. The charismatic legitimisation that has characterised much late twentieth-century and early twenty-first century published domestic advice is likely to continue to be important in online channels as people accept advice online both from friends and family and from advice professionals who have achieved celebrity status, such as Martha Stewart in the USA and Australia's Donna Hay. The domestic advice literature I have examined has, like its antecedents, depended on the authority of a persuasive and entertaining author, imbued with relevant expertise in the form of experience and/or qualifications and with access to the infrastructure of the publishing industry and the privileged voice or forum it provides. Twenty-first century published domestic advice is undergoing something akin to market deregulation. Published advice will increasingly take the form of peer advice. In this way, the inherent imbalance between the advisor and her or his reader will collapse and the hegemonic solutions I have analysed here will hopefully be replaced with more equitable recommendations for the material and social home.

References

A Lady (1695) *The Whole Duty of a Woman: or A Guide to the Female Sex. From the Age of Sixteen, to Sixty, &c. Being directions, how women of all qualities and conditions, ought to behave themselves in the various circumstances of this life ... With the whole art of cookery ... Written by a lady*, London: printed for J. Gwillim.

A Lady (1856) *A Manual of Etiquette for Ladies: or, True Principles of Politeness. By a Lady*, London: T. Allman & Son.

A Lady in Society (1907) *The New Book of Etiquette. By a Lady in Society*, London: Cassell & Co.

A Lady of New York (1894) *Etiquette for Ladies: A Manual of the Most Approved Rules of Conduct in Polished Society for Married and Unmarried Ladies*, Philadelphia: G. B. Zieber.

A Society Lady (1923) *The A. B. C. of Etiquette by a Society Lady*, London: Dranes.

A Woman of the World (1922) *Cassell's Book of Etiquette, by 'A Woman of the World'*, London: Cassell and Co.

Abbott-Chapman, Joan and Margaret Robertson (2001) 'Youth, Leisure and Home: Space, Place and Identity', *Loisir et société/Society and Leisure*, vol. 24, no. 2 (Autumn): 485–506.

Abercrombie, Stanley ([1995] 2000) *George Nelson: The Design of Modern Design*, Cambridge, MA: MIT Press.

About.com (2012) 'Teen Advice Forum', http://forums.about.com/n/pfx/forum. aspx?webtag=ab-teenadvice. Accessed 1 October 2012.

Abrams, Mark (1959) *The Teenage Consumer*, London: London Press Exchange.

Acton, Eliza (1845) *Modern Cookery, in all its Branches: Reduced to a System of Easy Practice, for the Use of Private Families, Illustrated with Numerous Woodcuts*, third edition, London: Longman, Brown, Green and Longman.

Adorno, Theodor W. ([1957] 2002) 'The Stars Down to Earth: The *Los Angeles Times* Astrology Column', in *Adorno: The Stars Down to Earth*, ed. Stephen Crook, London: Routledge, 46–171. [*Jahrbuch für Amerikastudien* II, Heidelberg, reproduced in *Telos*, no. 19 (Spring 1974): 13–90.]

Adorno, Theodor and Max Horkheimer (1979) *Dialectic of Enlightenment*, trans. J. Cumming, London: Verso.

Advertising Age (1999) 'Betty Crocker', *Special Report: The Advertising Century*, http://adage.com/article/special-report-the-advertising-century/betty-crocker/140173/. Accessed 20 August 2013.

Agogos (Charles William Day) (1834) *Hints on Etiquette and the Usages of Society with a Glance at Bad Habits*, London: Messrs. Longman, Rees, Orme, Brown, Green and Longman.

Albert R. Mann Library (2012) *Home Economics Archive: Research, Tradition and History (HEARTH)*, Ithaca, NY: Albert R. Mann Library, Cornell University. http://hearth.library.cornell.edu (version January 2005).

Aldrich, Elizabeth (1991) *From the Ballroom to Hell: Grace and Folly in Nineteenth-Century Dance*, Evanston, IL: Northwestern University Press.

Alexander, Jane (1999) *The Illustrated Spirit of the Home: How to Make Your Home a Sanctuary*, London: Thorsons.

Allen, Betty and Mitchell Pirie Briggs ([1937] 1945, 1950) *Behave Yourself! Etiquette for American Youth*, New York: J. B. Lippincott Company.

Allen, Betty and Mitchell Pirie Briggs ([1942] 1950) *If You Please! A Book of Manners for Young Moderns*, drawings by Charles Malcolm Allen, New York: J. B. Lippincott Company.

Allen, Betty and Mitchell Pirie Briggs ([1957] 1964, 1971) *Mind Your Manners*, Chicago, IL: Lippincott.

Ambasz, Emilio (1972) *Italy: The New Domestic Landscape*, New York: The Museum of Modern Art in collaboration with Centro Di, Florence.

American Antiquarian Society (2004) 'Portraits!: Waldo Lincoln', http://www.americanantiquarian.org/Exhibitions/Portraits/waldolincoln.htm. Last updated 10 December 2004.

American Antiquarian Society (2005) 'Cookbooks', http://www.americanantiquarian.org/cookbooks.htm/. Last updated 31 January 2005.

American Youth Commission (1942) *Youth and the Future*, Washington, DC: American Council on Education.

An American Gentleman (1847) *In True Politeness: A Hand-Book of Etiquette for Gentlemen by An American Gentleman*, New York: Leavitt and Allen.

Andrews, Maggie (2012) *Domesticating the Airwaves: Broadcasting, Domesticity and Femininity*, London: Continuum.

Anonymous (2004) 'Obituary: The Duke of Devonshire', *The Economist*, 13 May, http://www.economist.com/node/2668109. Accessed 21 August 2012.

Anson, Lady Elizabeth (1986) *Party Planners Book*, London: Weidenfeld & Nicolson.

Anthony, Hugh (pseudonym) (1945) *Houses: Permanence and Prefabrication*, London: Pleiades Books.

Anthony, Hugh (pseudonym) (1946) *Homes by the Million: An Account of the Housing Achievements in the USA 1940–1945*, Harmondsworth: Penguin.

Arditi, Jorge (1996) 'The Feminization of Etiquette Literature: Foucault, Mechanisms of Social Change, and the Paradoxes of Empowerment', *Sociological Perspectives*, vol. 39, no. 3: 417–435.

Arditi, Jorge (1998) *A Genealogy of Manners: Transformations of Social Relations in France and England from the Fourteenth to the Eighteenth Century*, Chicago, IL: University of Chicago Press.

Arditi, Jorge (1999) 'Etiquette Books, Discourse and the Deployment of an Order of Things', *Theory, Culture and Society*, vol. 16, no. 4: 25–48.

Armstrong, Nancy and Leonard Tennenhouse, eds. (1987) *The Ideology of Conduct: Essays in Literature and the History of Sexuality*, London: Methuen.

Arnett, Jeffrey Jensen (2006) 'G. Stanley Hall's *Adolescence*: Brilliance and Nonsense', *History of Psychology*, vol. 9, no. 3: 186–197.

Ashworth, Holly (2012) '10 Cool Teenage Room Ideas', http://teenadvice.about. com/od/entertainment/tp/cool_teenage_room_ideas.htm. Accessed 1 October 2012.

Atha, Christine (2012) 'Dirt and Disorder: Taste and Anxiety in the Homes of the British Working Class', in *Atomic Dwelling: Anxiety, Domesticity and Postwar Architecture*, ed. Robin Schuldenfrei, Abingdon, Oxon: Routledge, 207–226.

Atkinson, Anthony Barnes (1980) *Wealth, Income and Inequality*, Oxford: Oxford University Press.

Attar, Dena (1990) *Wasting Girls' Time: The History and Politics of Home Economics*, London: Virago.

Attfield, Judy (1997) 'Design as a Practice of Modernity: A Case Study of the Coffee Table in the Mid-Century Domestic Interior', *Journal of Material Culture*, vol. 2, no. 3: 267–289.

Attfield, Judy (1999) 'Bringing Modernity Home: Open Plan in the British Domestic Interior', in *At Home: An Anthropology of Domestic Space*, ed. Irene Cieraad, Syracuse, NY: Syracuse University Press, 73–82.

Austen, Diana and Catherine Davies (1976) *Good Housekeeping Kitchens*, London: Ebury Press/National Magazine Co.

Austin, Joe and Michael Nevin Willard, eds. (1998) *Generations of Youth*, New York: NYU Press.

Aynsley, Jeremy and Kate Forde, eds. (2007) *Design and the Modern Magazine*, Manchester: Manchester University Press.

Bain, Priscilla (1986) 'Recounting Chickens, or Hannah Further Scrutinised', *Petits Propos Culinaires*, no. 23: 28.

Bainbridge, David (2009) *Teenagers: A Natural History*, Vancouver: Greystone Books and London: Portobello Books.

Baker, David (2005) 'Rock Rebels and Delinquents: The Emergence of the Rock Rebel in 1950s "Youth Problem" Films', *Continuum: Journal of Media and Cultural Studies*, vol. 19, no. 1 (March): 39–54.

Baldick, Chris (2008) *The Oxford Dictionary of Literary Terms*, third edition, Oxford: Oxford University Press.

Banner, Stephen (2011) *American Property: A History of How, Why and What We Own*, Cambridge, MA: Harvard University Press.

Barbatsis, Gretchen (1983) 'Soap Opera as Etiquette Book: Advice for Interpersonal Relationships', *Journal of American Culture*, vol. 6, no. 3 (Fall): 88–91.

Barber, Edith Michael (1952) *The Short-Cut Cook Book: A Modern Sampler of Budget Recipes and Menus*, New York: Sterling Publishing Co.

Barber, Edith Michael ([1953] 1956) *Short Cut to Etiquette*, illus. Doug Anderson, Kingswood, Surrey: The World's Work [New York: Sterling Publishing Co.].

Barclay, Marion Stearns and Frances Champion (1961) *Teen Guide to Homemaking*, New York and London: McGraw-Hill Book Company Inc.

Barker, Jean (1968) *Your Own Work*, illus. Hugh Marshall, London and Harlow: Longmans, Green and Co.

Barker, Linda (1997) *Changing Rooms*, London: BBC Books.

Barker, Linda (2000) *Finishing Touches: Styling Secrets to Transform your Home*, London: BBC Worldwide.

Barrie, Heather (1950) *Practical Homecraft*, London: Thorsons Publishers Ltd.

Barthes, Roland ([1967] 1985) *The Fashion System,* trans. Matthew Ward and Richard Howard, London: Jonathan Cape [*Système de la mode,* Paris: Editions du Seuil].

Baruch, Dr Dorothy W. (1953) *How to Live with Your Teenager,* illus. Lois Fisher, New York, Toronto, London: McGraw-Hill.

Baudrillard, Jean ([1968] 1996), *The System of Objects,* trans. James Benedict, London: Verso [*Le système des objets,* Paris: Editions Gallimard].

Baudrillard, Jean ([1970] 1998) 'Towards a Theory of Consumption', in *The Consumer Society: Myths and Structures,* London: Sage [*La société de consommation,* Paris: Editions Denoël], 69–86.

Bauman, Lawrence with Robert Riche (1986) *The Nine Most Troublesome Teenage Problems and How to Solve Them,* Secaucus, NJ: Lyle Stuart Inc.

Bazal Productions (1999) *Changing Rooms* 'Seasonal special', directed by Andrew Anderson and Linda Maher, produced by Susannah Walker.

BBC News (2002) 'Duke who "remade" Woburn mourned' (20 October 2002), http://news.bbc.co.uk/1/hi/england/2373801.stm.

Beck, Simone, Louisette Bertholle and Julia Child (1961) *Mastering the Art of French Cooking,* New York: Knopf.

Bedford, John, Duke of, (1959) *A Silver-Plated Spoon,* London: Cassell & Co.

Bedford, John, Duke of, ed. (1968) *The Flying Duchess: The Diaries and Letters of Mary, Duchess of Bedford,* London: Macdonald and Co.

Bedford, John, Duke of, and George Mikes (1965) *The Duke of Bedford's Book of Snobs,* illus. Nicolas Bentley, London: Peter Owen.

Bedford, John, Duke of, in collaboration with George Mikes (1971) *How to Run a Stately Home,* illus. ffolkes, London: André Deutsch.

Bedford, Nicole de ([1974] 1975) *Nicole Nobody: The Autobiography of the Duchess of Bedford,* London: W. H. Allen & Co. Ltd.

Beecher, Catharine E. (1832) *Arithmetic Simplified ... In Three Parts ... By Catharine E. Beecher,* Hartford, CT: D. F. Robinson & Co.

Beecher, Catharine E. ([1841] 1842) *A Treatise on Domestic Economy, For The Use Of Young Ladies at Home, and at School. By Miss Catharine E. Beecher,* Boston, MA: Marsh, Capen, Lyon & Webb [Boston: T.H. Webb & Co.].

Beecher, Catharine E. ([1841] 1977) *A Treatise on Domestic Economy,* with an introduction by Kathryn Kish Sklar, New York: Schocken Books.

Beecher, Catharine E. (1842) *Letters to Persons who are Engaged in Domestic Service,* New York: Leavitt & Trow.

Beecher, Catharine E. (1845) *The Duty of American Women to their Country,* New York: Harper & Brothers.

Beecher, Catharine E. ([1846] 2001) *Miss Beecher's Domestic Receipt-Book: Designed as a Supplement to her Treatise on Domestic Economy,* ed. Janice Bluestein Longone, Mineola, NY: Dover Publications [New York: Harper & Brothers, ca. 1846 and 1858].

Beecher, Catharine E. (1857) *Common Sense Applied to Religion; or, The Bible and the People,* New York: Harper & Brothers and Montreal: B. Dawson.

Beecher, Catharine E. (1871) *Woman's Suffrage and Woman's Profession,* Hartford, CT: Brown & Gross.

Beecher, Catharine E. (1873) *Miss Beecher's Housekeeper and Healthkeeper: Containing Five Hundred Recipes for Economical and Healthful Cooking; Also, Many Directions for Securing Health and Happiness,* New York: Harper & Brothers.

Beecher, Catharine E. and Harriet Beecher Stowe ([1869] 1991) *The American Woman's Home: or, Principles of Domestic Science; Being a Guide to the Formation and Maintenance of Economical, Healthful, Beautiful, and Christian Homes*, Hartford, CT: The Stowe-Day Foundation [New York: J. B. Ford and Co., and Boston, MA: H.A. Brown & Co., 1869; reissued New York: Arno Press, 1971].

Beecher Stowe, Harriet ([1852] 1992) *Uncle Tom's Cabin*, New York: Vintage Books.

Beeton, Mrs Isabella Mary, ed. (1859–1861) *Beeton's Book of Household Management*, London: S. O. Beeton.

Bell, David and Joanne Hollows, eds. (2005) *Ordinary Lifestyles: Popular Media, Consumption and Taste*, Maidenhead: Open University Press.

Bell, Howard M. (1938) *Youth Tell Their Story*, conducted for the American Youth Commission, Washington, DC: American Council on Education.

Benson, John (1989) *The Working Class in Britain, 1850–1939*, London: Longman.

Bentley, Nicolas (1938a) *The Week-End Wants of a Guest. A Memorandum Book. Arranged by N. Bentley, who also drew the pictures*, London: Cobden-Sanderson.

Bentley, Nicolas (1938b) *The Week-End Worries of a Hostess. A Memorandum Book. Arranged by N. Bentley, who also drew the pictures*, London: Cobden-Sanderson.

Bentley, Nicholas (1960) *A Version of the Truth*, London: André Deutsch.

Bentley, Nick (2005) 'The Young Ones: A Reassessment of the British New Left's Representation of 1950s Youth Subcultures', *European Journal of Cultural Studies*, vol. 8, no. 1: 65–83.

Berger, John (1972) *Ways of Seeing*, Harmondsworth: Penguin.

Bertram, Anthony (1938) *Design*, Harmondsworth: Penguin.

Betjeman, Sir John (1933) *Ghastly Good Taste: The Depressing Story of the Rise and Fall of British Architecture*, second edition, London: Chapman & Hall.

Bird, Eric and Kenneth Holmes (1955) *Decorating for the Amateur*, London: The Studio.

Birnbach, Lisa, ed. (1980) *The Official Preppy Handbook*, New York: Workman Publishing.

Blood, Gertrude Elizabeth (1893) *Etiquette of Good Society*, London: Cassell & Co.

Bolton, Mary and John Bolton (1968) *The Complete Book of Etiquette*, London: W. Foulsham & Co. Ltd.

Borelli, Laird O'Shea (1997) 'Dressing Up and Talking About It: Fashion Writing in *Vogue* from 1968 to 1993', *Fashion Theory*, vol. 1, no. 3: 247–259.

Bourdieu, Pierre ([1972] 1977) *Outline of A Theory of Practice*, Cambridge Studies in Social Anthropology, no. 16, trans. by Richard Nice, Cambridge: Cambridge University Press [*Esquisse d'une théorie de la pratique*, Geneva: Droz].

Bourdieu, Pierre ([1979] 1986) *Distinction: A Social Critique of the Judgment of Taste*, trans. by Richard Nice, London: Routledge [*La Distinction*, Paris: Les Editions de Minuit].

Bourke, Joanna (1994) *Working Class Cultures in Britain 1890–1960: Gender, Class and Ethnicity*, London: Routledge.

Bowden, Sue and Avner Offner (1996) 'The Technological Revolution that Never Was: Gender, Class and the Diffusion of Electrical Appliances in Interwar England', in *The Sex of Things: Gender and Consumption in Historical Perspective*, ed. Victoria de Grazia and Ellen Furlough, Berkeley, CA: University of California Press, 244–274.

Bracken, Peg (1960) *The I Hate to Cook Book*, drawings by Hilary Knight, New York: Harcourt, Brace.

Bracken, Peg ([1962] 1963) *The I Hate to Housekeep Book: When and How to Keep House without Losing Your Mind*, drawings by Hilary Knight, London: Arlington Books [New York: Harcourt, Brace & World].

Bracken, Peg ([1964] 1969) *Instant Etiquette Book*, decorated by Hilary Knight, London: Sphere [London: Arlington Books].

Bracken, Peg (1964) *I Try to Behave Myself: Peg Bracken's Etiquette Book*, drawings by Hilary Knight, New York: Harcourt, Brace & World.

Bracken, Peg (1966) *Appendix to The I Hate to Cook Book*, New York: Harcourt, Brace and World.

Bracken, Peg ([1967] 1980) *The I Still Hate to Cook Book*, decorated by Hilary Knight, ed. Ruth Martin, London: Corgi [London: Arlington Books].

Bracken, Peg (1976) *The I Hate to Cook Almanack: A Book of Days*, New York: Harcourt Brace Jovanovich.

Bracken, Peg (1977) *The I Hate to Cook Book of The Year: A Book of Days*, London: Arlington Books.

Bracken, Peg (1981) *A Window Over the Sink: A Mainly Affectionate Memoir*, drawings by Paul Bacon, New York: Harcourt, Brace, Jovanovich.

Bracken, Peg (1986) *The Compleat I Hate to Cook Book*, drawings by Hilary Knight, San Diego, CA: Harcourt Brace Jovanovich and London: Arlington.

Bracken, Peg (2010) *The I Hate to Cook Book*, updated and revised fiftieth anniversary edition, New York: Grand Central Publishing.

Bracken, Peg and Emily Bracken (1997) *On Getting Old for the First Time*, Wilsonville, OR: Book Partners.

Brandt, Mary L. (1955) *How to Plan Your Bedroom*, New York: Greenburg.

Braudel, Fernand (1969) *On History*, trans. Sarah Matthews, Chicago, IL: University of Chicago Press.

Braverman, Harry (1974) *Labour and Monopoly Capital: The Degradation of Work in the Twentieth Century*, New York and London: Monthly Review Press.

Brett, Lionel (1947) *The Things We See No. 2: Houses*, West Drayton, Middlesex: Penguin Books.

Brett, Simon (1984) *Bad Form Or How Not to Get Invited Back*, illus. Tony Matthews, London: Elm Tree Books.

Briggs, Asa (1994) 'Introduction', in *The Culture of Youth*, London: Hamlyn.

Briggs, Desmond (1968) *Entertaining Single-Handed*, Harmondsworth: Penguin.

Brown, Helen Gurley ([1962] 1963) *Sex and the Single Girl*, London: Frederick Muller Limited, [New York: B. Geis Associates, Random House].

Brown, Helen Gurley (2000) *I'm Wild Again: Snippets from My Life and a Few Brazen Thoughts*, New York: St Martin's Press.

Brunt, Rosalind (1982) '"An Immense Verbosity": Permissive Sexual Advice in the 1970s', in *Feminism, Culture and Politics*, ed. Rosalind Brunt and Caroline Rowan, London: Lawrence & Wishart, 143–170.

Buckingham, David and Rebekah Willet, eds. (2006) *Digital Generations: Children, Young People, and New Media*, Mahwah, NJ: Lawrence Erlbaum.

Bullivant, Lucy (1986) '"Design for Better Living" and the Public Response to *Britain Can Make It*', in *Did Britain Make It? British Design in Context 1946–1986*, ed. Penny Sparke, London: The Design Council, 145–155.

Bullock, Nicholas (1988) 'First the Kitchen – then the Façade', *Journal of Design History*, vol. 1, nos. 3–4: 177–192.

Burkitt, Ian (1991) *Social Selves: Theories of the Social Formation of Personality*, London: Sage.

Byers, Anthony ([1981] 1988) *The Willing Servants: A History of Electricity in the Home*, London: The Electricity Council.

Caldwell, Beth O. (2004) 'One of my all time favorite books', 15 November, online review, www.amazon.com.

Calhoun, Craig, Edward LiPuma and Moishe Postone, eds. (1993) *Bourdieu: Critical Perspectives*, Cambridge: Polity Press.

Callahan, Genevieve and Lou Richardson (1966) *Home Economics Show-How and Showmanship*, Ames, IA: Iowa State University Press.

Cannadine, David (1990) *The Decline and Fall of the British Aristocracy*, New Haven, CT and London: Yale University Press.

Card, Orson Scott (1977) *Listen Mom and Dad: Young Adults Look Back on their Upbringing*, Salt Lake City, UT: Bookcraft, Inc.

Carter, Fan (2005) 'It's a Girl Thing: Teenage Magazines, Lifestyle and Consumer Culture', in *Ordinary Lifestyles: Popular Media, Consumption and Taste*, ed. David Bell and Joanne Hollows, Maidenhead: Open University Press, 173–186.

Cassell's Saturday Journal (1912) 'The Searchlight on the Middle Classes', comprising 'Middle-Class Recreations' (6 April), 'Middle-Class Parents' (27 April) and 'Middle-Class Literature' (4 May).

Cavan, Sherri (1970) 'The Etiquette of Youth', in *Social Psychology Through Symbolic Interaction*, ed. G. P. Stone and H. A. Farberman, Waltham, MA: Ginn-Blaisdell, 554–565.

Caxton, William ([1477–1478] 1999) *Book of Curtesye*, Extra Series, no. 3, ed. F. J. Furnivall, London: Early English Text Society, 1868, reissued London: Boydell & Brewer.

Chamberlain, Valerie, Peyton Bailey Budinger and Jan Perry Jones (1982) *Teen Guide*, fifth edition, New York: Webster Division/McGraw-Hill.

Chaney, David (1996) *Lifestyles*, London: Routledge.

Chartier, Roger (1988) *Cultural History: Between Practices and Representations*, trans. Lydia G. Cochrane, Cambridge: Polity.

Chesterfield, Lord (1774) *Letters Written by the ... Earl of Chesterfield to his Son Philip Stanhope ... Together with Several Other Pieces on Various Subjects. Published by Mrs. Eugenia Stanhope*, 2 vol., London: J. Dodsley.

Chiazzari, Suzy (1998) *The Healing Home: Creating the Perfect Place to Live with Colour, Aroma, Light and Other Natural Elements*, London: Ebury Press.

Christensen, Pia, Alison James and Chris Jenks (2000) 'Home and Movement: Children Constructing "Family Time"', in *Children's Geographies: Playing, Living Learning*, ed. Sarah L. Holloway and Gill Valentine, London and New York: Routledge, 139–155.

Clapp, James A. (2007) 'Growing Up Urban: The City, the Cinema, and American Youth', *Journal of Popular Culture*, vol. 40, no. 4: 601–629.

Clifford, Jane (1985) *Laura Ashley Decorates a London House*, London: Laura Ashley Limited.

Clifford-Poston, Andrea (2005) *Tweens: What to Expect from – and How to Survive – Your Child's Pre-Teen Years*, Oxford: Oneworld.

Cohen, Phil and Pat Ainley (2000) 'In the Country of the Blind? Youth Studies and Cultural Studies in Britain', *Journal of Youth Studies*, vol. 3, no. 1: 79–95.

Cohen, Stanley (1972) *Folk Devils and Moral Panics*, London: MacGibbon and Kee.

Cole, Mrs Mary ([1788] 1791) *The Lady's Complete Guide; or, Cookery in All its Branches*, third edition, London: G. Kearsley.

Coleman, David (2000) 'Population and Family', in *Twentieth-Century British Social Trends*, ed. A. H. Halsey with Josephine Webb, London and Basingstoke: Macmillan, 27–93.

Coleman, James S. and Torsten Husén (1985) *Becoming Adult in a Changing Society*, Paris: Centre for Educational Research and Innovation (CERI) and Organisation for Economic Co-operation and Development.

Collins, Randall (1988) 'Theoretical Continuities in Goffman's Work', in *Erving Goffman: Exploring the Interaction Order*, ed. Paul Drew and Anthony Wootton, Cambridge: Polity, 41–63.

Comstock, George and Erica Scharrer (2007) *Media and the American Child*, Burlington, MA: Academic Press.

Conran, Shirley ([1975] 1977) *Superwoman*, London: Penguin.

Conran, Shirley (1977) *Superwoman 2*, London: Sidgwick & Jackson.

Conran, Terence (1974) *The House Book*, London: Mitchell Beazley.

Conran, Terence (1985) *Terence Conran's New House Book*, London: Conran Octopus.

Conran, Terence and Elizabeth Wilhide (2003) *The Ultimate House Book*, ed. Elizabeth Wilhide, London: Conran Octopus.

Conway, Amy (1997) *Good Things: The Best of Martha Stewart Living*, New York: Martha Stewart Living Omnimedia LLC.

Cook, Chris and John Stevenson (1996) *The Longman Companion to Britain since 1945*, London: Longman.

Cook, Harold J. (1994) 'Good Advice and Little Medicine: The Professional Authority of Early Modern English Physicians', *Journal of British Studies*, vol. 33: 1–31.

Cook, Peter, ed. (1999) *Archigram*, New York: Princeton Architectural Press.

Core, Philip (1984) *The Original Eye: Arbiters of Twentieth-Century Taste*, London: Quartet.

Coser, Lewis A. (1977) *Masters of Sociological Thought: Ideas in Historical and Social Context*, second edition, New York: Harcourt Brace Jovanovich.

Coveney, John (2000) *Food, Morals and Meanings: The Pleasure and Anxiety of Eating*, London: Routledge.

Cowan, Ruth Schwartz ([1983] 1989) *More Work for Mother: The Ironies of Household Technology from the Open Hearth to the Microwave*, London: Free Association Books [New York: Basic Books].

Creighton, Thomas H. and other editors of *Progressive Architecture* (1947) *Homes*, New York: Reinhold Publishing Corp.

Crocker, Betty (1934) *Vitality Demands Energy: 109 Smart New Ways to Serve Bread, our Outstanding Energy Food*, Minneapolis, MN: General Mills.

Crocker, Betty (1959) *Guide to Easy Entertaining*, illus. Peter Spier, New York: Golden Press.

Crompton, Rosemary and Kay Sanderson (1990) *Gendered Jobs and Social Change*, London: Unwin Hyman.

Cronstrom, Kendell (2004) *Real Simple: The Organized Home*, New York: Real Simple Books.

Cross, Barbara M., ed. (1965) *The Educated Woman in America: Selected Writings of Catharine* [sic] *Beecher, Margaret Fuller, and M. Carey Thomas*, New York: Teachers College Press.

Cross, Gary (1997) *Kids' Stuff: Toys and the Changing Worlds of American Childhood*, Cambridge, MA: Harvard University Press.

Currell, Sue (2006) 'Depression and Recovery: Self-Help and America in the 1930s', in *Historicizing Lifestyle: Mediating Taste, Consumption and Identity from the 1900s to 1970s*, ed. David Bell and Joanne Hollows, London: Ashgate, 131–144.

Currie, Dawn H. (1999) *Girl Talk: Adolescent Magazines and their Readers*, Toronto: University of Toronto Press.

Curtin, Michael (1985) 'A Question of Manners: Status and Gender in Etiquette and Courtesy', *Journal of Modern History*, vol. 57, no. 3: 395–423.

Curtin, Michael (1987) *Propriety and Position: A Study of Victorian Manners*, New York: Garland.

Cwerner, Saulo B. and Alan Metcalfe (2003) 'Storage and Clutter: Discourses and Practices of Order in the Domestic World', *Journal of Design History*, vol. 16, no. 3: 229–239.

Daily Express (1937) *The Housewife's Book*, London: Syndicated Publishing Company for Express Newspapers.

Damien, Paul (2008) *Help! Debunking the Outrageous Claims of Self-Help Gurus*, Austin, TX: Synergy Books.

Daunton, Martin and Matthew Hilton, eds. (2001) *The Politics of Consumption: Material Culture and Citizenship in Europe and America*, Oxford: Berg.

David, Elizabeth (1950) *A Book of Mediterranean Food*, London: John Lehmann.

Davidoff, Leonore (1973) *The Best Circles: Society Etiquette and the Season*, London: Croom Helm.

Davidson, Alan, ed. (1999) 'Cole, Mrs Mary', in *The Oxford Companion to Food*, Oxford: Oxford University Press, 203.

Davies, Kevin (1998) 'Finmar and the Furniture of the Future: The Sale of Alvar Aalto's Plywood Furniture in the UK, 1934–1939', *Journal of Design History*, vol. 11, no. 2: 145–156.

Davin, Anna (1979) '"Mind That You Do as You Are Told": Reading Books for Board School Children, 1870–1902', *Feminist Review*, vol. 3: 89–98.

De Syllas, Phoebe and Dorothy Meade (1965) *Design to Fit the Family*, illus. John Smith, a Penguin Handbook PH114, Harmondsworth: Penguin.

De Wolfe, Elsie (1913) *The House in Good Taste*, New York: Century Co.

Delgado, Celeste Fraser (1995) 'Housekeeping Books', in *The Oxford Companion to Women's Writing in the United States*, ed. Cathy N. Davidson and Linda Wagner-Martin, Oxford: Oxford University Press.

Demant Jakob and Jeanette Østergaard (2007) 'Partying as Everyday Life: Investigations of Teenagers' Leisure Life', *Journal of Youth Studies*, vol. 10, no. 5: 517–537.

Dempsey, Mike (2001) 'The Graphic Economist: Keith Cunningham Brought the Eye of a Fine Artist to Graphic Design', *Design Week* (16 August).

Denvir, Catrina, Nigel J. Balmer and Pascoe Pleasence (2011) 'Surfing the Web – Recreation or Resource? Exploring how Young People in the UK use the Internet as an Advice Portal for Problems with a Legal Dimension', *Interacting with Computers*, vol. 23, no. 1: 96–104.

Dickson, Elizabeth and Margaret Colvin (1982) *The Laura Ashley Book of Home Decorating*, London: Octopus Books.

Dickson, Elizabeth, Margaret Colvin, Dorothea Hall and Peter Collenette (1985) *The Laura Ashley Book of Home Decorating*, London: Octopus Books.

Diller, Phyllis (1966) *Phyllis Diller's Housekeeping Hints*, illus. Susan Perl, Garden City, NY: Doubleday and Company, Inc.

Docherty, David, David Morrison and Michael Tracey (1987) *The Last Picture Show? Britain's Changing Film Audiences*, London: BFI Publishing.

Dolby, Sandra K. (2005) *Self-Help Books: Why Americans Keep Reading Them*, Urbana and Chicago, IL: University of Illinois Press.

Douglas, George H. (1991) *The Smart Magazines*, Hamden, CT: Archon Books.

Dow Chemicals (1959) 'DOW CHEMICALS *and paint*. Paints made with Dow latex offer many sales advantages...' advertisement, *Paint Manufacture* (June).

Drachman, Virginia G. (2005) *Enterprising Women: 250 Years of American Business*, Chapel Hill, NC: University of North Carolina Press.

Draper, Dorothy (1939) *Decorating is Fun!*, New York: Doubleday, Doran & Company.

Dreyfuss, Henry (1960) *Measure of Man: Human Factors in Design*, New York: Whitney Library of Design.

Dyhouse, Carol (1981) *Girls Growing Up in Late Victorian and Edwardian England*, London: Routledge & Kegan Paul.

Eastlake, Charles Locke (1868) *Hints on Household Taste in Furniture, Upholstery and other Details*, second edition, revised, London: Longmans & Co.

Edgell, Stephen (1993) *Class*, London: Routledge.

Editors of *Esquire* Magazine with S. and R. Welch ([1935] 1965) *Esquire Party Book*, London: Arthur Baker Ltd.

Editors of *Esquire*, The Magazine for Men (1953) *Esquire Etiquette: A Guide to Business, Sports and Social Conduct by the Editors of Esquire Magazine*, New York, Philadelphia, PA: J. B. Lippincott Co. (advisory editors: Phil Bernstein and others).

Editors of *Vogue* (1934) *Vogue's Book of Etiquette*, Garden City, NY: Doubleday, Doran & Co.

Edwardes, Margery and Gillian Smedley ([1970] 1975) *Running a Home is Fun*, London: Ebury Press/National Magazine Co.

Edwards, Anne and Drusilla Beyfus ([1956] 1957) *Lady Behave: A Guide to Modern Manners*, London: Cassell & Company Ltd.

Ehrenreich, Barbara and Deirdre English ([1978] 1989) *For Her Own Good: 150 Years of the Experts' Advice to Women*, New York, NY: Doubleday.

Eichler, Lillian ([1921] 1922) *The Book of Etiquette*, New York: Triangle Books.

Eide, Martin and Graham Knight (1999) 'Public/Private Service: Service Journalism and the Problems of Everyday Life', *European Journal of Communication Studies*, vol. 14, no. 4: 525–547.

Eley, Geoff ([1993] 1995) 'Nations, Publics, and Political Cultures: Placing Habermas in the Nineteenth Century', in *Habermas and the Public Sphere*, ed. Craig Calhoun, London: MIT Press, 289–296.

Elias, Norbert ([1939] 1994) *The Civilizing Process*, vol. 1 'The History of Manners', Oxford: Blackwell.

Elias, Norbert ([1969] 1983) *The Court Society*, trans. Edmund Jephcott, Oxford: Basil Blackwell.

Espejo, Roman, ed. (2003) *America's Youth*, Opposing Viewpoints Series, Farmington Hills, MI: Greenhaven Press.

Expertvillage.com (2006) 'Making a Good Impression at a Dinner Party: Using a Napkin Properly at the Dinner Table', http://www.youtube.com/watch?v=iRPH8 o9N2MA&feature=fvst. Accessed 24 July 2010.

Faber, Adele and Elaine Mazlish ([1980] 2001) *How to Talk so Kids will Listen and Listen so Kids will Talk,* London: Piccadilly [New York: Rawson, Wade Publishers].

Faber, Adele and Elaine Mazlish (2005) *How to Talk so Teens will Listen and Listen so Teens will Talk,* New York: HarperCollins and London: Piccadilly Press.

Farrell, Amy Erdman (1998) *Yours in Sisterhood:* Ms *Magazine and the Promise of Popular Feminism,* Chapel Hill: University of North Carolina Press.

Fenwick, Millicent (1948) *Vogue's Book of Etiquette,* New York: Simon & Schuster.

Ferreday, Debra (2010) 'Reading Disorders: Online Suicide and the Death of Hope', *Journal for Cultural Research,* vol. 14, no. 4: 409–426.

Ferry, Emma (2003) '"Decorators May be Compared to Doctors": An Analysis of Rhoda and Agnes Garrett's *Suggestions for House Decoration in Painting, Woodwork and Furniture* (1876)', *Journal of Design History,* vol. 16, no. 1: 15–34.

Fielding, Helen (1996) *Bridget Jones's Diary,* London: Picador.

Fielding, Helen (1999) *Bridget Jones: The Edge of Reason,* London: Picador.

Fielding, Helen (2001) *Bridget Jones's Guide to Life,* London: Picador.

Fischer, Claude S. (1992) *America Calling: A Social History of the Telephone to 1940,* Berkeley, CA: University of California Press.

Fisher, Rosie (1984) *Rooms to Grow Up In,* London: New Burlington Books.

Fleming, C. M. (1963) *Adolescence: Its Social Psychology,* London: Routledge Keegan Paul.

Fletcher, Adele Whitely (1963) *How to Decorate with Accessories,* The Amy Vanderbilt Success Program for Women, Garden City, NY: Nelson Doubleday, Inc.

Fletcher, Anthony and Stephen Hussey (1999) *Childhood in Question: Children, Parents and the State,* Manchester: Manchester University Press.

Flinchum, Russell (1997) *Henry Dreyfuss, Industrial Designer: The Man in the Brown Suit,* New York: Rizzoli.

Ford, James and Katherine Morrow Ford (1940) *The Modern House in America,* New York: Architectural Book Publishing Company.

Ford, James and Katherine Morrow Ford (1942) *Design of Modern Interiors,* New York, NY: Architectural Book Publishing Company.

Forino, Imma (2013) 'Kitchens: From Warm Workshop to Kitchenscape', in *Domestic Interiors: Representing Homes from the Victorians to the Moderns,* ed. Georgina Downey, London: Bloomsbury, 91–110.

Forty, Adrian (1986) *Objects of Desire: Design and Society, 1750–1980,* London: Thames & Hudson.

Foucault, Michel ([1969] 1972) *The Archaeology of Knowledge,* trans. A. M. Sheridan-Smith, London: Tavistock.

Foucault, Michel (1979) *Discipline and Punish: The Birth of the Prison,* trans. Alan Sheridan, New York: Vintage Books.

Foucault, Michel (1990) 'Politics and Reason', in *Michel Foucault: Politics, Philosophy, Culture. Interviews and Other Writings 1977–1984,* ed. Lawrence Kritzman, trans. Alan Sheridan *et al.,* New York and London: Routledge, 57–85.

Fowler, Damon Lee, ed. (2005) *Dining at Monticello: In Good Taste and Abundance,* Thomas Jefferson Foundation, Inc.

Fowler, David (1996) *The First Teenagers: The Lifestyle of Young Wage-Earners in Interwar Britain*, London: Routledge.

Fowler, David (2008) *Youth Culture in Modern Britain, c. 1920–c. 1970*, London: Palgrave Macmillan.

Francatelli, Charles Elmé ([1852] 1862) *Plain Cookery Book for the Working Classes*, second edition, London: Bosworth and Harrison.

Frederick, Christine (1913) *The New Housekeeping: Efficiency Studies in Home Management*, Garden City, NY: Doubleday.

Frederick, Christine (1920) *Scientific Management in the Home*, London: G. Routledge & Sons.

Frederick, Christine ([1923] 1919) *Household Engineering: Scientific Management in the Home*, Chicago, IL: American School of Home Economics.

Frederick, Christine (1929) *Selling Mrs. Consumer*, New York: The Business Bourse.

Frederick, Christine (1932) *The Ignoramus Book of Housekeeping*, New York: Sears Publishing.

Freeman, June (2004) *The Making of the Modern Kitchen*, Oxford: Berg.

Friedan, Betty ([1963] 1982) *The Feminine Mystique*, Harmondsworth: Penguin [New York: W. W. Norton, London: Victor Gollancz Ltd.].

Friedman, Alice T. (1996) 'Domestic Difference: Edith Farnsworth, Mies van der Rohe and the Gendered Body', in *Not at Home: The Suppression of Domesticity in Modern Art and Architecture*, ed. Christopher Reed, London: Thames & Hudson, 179–192.

Fryer, Peter (1963) *Mrs. Grundy: Studies in English Prudery*, London: Dobson.

Galbraith, J. K. ([1958] 1962) *The Affluent Society*, Harmondsworth: Penguin, London: Hamish Hamilton.

Garner, Ana, Helen M. Sterk and Shawn Adams (1998) 'Narrative Analysis of Sexual Etiquette in Teenage Magazines', *Journal of Communication*, vol. 48, no. 4: 59–78

Gartrell, Ellen (2000) 'Advertising Cookbooks', John W. Hartman Center for Sales, Advertising and Marketing History, Duke University, *The Emergence of Advertising in America, 1850–1930*, http://library.duke.edu/rubenstein/scriptorium/eaa/cookbooks.html. Accessed 20 August 2013.

Gelber, Steven M. (1999) *Hobbies: Leisure and the Culture of Work in America*, New York and Chichester, West Sussex: Columbia University Press.

Gelson, Hilary (1976) *Children about the House*, A Design Centre Book, London: The Design Council.

Gerth, H. and C. Wright Mills (1946) *From Max Weber: Essays in Sociology*, New York: Oxford University Press.

Giddens, Anthony (1981) *The Class Structure of the Advanced Societies*, second edition, London: Hutchinson.

Giddens, Anthony (1991) *Modernity and Self-Identity*, Cambridge: Polity Press.

Gilbert, Dennis, and Joseph A. Kahl (1987) *The American Class Structure*, third edition, Belmont, CA: Wadsworth.

Gilbreth, Frank B. Jr. and Ernestine Gilbreth Carey (1948) *Cheaper by the Dozen*, illus. Donald McKay, New York: T.Y. Crowell Co.

Gilbreth, Lillian (1927) *The Home-Maker and Her Job*, New York and London: D. Appleton and Company.

Gilbreth, Lillian M. (1998) *As I Remember: An Autobiography*, Norcross, GA: Engineering & Management Press.

Gilbreth, Lillian M., Orpha Mae Thomas and Eleanor Clymer ([1954] 1959) *Management in the Home: Happier Living through Saving Time and Energy*, illus. Ingrid Fetz, New York: Dodd, Mead.

Gilliatt, Mary (1967) *English Style*, London: Bodley Head.

Gilliatt, Mary (1981) *The Decorating Book*, London: Michael Joseph.

Gilliatt, Mary (1984a) *Mary Gilliatt's Mix and Match Decorating Book*, London: Michael Joseph.

Gilliatt, Mary (1984b) *Making the Most of Children's Rooms: A Creative Guide to Home Design*, London: Orbis for Marks & Spencer.

Gilliatt, Mary (1985) *Setting Up Home*, London: Orbis.

Gillis, John R. (1981) *Youth and History: Tradition and Change in European Age Relations, 1770–Present*, New York: Academic Press.

Gillis, John R. (1996) Review of Porter and Hall (1995), *American Historical Review*, vol. 101, no. 4: 1210.

Glasse, Hannah ([1747] 1974) *The Whole Art of Cookery Made Plain and Easy*, London: the Author.

Goffman, Erving ([1959] 1990) *The Presentation of Self in Everyday Life*, London: Penguin.

Goldscheider, Frances K., Dennis Hogan and Regina Bures (2001) 'A Century (Plus) of Parenthood: Changes in Living with Children, 1880–1990', *History of the Family*, vol. 6: 477–494.

Goldstein, Carolyn M. (1998) *Do it Yourself: Home Improvement in 20th-Century America*, New York: Princeton Architectural Press and Washington, DC: National Building Museum.

Goldthorpe, John H., David Lockwood, Frank Bechhofer and Jennifer Platt (1968–1969) *The Affluent Worker*, 3 vols., London: Cambridge University Press

Good, Elizabeth (1969) *Tableware: A Design Centre Publication*, London: Macdonald & Co. in association with the Council of Industrial Design.

Good Housekeeping Institute ([1944] 1945 1946) *The Book of Good Housekeeping*, London and Chesham: Gramol Publications Ltd.

Good Housekeeping Institute in association with Smith's Crisps (1961) *It's Your Party: A Book of Successful Entertaining*, London: The National Magazine Co.

Gordon, Michael (1971) 'From an Unfortunate Necessity to a Cult of Mutual Orgasm: Sex in American Marital Education Literature 1830–1940', *Studies in the Sociology of Sex*, ed. J. Henslin, New York: Appleton Century Crofts, 53–77.

Gould, Madelyn S., Jimmie Lou Harris Munfakh, Keri Lubell, Marjorie Kleinman and Sarah Parker (2002) 'Seeking Help from the Internet during Adolescence', *Journal of the American Academy of Child and Adolescent Psychiatry*, vol. 41, no. 10 (October): 1182–1189.

Green, Shirley (1973) *Doing Up Your Home*, Good Housekeeping Family Library, London: Ebury Press/National Magazine Co.

Greenhalgh, Paul (1995) 'The English Compromise: Modern Design and National Consciousness 1870–1940', in *Designing Modernity: The Arts of Reform and Persuasion 1885–1945*, ed. Wendy Kaplan, New York: Thames & Hudson, 111–139.

Guardian, The (1969) *The Permissive Society: The Guardian Inquiry*, London: Panther Books and *The Guardian*.

Gunn, Simon and Rachel Bell (2003) *Middle Classes: Their Rise and Sprawl*, London: Orion Books.

Haber, Samuel ([1964] 1973) *Efficiency and Uplift: Scientific Management in the Progressive Era*, Midway reprint, Chicago, IL and London: University of Chicago Press.

Habermas, Jurgen ([1962] 1974) 'The Public Sphere', *New German Critique*, no. 3: 49–55 [*Strukturwandel der Offentlichkeit*, Neuwied].

Hall, G. Stanley (1904) *Adolescence*, New York: D. Appleton and Co.

Hall, Stuart (1959) 'Absolute Beginnings', *Universities and Left Review*, vol. 7: 17–25.

Hall, Stuart and Tony Jefferson (1975) *Resistance through Rituals: Youth Subcultures in Post-War Britain*, London: Hutchinson University Library in Association with the Centre for Contemporary Cultural Studies.

Halpern, Sue M. (2003) 'Evangelists for Kids', *New York Review of Books*, vol. 50, no. 9 (29 May): 20–22.

Halsey, A. H. (1972) *Trends in British Society since 1900*, London and Basingstoke: Macmillan.

Halsey, A. H. (2000) 'Introduction', in *Twentieth-Century British Social Trends*, ed. A. H. Halsey and Josephine Webb, London and Basingstoke: Macmillan.

Hammerton, Sir John Alexander, ed. (1933) *Home-Lovers Encyclopedia*, London: The Amalgamated Press Ltd.

Hanisch, Carol ([1969] 1970) 'The Personal is Political', in *Notes from the Second Year: Women's Liberation: Major Writings of the Radical Feminists*, ed. Shulamith Firestone and Anne Koedt, New York: Radical Feminism; reprinted in Jerome Agel, ed. (1971) *The Radical Therapist*, New York: Ballantine, 152–157.

Hardyment, Christina ([1983] 2007) *Dream Babies: Childcare Advice from John Locke to Gina Ford*, London: Frances Lincoln.

Hardyment, Christina (1995) *Slice of Life: The British Way of Eating Since 1945*, London: BBC Books.

Hartmann, Susan M. (1998) *The Other Feminists: Activists in the Liberal Establishment*, New Haven, CT: Yale University Press.

Hayden, Dolores (1978) 'Two Utopian Feminists and their Campaigns for Kitchenless Houses', *Signs*, vol. 4, no. 2 (Winter): 274–290.

Hebdige, Dick (1981) 'Towards a Cartography of Taste 1935–1962', *Block*, vol. 4: 44–64.

Hebdige, Dick (1988) 'Hiding in the Light: Youth Surveillance and Display', in *Hiding in the Light*, London: Routledge.

Heßler, Martina (2009) 'The Frankfurt Kitchen: The Model of Modernity and the "Madness" of Traditional Users, 1926 to 1933', in *Cold War Kitchen: Americanization, Technology and European Users*, ed. Ruth Oldenziel and Karin Zachman, Cambridge, MA: MIT Press, 163–184.

Hemans, Felicia ([1827] 2000) 'The Homes of England', originally published in *Blackwood's Magazine*, 1827, reproduced in *Felicia Hemans: Selected Poems, Letters, Reception Materials*, ed. Susan J. Wolfson, New Jersey: Princeton University Press, 405.

Henderson, Susan R. (1996) 'A Revolution in the Woman's Sphere: Grete Lihotsky and the Frankfurt Kitchen', in *Architecture and Feminism*, ed. Debra Coleman, Elizabeth Danze and Carol Henderson, New York: Princeton Architectural Press, 221–253.

Hennessee, Judith (1998) *Betty Friedan*, London: Rivers Oram Press.

Hepworth, Mike (1999) 'Privacy, Security and Respectability: The Ideal Victorian Home', in *Ideal Homes?*, ed. Tony Chapman and Jenny Hockey, London: Routledge.

Highmore, Ben (2002a) *Everyday Life and Cultural Theory: An Introduction*, London: Routledge.

Highmore, Ben, ed. (2002b) *The Everyday Life Reader*, London: Routledge.

Hilkey, Judy (1997) *Character is Capital: Success Manuals and Manhood in Gilded Age America*, Chapel Hill, NC: University of North Carolina Press.

Hilton, Matthew (2001) 'Consumer Politics in Postwar Britain', in *The Politics of Consumption: Material Culture and Citizenship in Europe and America*, ed. Martin Daunton and Matthew Hilton, Oxford: Berg, 241–250.

Hilton, Matthew (2003) *Consumerism in Twentieth-Century Britain: The Search for a Historical Movement*, Cambridge: Cambridge University Press.

Hine, Thomas (1986) *Populuxe*, New York: Knopf.

Hinnant, Amanda (2005) *Real Simple: Solutions*, New York, NY: Real Simple Books.

Hiscock, Kevin (2000) 'Modernity and the "English" Tradition: Betjeman at *The Architectural Review*', *Journal of Design History*, vol. 13, no. 3: 193–212.

HMSO (1991) *Social Trends*, 21.

Hobsbawm, Eric (1981) 'The Forward March of Labour Halted?', in *The Forward March of Labour Halted?*, ed. Martin Jacques and Francis Mulhern, London: NLB in association with *Marxism Today*.

Hochschild, Arlie Russell (1983) *The Managed Heart: The Commercialization of Human Feeling*, Berkeley, CA: The University of California Press.

Hochschild, Arlie Russell (1994) 'The Commercial Spirit of Intimate Life and the Abduction of Feminism: Signs from Women's Advice Books', *Theory, Culture and Society*, vol. 11, no. 1: 1–24.

Hodkinson, Paul and Sian Lincoln (2008) 'Online Journals as Virtual Bedrooms? Young People, Identity and Personal Space', *YOUNG*, vol. 16, no. 1: 27–47.

Hoeller, Hildegarde (2007) 'Branded from the Start: The Paradox of (the) American (Novel of) Manners', in *Etiquette: Reflections on Contemporary Comportment*, ed. Ron Scapp and Brian Seitz, Albany, NY: State University of New York Press, 135–150.

Hoggart, Richard (1958) *The Uses of Literacy*, London: Pelican.

Holden, Edith (1977) *The Country Diary of an Edwardian Lady*, London: Michael Joseph, Exeter: Webb and Bower.

Holder, Julian (2009) 'The Nation State or the United States? The Irresistible Kitchen of the British Ministry of Works, 1944–1951', in *Cold War Kitchen: Americanization, Technology and European Users*, ed. Ruth Oldenziel and Karin Zachman, Cambridge, MA: MIT Press, 235–258.

Holland, Patricia (2004) *Picturing Childhood: The Myth of the Child in Popular Imagery*, London: I. B. Tauris.

Hollowood, Bernard (1947) *The Things We See, No. 4: Pottery and Glass*, West Drayton, Middlesex: Penguin Books.

Hollows, Joanne (2002) 'The Bachelor Dinner: Masculinity, Class and Cooking in *Playboy*, 1953–1961', *Continuum: Journal of Media and Cultural Studies*, vol. 16: 143–155.

Hollows, Joanne (2005) 'Feeling Like a Domestic Goddess: Postfeminism and Cooking', *European Journal of Cultural Studies*, vol. 6, no. 2: 179–202.

Horne, Alan (1944) *The Dictionary of 20th Century British Book Illustrators*, Woodbridge: Antique Collectors Club.

Horowitz, Daniel (1998) *Betty Friedan and the Making of the Feminine Mystique: The American Left, The Cold War, and Modern Feminism*, Amherst, MA: University of Massachusetts Press.

House-Building Industries' Standing Committee (1946) *Demonstration Permanent Houses 1946*, London: House Building Industries Standing Committee.

Hoy, Suellen (1995) *Chasing Dirt: The American Pursuit of Cleanliness*, Oxford: Oxford University Press.

Hulbert, Ann (2003) *Raising America: Experts, Parents, and a Century of Advice about Children*, New York: Knopf.

Humble, Nicola (2000) 'Introduction', in *Mrs Beeton's Book of Household Management*, Oxford: Oxford University Press, abridged edition.

Humm, Maggie (1995) *The Dictionary of Feminist Theory*, second edition, Columbus, OH: Ohio University Press.

Hunter, Lynette (1999) 'English Cookery Books: Of the Period 1500–1700', in *Oxford Companion to Food*, ed. Alan Davidson, Oxford: Oxford University Press, 276–280.

Jackson, Linda A. (2008) 'Adolescents and the Internet', in *The Changing Portrayal of Adolescents in the Media Since 1950*, ed. Patrick E. Jamieson and Daniel Romer, Oxford: Oxford University Press, 377–411.

Jackson, Shirley (1952) *Life Among the Savages*, New York: Farrar, Straus and Young (London: Michael Joseph, 1954).

Jackson, Shirley (1957) *Raising Demons*, New York: Farrar, Straus and Cudahy.

Jacobson, Lisa (2004) *Raising Consumers: Children and the American Mass Market in the Early Twentieth Century*, New York: Colombia University Press.

James, Nicky (1989) 'Emotional Labour: Skill and Work in the Social Regulation of Feelings', *The Sociological Review*, vol. 37: 15–42.

Jameson, Frederic (1991) *Postmodernism, or, The Cultural Logic of Late Capitalism*, London: Verso.

Jarvis, Alan (1946) *The Things We See No. 1: Indoors and Out*, West Drayton, Middlesex: Penguin Books.

Jeremiah, David (2000) *Architecture and Design for the Family in Britain, 1900–70*, Manchester: Manchester University Press.

Jones, Michelle (2003) 'Design and the Domestic Persuader: Television and the British Broadcasting Corporation's Promotion of Postwar "Good Design"', *Journal of Design History*, vol. 16, no. 4: 307–318.

Jones, Steve and Ben Taylor (2001) 'Food Writing and Food Cultures: The case of Elizabeth David and Jane Grigson', *European Journal of Cultural Studies*, vol. 4, no. 2: 171–188.

Justin, Margaret M. and Lucile Osborn Rust (1947) *Today's Home Living*, Chicago, IL, Philadelphia, PA, New York: J. B. Lippincott Company.

Kaufmann, Jean-Claude ([1992] 1998) *Dirty Linen: Couples and their Laundry*, trans. Helen Alfrey, London: Middlesex University Press [*La trame conjugale: analyse du couple by son ligne*, Paris: Editions Nathan].

Kavanaugh, Dorriet, ed. (1978) *Listen to Us: The Children's Express Report*, New York: Workman Publishing.

Kent, Katherine (1937) 'A Room of Their Own', *Scribner's Magazine*, vol. CI, no. 5 (May): 90–91.

Kerber, Linda K. (1988) 'Separate Spheres, Female Worlds, Woman's Place: The Rhetoric of Women's History', *Journal of American History*, vol. 75: 9–39.

Kimber, Richard (2010) 'Political Science Resources', http://www.politicsresources.net/area/uk/ge45/results.htm. Last Modified 13 February 2010.

Kirkham, Pat (1998) 'Humanizing Modernism: The Crafts, "Functioning Decoration" and the Eameses', *Journal of Design History*, vol. 11, no. 1: 15–29.

Kirkham, Pat and Penny Sparke (2000) '"A Woman's Place..."? Women Interior Designers', in *Women Designers in the USA, 1900–2000: Diversity and Difference*, ed. Pat Kirkham, New Haven, CT and London: Yale University Press, 305–316.

Kitchens, Rachael (2007) 'The Informalization of the Parent–Child Relationship: An Investigation of Parenting Discourses Produced in Australia in the Inter-War Years', *Journal of Family History*, vol. 32, no. 4: 459–478.

Laclau, Ernesto and Chantal Mouffe (1985) *Hegemony and Socialist Strategy: Towards a Radical Democratic Politics*, trans. Winston Moore and Paul Cammack, London: Verso.

Lambert, Angela (1989) *1939: The Last Season of Peace*, London: Weidenfeld & Nicolson.

Lancaster, Bill (1995) *The Department Store: A Social History*, London and New York: Leicester University Press.

Lancaster, Jane (2006) *Making Time: Lillian Moller Gilbreth – A Life Beyond "Cheaper by the Dozen"*, Lebanon, NH: Northeastern University Press.

Lancaster, Osbert ([1938] 1956) *Pillar to Post: Architecture without Tears*, new enlarged edition, London: John Murray.

Lancaster, Osbert (1939) *Homes Sweet Homes*, London: John Muarry.

LaRossa, Ralph (1997) *The Modernization of Fatherhood: A Social and Political History*, Chicago, IL: University of Chicago Press.

LaRossa, Ralph (2004) 'The Culture of Fatherhood in the Fifties: A Closer Look', *Journal of Family History*, vol. 29: 47–70.

Lasch, Christopher (1977) *Haven in a Heartless World: The Family Besieged*, New York: Basic Books.

Lawson, Sarah (2003) *Coping with Teenagers*, London: Sheldon Press.

Lears, T. J. Jackson (1983) 'From Salvation to Self-Realization: Advertising and the Therapeutic Roots of the Consumer Culture, 1880–1930', in *The Culture of Consumption: Critical Essays in American History 1880–1980*, ed. Richard Wightman Fox and T. J. Jackson Lears, Pantheon Books: New York, 3–38.

Leavitt, Sarah A. (2002) *From Catharine Beecher to Martha Stewart: A Cultural History of Domestic Advice*, Chapel Hill, NC and London: University of North Carolina Press.

Lees-Maffei, Grace (2001) 'From Service to Self-Service: Etiquette Writing as Design Discourse 1920–1970', *Journal of Design History*, vol. 14, no. 3: 187–206.

Lees-Maffei, Grace (2003) 'Studying Advice: Historiography, Methodology, Commentary, Bibliography', *Journal of Design History*, vol. 16, no. 1: 1–14.

Lees-Maffei, Grace (2007) 'Accommodating "Mrs Three in One": Homemaking, Home Entertaining and Domestic Advice Literature in Post-War Britain', *Women's History Review*, vol. 16, no. 5: 723–754.

Lees-Maffei, Grace (2008) 'Introduction: Professionalization as a Focus in Interior Design History', *Journal of Design History*, vol. 21, no. 1: 1–18.

Lees-Maffei, Grace (2009) 'The Production–Consumption–Mediation Paradigm', *Journal of Design History*, vol. 22: 4: 351–376.

Lees-Maffei, Grace (2011) 'Dressing the Part(y): 1950s Domestic Advice Books and the Studied Performance of Informal Domesticity in the UK and the US', in *Performance, Fashion and the Modern Interior*, ed. Fiona Fisher, Trevor Keeble, Patricia Lara-Betancourt and Brenda Martin, Oxford: Berg, 183–196.

Lees-Maffei, Grace (2012) 'Small Change? Emily Post's Etiquette', in *Must Read: Rediscovering American Bestsellers*, ed. Sarah Churchwell and Thomas Ruys-Smith, London: Continuum, 217–248.

Leman, Joy (1980) '"The Advice of a Real Friend": Codes of Intimacy and Oppression in Women's Magazines 1937–1955', *Women's Studies International Quarterly*, vol. 3: 63–78

Leslie, Fiona (2000) *Designs for 20th-Century Interiors*, London: V&A Publications.

Lewis, Tania (2008) *Smart Living: Lifestyle Media and Popular Expertise*, New York: Peter Lang Publishing, Inc.

Library of Congress (2011) 'Good Housekeeping', *Today in History: May 2nd*, http://memory.loc.gov/ammem/today/may02.html. Last updated 1 October 2011.

Life (1959) 'New, $10 Billion Power: The US Teen-Age Consumer', 31 August.

Light, Alison (1991) *Forever England: Femininity, Literature and Consumption between the Wars*, London: Routledge.

Lincoln, Mary Johnson ([1884] 1996) *Boston Cooking School Cook Book: A Reprint of the 1884 Classic*, Mrs. D. A. Lincoln with a new introduction by Janice Bluestein Longone, Mineola, NY: Dover Publications.

Lincoln, Sian (2004) 'Teenage Girls' "Bedroom Culture": Codes versus Zones', in *After Subculture: Critical Studies in Contemporary Youth Culture*, ed. Andy Bennett and Keith Kahn-Harris, London: Palgrave Macmillan, 94–106.

Lincoln, Sian (2005) 'Feeling the Noise: Teenagers, Bedrooms and Music', *Leisure Studies*, vol. 24, no. 4: 399–414.

Lindenfield, Gael (2001) *Confident Teens: How to Raise a Positive, Confident and Happy Teenager*, London: Thorsons, HarperCollins.

Lister, Martin, John Dovey, Seth Giddings, Iain Grant and Kieran Kelly (2003) *New Media: A Critical Introduction*, London: Routledge.

Livingstone, Sonia (2009) *Children and the Internet*, Cambridge: Polity Press.

Lloyd, Helen (1999) 'Are Current Visitor Numbers at Historic Properties Sustainable? A Case Study from Bateman's, the Home of Rudyard Kipling', *Views*, vol. 29 (Winter): 29–30.

Loehlin, Jennifer Ann (1999) *From Rugs to Riches: Housework, Consumption and Modernity in Germany*, Oxford: Berg.

Longhurst, Robyn (1999) 'Pregnant Bodies, Public Scrutiny: "Giving" Advice to Pregnant Women', in *Embodied Geographies: Spaces, Bodies and Rites of Passage*, ed. Elizabeth Kenworthy Teather, London: Routledge, 78–90.

Longone, Janice (1998–1999) 'From the Kitchen', *American Magazine and Historical Chronicle*, vol. 4, no. 2: 450–451.

Longone, Janice (1999) 'American Cookbooks', in *Oxford Companion to Food*, ed. Alan Davidson, Oxford: Oxford University Press, 15–17.

Lord Chancellor's Department (1967) *Report of the Committee in the Age of Majority* [Latey Report], London: HMSO.

Lott, Jane (1989) *Children's Rooms*, A Mothercare Book, London: Conran Octopus and Prentice Hall.

Lowenstein, Eleanor ([1954] 1972) *American Cookery Books 1742–1860*, third edition, Worcester, MA: American Antiquarian Society.

Lowrie, Joyce (1965) *Practical Homemaking*, London: Oldbourne.

Lucraft, Fiona (1997) 'A Study of *The Compleat Confectioner* by Hannah Glasse (*c.* 1760), Part One', *Petits Propos Culinaires*, vol. 56: 23–36.

Lynes, Russell ([1949] 1980) *The Tastemakers: The Shaping of American Popular Taste*, New York: Dover.

Lynes, Russell ([1956] 1991) 'Introduction', in *Noblesse Oblige: An Inquiry into the Identifiable Characteristics of the English Aristocracy*, ed. Nancy Mitford, New York: Harper & Brothers, reprinted in Russell Lynes, *Life in the Slow Lane: Observations on Art, Architecture, Manners and Other Such Spectator Sports*, New York: Cornelia & Michael Bessie Books, 36–41.

Lyons, Pam (1967) *Today's Etiquette*, illus. Belinda Lyon, London: Bancroft and Co. Ltd.

MacCarthy, Fiona (1972) *All Things Bright and Beautiful: Design in Britain 1830 to Today*, London: George Allen and Unwin.

McCloud, Kevin (1990) *Kevin McCloud's Decorating Book*, London: Dorling Kindersley.

McCracken, Grant (1990) *Culture and Consumption: New Approaches to the Symbolic Character of Consumer Goods and Activities*, Bloomington, IN: Indiana University Press.

MacFarlane, Aiden and Ann McPherson (1999) *Teenagers: The Agony, the Ecstasy, the Answers*, London: Little, Brown and Company.

McGaw, Judy A. (1989) 'No Passive Victims, No Separate Spheres: A Feminist Perspective on Technology's History', in *In Context: History and the History of Technology (Essays in Honor of Melvin Kranzberg)*, ed. Stephen H. Cutcliffe and Robert C. Post, Bethlehem, PA: Lehigh University Press and London: Associated University Presses.

McGee, Micki (2005) *Self-Help, Inc: Makeover Culture in American Life*, New York: Oxford University Press.

McInnes, Colin ([1959] 1964) *Absolute Beginners*, Harmondsworth: Penguin.

McKellar, Susie (1999) '"The Beauty of Stark Utility": Rational Consumption in America – *Consumer Reports: 1936–1954*', in *Utility Reassessed: The Role of Ethics in the Practice of Design*, ed. Judy Attfield, Manchester: Manchester University Press, 73–89.

McKellar, Susie (2002) '"Seals of Approval": Consumer Representation in 1930s' America', *Journal of Design History*, vol. 15, no. 1: 1–14.

McKibbin, Ross (1998) *Classes and Cultures: England 1918–1951*, Oxford: Oxford University Press.

MacKinnon, Kenneth (2004) 'The Family in Hollywood Melodrama: Actual or Ideal?', *Journal of Gender Studies*, vol. 13, no. 1 (March): 29–36.

Maclean, Sarah (1962) *The Pan Book of Etiquette and Good Manners*, London: Pan.

McRobbie, Angela and Jenny Garber (1991) 'Girls and Subcultures', in *Feminism and Youth Culture: From Jackie to Just Seventeen*, London: Macmillan, 1–15.

Maffei, Nicolas P. (2000) 'John Cotton Dana and the Politics of Exhibiting Industrial Art in the US, 1909–1929', *Journal of Design History*, vol. 13, no. 4: 301–318.

Maffei, Nicolas P. (2003) 'The Search for an American Design Aesthetic: From Art Deco to Streamlining', in *Art Deco 1910–1939*, ed. Charlotte Benton, Tim Benton and Ghislaine Wood, London: V&A Publications, 361–369.

Mandler, Peter (1997) *The Fall and Rise of the Stately Home*, New Haven, CT and London: Yale University Press.

Mann, Sandi, Paul Seager and Jonny Wineberg (2008) *Surviving the Terrible Teens: How to Have a Teenager and Stay Sane*, Devon: White Ladder Press.

Marchand, Roland (2001) *Creating the Corporate Soul*, Berkeley, CA: University of California Press.

Marcuse, Herbert ([1964] 1972) *One Dimensional Man*, London: Abacus.

Marcuse, Herbert (1969) *An Essay on Liberation*, Boston, MA: Beacon Press and London: Allen Lane, The Penguin Press.

Marks, Susan (2008) *Finding Betty Crocker: The Secret Life of America's First Lady of Food*, Minneapolis, MN: University of Minnesota Press.

Markun, Leo (1930) *Mrs. Grundy: A History of Four Centuries of Morals Intended to Illuminate Present Problems in Great Britain and the United States*, New York and London: D. Appleton and Company.

Martha Stewart Living Omnimedia (2011) 'Investor Relations', http://phx.corporate-ir.net/phoenix.zhtml?c=96022&p=irol-irhome. Accessed 21 July 2012.

Martha Stewart Living Omnimedia (2012a) dreamers.marthastewart.com. Accessed 10 July 2012.

Martha Stewart Living Omnimedia (2012b) http://www.facebook.com/Dreamers IntoDoers. Accessed 10 July 2012.

Martin, J. L. and Sadie Speight (1939) *The Flat Book*, London: Heinemann.

Marwick, Arthur (1991) *Culture in Britain since 1945*, Oxford: Basil Blackwell.

Marwick, Arthur (1996) *British Society since 1945*, third edition, Penguin Social History of Britain, Harmondsworth: Penguin.

Marx, Karl and Friedrich Engels ([1848] 1998) *The Communist Manifesto*, Oxford World's Classics edition, ed. David McLellan, Oxford: Oxford University Press.

Mason, Ann and Marian Meyers (2001) 'Living with Martha Stewart Media: Chosen Domesticity in the Experience of Fans', *Journal of Communication*, vol. 51, no. 4: 801–823.

Massoni, Kelley (2006) '"Teena Goes to Market": *Seventeen* Magazine and the Early Construction of the Teen Girl (as) Consumer', *Journal of American Culture*, vol. 29, no. 1: 31–42.

Matthews, Glenna (1987) *'Just a Housewife': The Rise and Fall of Domesticity in America*, New York: Oxford University Press.

Matthews, Peter (1969) *Workrooms: A Design Centre Publication*, London: Macdonald & Co. in association with the Council of Industrial Design.

Mays, John Barron (1965) *The Young Pretenders: A Study of Teenage Culture in Contemporary Society*, London: Michael Joseph.

Mechling, Jay (1975) 'Advice to Historians on Advice to Mothers', *Journal of Social History*, vol. 9: 44–57.

Merivale, Margaret ([1938] 1944) *Furnishing the Small Home*, London: The Studio.

Merril, Hugh (1995) *Esky: The Early Years at Esquire*, New Brunswick, NJ: Rutgers University Press.

Miall, Agnes M. (1950) *Modern Etiquette*, London: C. Arthur Pearson.

Miller, Derek (1969) *The Age Between: Adolescents in a Disturbed Society*, London: Cornmarket Hutchinson.

Miller, J. Hillis (1990) 'Narrative', in *Critical Terms for Literary Study*, ed. Frank Lentricchia and Thomas McLaughlin, Chicago, IL and London: University of Chicago Press, 66–79.

Miller, Tim (2010) 'The Birth of the Patio Daddy-O: Outdoor Grilling in Postwar America', *Journal of American Culture*, vol. 33, no. 1 (March): 5–11.

Miller, Toby and Alec McHoul (1998) 'Self Help/Therapy', in *Popular Culture and Everyday Life*, Toby Miller and Alec McHoul, London: Sage, 90–133.

Mills, C. Wright (1951) *White Collar: The American Middle Classes*, Oxford: Oxford University Press.

Mills, C. Wright ([1956] 1999) *The Power Elite*, New York: Oxford University Press.

Miss Abigail (2012) 'Miss Abigail's Time Warp Advice', http://www.missabigail.com/.

Mitchell, Claudia and Jacqueline Reid-Walsh (2002) 'Physical Spaces: Children's Bedrooms as Cultural Texts', in *Researching Children's Popular Culture: The Cultural Spaces of Childhood*, London: Routledge, 113–140.

Mitford, Jessica (1963) *The American Way of Death*, New York: Simon & Schuster.

Mitford, Jessica (1973) *Kind and Usual Punishment: The Prison Business*, New York: Knopf.

Mitford, Nancy, ed. ([1956] 2002) *Noblesse Oblige: An Enquiry into the Identifiable Characteristics of the English Aristocracy*, with contributions by Alan Strode Campbell Ross, Evelyn Waugh, 'Strix', Christopher Sykes, John Betjeman and others and cartoons by Osbert Lancaster, Oxford: Oxford University Press [London: Hamish Hamilton].

Mock, Elizabeth B. (1945) *Tomorrow's Small House*, New York: The Museum of Modern Art.

Mock, Elizabeth B. (1946) *If You Want to Build a House*, New York: The Museum of Modern Art.

Moran, Jeffrey (2000) *Teaching Sex: The Shaping of Adolescence in the 20th Century*, Cambridge, MA: Harvard University Press.

Morgan, Marjorie (1991) 'Puffery Prevails: Etiquette in 19th-Century England', *History Today*, vol. 41, no. 8 (August): 23–30.

Morgan, Marjorie (1994) *Manners, Morals and Class in England 1774–1858*, Basingstoke: Macmillan.

Morley, Christine (1990) 'Homemakers and Design Advice in the Postwar Period', in *Household Choices*, ed. Charles Newton and Tim Putnam, London: Futures Publications, 89–97.

Morley, Christopher (1932) 'Editorial', *General Electric Hour* (19 December), NBC, in Norman Bel Geddes's Scrapbook 'Industrial Design Publicity, Personal' box 982.1a, Philco. Harry Ransom Humanities Research Center, University of Texas, Austin, TX.

Morley, David (1992) *Television, Audiences, and Cultural Studies*, London and New York: Routledge.

Morris, William ([1880] 1882) 'The Beauty of Life' lecture, Birmingham Society of Arts and School of Design, 19 February 1880, published in William Morris, *Hopes and Fears for Art: Five Lectures Delivered in Birmingham, London, and Nottingham, 1878–1881*, London: Ellis and White.

Moskowitz, Eva (1996) '"It's Good to Blow Your Top": Women's Magazines and a Discourse of Discontent, 1945–1965', *Journal of Women's History*, vol. 8, no. 3 (Fall): 66–98.

Mosley, The Honourable Lady, (Diana Mitford) (1978) 'Nancy Obliged', in *U & Non-U Revisited*, ed. Richard Buckle, London: Debrett's Peerage Ltd.

Muggeridge, Malcolm (1995) 'Bentley, Nicolas', in *Dictionary of National Biography*, Oxford: Oxford University Press.

Munro, Sheila (1998) *Communicating with Your Teenager for Parents*, London: Piccadilly Press.

Munroe, Moira and Ruth Madigan (1999) 'Negotiating Space in the Family Home', in *At Home: An Anthropology of Domestic Space*, ed. Irene Cieraad, Syracuse, NY: Syracuse University Press, 107–118.

Murray, Suellen (1988) '"Keeping Their Secret Safe": Menstrual Etiquette in Australia 1900–1960', *Hecate*, vol. 24, no. 1: 62–80.

Murray, Sylvie (2003) *The Progressive Housewife: Community Activism in Suburban Queens, 1945–1965*, Politics and Culture in Modern America, Philadelphia, PA: University of Philadelphia Press.

Museum of Modern Art ([1934] 1994) *Machine Art*, sixtieth anniversary edition, New York: The Museum of Modern Art.

Myerson, Jeremy (1985) *Better Lighting*, The Habitat Home Decorator, London: Conran Octopus.

Naylor, Gillian (1988) *William Morris by Himself: Designs and Writings*, London: Macdonald & Co.

Neagle, Anna ([1974] 1979) *There's Always Tomorrow*, London: W. H. Allen [Litton: Magna Books, 1976 and London: Futura Publications].

Nelson, Claudia (1995) *Invisible Men: Fatherhood in Victorian Periodicals, 1850–1910*, Athens, GA and London: University of Georgia Press.

Nelson, George (1934) 'Both Fish and Foul', *Fortune*, (February) 4.

Nelson, George and Henry Wright (1945) *Tomorrow's House: A Complete Guide for the Home Builder*, third printing, New York: Simon & Schuster, London: The Architectural Press.

Nemy, Enid (1997) 'In an Age of Finger Food, a New Emily Post', *New York Times* (20 April).

Neuhaus, Jessamyn (2009) '"Is it Ridiculous For Me to say I Want to Write?" Domestic Humor and Redefining the 1950s Housewife Writer in Fan Mail to Shirley Jackson', *Journal of Women's History*, vol. 21, no. 2: 115–137.

New York Herald Home Institute (1941) *America's Housekeeping Book*, New York: Charles Scribner's Sons.

Newton, Sarah (2007) *Help! My Teenager is an Alien*, London: Michael Joseph.

Nicol, Margaret (1952) *Homecraft and Homemaking*, Edinburgh: McDougall's Educational Co. Ltd.

Nietzsche, Friedrich ([1887] 1996) *On the Genealogy of Morals, a Polemic: By Way of Clarification and Supplement to my Last Book Beyond Good and Evil*, trans. Douglas Smith, Oxford: Oxford University Press.

Oddy, Derek J. (2003) *From Plain Fare to Fusion Food: British Diet from the 1890s to the 1990*, Woodbridge: The Boydell Press.

OED Online (2012) 'Patio, n.', Oxford: Oxford University Press. December 2012, http://www.oed.com/view/Entry/138835. Accessed 8 March 2013.

Ogata, Amy F. (2008–2009) 'Building Imagination in Postwar American Children's Rooms', *Studies in the Decorative Arts*, vol. XVI, no. 1 (Fall–Winter): 126–142.

Ohmann, Richard (1996) *Selling Culture: Magazines, Markets and Class at the Turn of the Century*, London, New York: Verso.

Oliver, Jamie (2012) *Jamie's 15-Minute Meals*, London: Michael Joseph.

Oram, Scott (2004) '"Constructing Contemporary": Common-Sense Approaches to "Going Modern" in the 1950s', in *Interior Design and Identity*, ed. Susie McKellar and Penny Sparke, Manchester: Manchester University Press, 174–190.

Orwell, George [1941] 1962) *The Lion and the Unicorn: Socialism and the English Genius*, London: Secker & Warburg.

Osgerby, Bill (1998) *Youth in Britain since 1945*, Oxford: Blackwell.

Osgerby, Bill (2001) *Playboys in Paradise: Masculinity, Youth and Leisure-Style in Modern America*, Oxford: Berg.

O'Sullivan, Tim (2005) 'From Television Lifestyle to Lifestyle Television', in *Ordinary Lifestyles: Popular Media, Consumption and Taste*, ed. David Bell and Joanna Hollows, Maidenhead: Open University Press, 21–34.

Ouellette, Laurie (1999) 'Inventing the Cosmo Girl: Class Identity and Girl-Style American Dreams', *Media, Culture and Society*, vol. 21, no. 3: 359–383.

Owen, Patricia J. (1946) *Furnishing to Fit the Family*, London: Council of Industrial Design.

Palmer, Gareth, ed. (2008) *Exposing Lifestyle Television: The Big Reveal*, Aldershot: Ashgate.

Parsons, Rob (2007) *Teenagers: What Every Parent Has to Know*, London: Hodder.

Parsons, Talcott (1942) 'Age and Sex in the Social Structure of the United States', *American Sociological Review*, vol. 7, no. 5 (October): 604–616.

Parsons, Talcott (1977) *Social Systems and the Evolution of Action Theory*, New York: The Free Press.

Patmore, Derek (1934) *Modern Furnishing and Decoration*, London: The Studio.

Patmore, Derek (1945) *Colour Schemes and Modern Furnishing*, London: The Studio.

Patten, Marguerite, Ambrose Heath, Constance Spry, Ann Smith, Kay Pennett, D. S. Panisett and Joan Whitgift (1958) *The 'Creda' Housecraft Manual: A Treasury of Useful Recipes and Household Information*, Stoke-on-Trent: Odhams Press Limited for the Simplex Electric Company Limited.

Paul, Annie Murphy (2001) 'Self-Help: Shattering the Myths', *Psychology Today*, vol. 34, no. 2: 60–68.

Peril, Lynn (2002) *Pink Think: Becoming a Woman in Many Uneasy Lessons*, New York and London: Norton.

Philips, Deborah (2005) 'Transformation Scenes: The Television Interior Makeover', *International Journal of Cultural Studies*, vol. 8, no. 2: 213–229.

Phillips, Derek (1969) *Flooring: A Design Centre Publication*, London: Macdonald & Co. in association with the Council of Industrial Design.

Phillips, Derek (1970) *Lighting: A Design Centre Publication*, London: Macdonald & Co. in association with the Council of Industrial Design.

Pink, Sarah (2007) 'Sensing Cittàslow: Slow Living and the Constitution of the Sensory City', *The Senses and Society*, vol. 2, no. 1 (March): 59–77.

Pleydell-Bouverie, Millicent Frances (1945) *Daily Mail Book of Britain's Postwar Homes*, London: Associated Newspapers Ltd.

Pollock, Linda (1983) *Forgotten Children*. Cambridge: Cambridge University Press.

Popiel, Jennifer J. (2004) 'Making Mothers: The Advice Genre and the Domestic Ideal, 1760–1830', *Journal of Family History*, vol. 29, no. 4: 339–350.

Porter, Roy and Lesley Hall (1995) *The Facts of Life: The Creation of Sexual Knowledge in Britain 1650–1950*, New Haven, CT: Yale University Press.

Post, Anna (2007) *Emily Post's Wedding Parties*, New York: Collins.

Post, Anna (2007–2010) 'What Would Emily Post Do?' (blog), http://annapost.typepad.com/.

Post, Elizabeth L. and Joan M. Coles (1986) *Emily Post Talks with Teens about Manners and Etiquette*, New York: Harper & Row.

Post, Emily (1922) *Etiquette in Society, in Business, in Politics and at Home*, New York: Funk & Wagnalls.

Post, Emily (1927) *Etiquette, 'The Blue Book of Social Usage'*, New York: Funk & Wagnalls.

Post, Emily ([1930] 1948) *The Personality of a House: The Blue Book of Home Charm*, New York and London: Funk & Wagnalls.

Post, Emily (1937) *Etiquette, 'The Blue Book of Social Usage'*, fifth edition, New York, London: Funk & Wagnalls

Post, Emily (Mrs. Price Post) (1940a) *Etiquette: 'The Blue Book of Social Usage'*, revised edition, New York and London: Funk & Wagnalls.

Post, Emily (1940b) *Children are People: How to Understand and Guide Your Children*, New York: Funk & Wagnalls.

Post, Lizzie (2007) *How Do You Work This Life Thing? Advice for the Newly Independent on Roommates, Jobs, Sex, & Everything that Counts*, New York: Collins.

Post, Peggy (2004) *Emily Post's Etiquette*, seventeenth edition, New York: HarperCollins.

Powers, H. Brewster and James W. Putnam, eds (1930) *Manners Make Men: A Practical and Sparkling Manual of Modern Etiquette Written By University Men*, Lawrence, KS: The Witan, University of Kansas.

Prizeman, John ([1966] 1970) *Kitchens: A Design Centre Publication*, London: Macdonald & Co. in association with the Council of Industrial Design.

Pugin, Augustus Welby Northmore (1841) *The True Principles of Pointed or Christian Architecture*, London: John Weale.

Purvis, June (1985) 'Domestic Subjects since 1870', in *Social Histories of the Secondary Curriculum*, ed. Ivor Goodson, London: Falmer.

Putnam, J. W., ed. (1939) *Lady Lore: A Swingtime Handbook for Girls*, Lawrence, KS: The Witan, University of Kansas.

Putnam, Tim (1993) 'Beyond the Modern Home: Shifting the Parameters of Residence', in *Mapping the Futures: Local Cultures, Global Change*, ed. Jon Bird, Barry Curtis, Tim Putnam, George Robertson and Lisa Tickner, London: Routledge, 150–165.

Rabinbach, Anson (1992) *The Human Motor: Energy, Fatigue and the Origins of Modernity*, Berkeley, CA and London: University of California Press.

Raby, Rebecca C. (2002) 'A Tangle of Discourses: Girls Negotiating Adolescence', *Journal of Youth Studies*, vol. 5, no. 4: 425–448.

Rashley, Lisa Hammond (2005) '"Work it Out with Your Wife": Gendered Expectations and Parenting Rhetoric Online', *NWSA Journal*, vol. 17, no. 1 (Spring): 58–92.

Rayner, Claire (1967) *For Children: A Design Centre Publication*, London: Macdonald & Co. in association with the Council of Industrial Design.

Reid, Susan E. (2005) 'The Khrushchev Kitchen: Domesticating the Scientific-Technological Revolution', *Journal of Contemporary History*, vol. 40: 289–316.

Reilly, Paul (1953) 'Don't be Afraid of Contemporary Design', *Daily Mail Ideal Home Book 1953–54*, ed. Frances Lake, London: Associated Newspapers, 126–130.

Richards, C. R. (1931) 'Modernism in Furniture', in *The Better Homes Manual*, ed. Blanche Halbert, Chicago, IL: Chicago University Press, 447–449.

Richardson, Lou and Genevieve Callahan ([1962] 1970) *How to Write for Homemakers*, Ames, IA: Iowa State University Press.

Riesman, David, with Reuel Denney and Nathan Glazer (1950) *The Lonely Crowd: A Study of the Changing American Character*, New Haven, CT: Yale University Press.

Rimke, Heidi Marie (2000) 'Governing Citizens through Self-Help Literature', *Cultural Studies*, vol. 14, no. 1: 61–78.

Robertson, Cheryl (1997) 'From Cult to Profession: Domestic Women in Search of Equality', in *The Material Culture of Gender*, ed. K. Martinez and Kenneth Ames, Winterthur, DE: Henry Francis du Pont Winterthur Museum, Hanover, distributed by University Press of New England.

Robertson, Howard (1947) *Reconstruction and the Home*, London: The Studio.

Robinson, Dwight E. and Dennis F. Strong (1970) Review of Emily Post (Mrs. Price Post), *Etiquette in Society, in Business, in Politics and at Home* (New York: Funk & Wagnalls, 1969) 1922 Replica Edition, with 'A New Preface to an Old Edition', and Elizabeth L. Post, *Emily Post's Etiquette*, twelfth revised edition (New York: Funk & Wagnalls, 1969) in *Pacific Northwest Quarterly* (July).

Robinson, Oliver (1960) *The Good Housekeeping Annual*, London: The National Magazine Company.

Robsjohn-Gibbings, T. H. (1944) *Goodbye, Mr. Chippendale*, New York: Knopf.

Robson, Neil (2004) 'Living Pictures Out of Space: The Forlorn Hopes for Television in Pre-1939 London', *Historical Journal of Film, Radio and Television*, vol. 24, no. 2: 223–232.

Rojek, Chris, (2000) 'Leisure and the Rich Today: Veblen's Thesis After a Century', *Leisure Studies*, vol. 19, no.1: 1–15.

Ross, Alan S. C. (1954) 'Linguistic Class Indicators in Present-Day English', *Neuphilologische Mitteilungen* (Helsinki), vol. 55, 113–149.

Ross, Alan. S. C., Philip Howard and Richard Buckle (1978) 'Language: U and Non-U, Double-U, E and Non-E', in *U & Non-U Revisited*, ed. Richard Buckle, London: Debrett's Peerage Ltd.

Ross, Ellen ([1980] 1981) '"The Love Crisis": Couples Advice Books of the Late 1970s', in *Women, Sex and Sexuality*, ed. Catherine R. Stimpson and Ethel Spector Person, Chicago, IL: Chicago University Press, 274–287 [first published in *Signs*, vol. 5].

Routh, Guy (1987) *Occupations of People in Great Britain 1801–1981*, London: Macmillan.

Rowbotham, Sheila (1973) *Hidden from History: 300 Years of Women's Oppression and the Fight Against It*, London: Pluto Press.

Rundell, Mrs. (1807) *A New System of Domestic Cookery by a Lady [i.e. Mrs. Rundell], To Which are now Added ... Illustrative Plates*, second edition, London: n.p.

Rundell, Mrs. (1815) *The New Family Receipt-Book, Containing Eight Hundred Truly Valuable Receipts in Various Branches of Domestic Economy*, new edition, London: n.p.

Rupp, Leila J. (2003) Forum: 'Women's History in the New Millennium: Rethinking Public and Private', *Journal of Women's History*, vol.15, no. 1: 10.

Russell, Gordon (1947) *The Things We See No. 3 – Furniture*, West Drayton, Middlesex: Penguin Books.

Russell, Gordon (1964) *Looking at Furniture*, London: Lund Humphries, revised edition 1964.

Rutherford, Janice Williams (2003) *Selling Mrs. Consumer: Christine Frederick and the Rise of Household Efficiency*, Athens, GA and London: University of Georgia Press.

Rutt, Anna Hong (1935) *Home Furnishing*, New York: J. Wiley & Sons and London: Chapman & Hall.

Ryle, Sarah (2002) '80 Years of Keeping a Title Tidy', *The Observer* (1 September): 6.

Salerno, Steve (2005) *Sham: How the Self-Help Movement Made America Helpless*, New York: Crown Publishers.

Salinger, Adrienne (1995) *In My Room: Teenagers in their Bedrooms*, San Francisco, CA: Chronicle Books.

Salmon, Geoffrey (1967), *Storage: A Design Centre Publication*, London: Macdonald & Co. (Publishers) Ltd in association with the Council of Industrial Design.

Santiesteban, Eugenia (2003) *Living with Kids: Ideas and Solutions for Family-Friendly Interiors*, Gloucester, MA: Rockport Publishers.

Savage, Jon (2007) *Teenage: The Creation of Youth, 1875–1945*, London: Chatto & Windus.

Scanlon, Jennifer (1995) *Inarticulate Longings: The "Ladies' Home Journal", Gender, and the Promises of Consumer Culture*, New York and London: Routledge.

Scanlon, Jennifer (2004) 'Old Housekeeping, New Housekeeping, or No Housekeeping? The Kitchenless Home Movement and the Women's Service Magazine', *Journalism History*, vol. 30 (April): 2–10.

Schenk, Beulah and Gladys Denny Schultz (1929) *The House That Runs Itself*, New York: The John Day Company.

Schlesinger, Arthur M. ([1946] 1968) *Learning How to Behave: A Historical Study of American Etiquette Books*, New York: Cooper Square Publishers [New York: Macmillan].

Seiter, Ellen (2005) *The Internet Playground: Children's Access, Entertainment and Mis-Education*, New York: Peter Lang.

Sennett, Richard (1973) 'Two on the Aisle', *New York Review of Books*, vol. 20, no. 17 (1 November): 29–31.

Sennett, Richard ([1977] 1992) *The Fall of Public Man*, New York and London: W.W. Norton & Company, 1992 [New York: Knopf].

Shales, Ezra (2010) *Made in Newark: Cultivating Industrial Arts and Civic Identity in the Progressive Era*, Piscataway, NJ: Rutgers University Press.

Shapiro, Laura (2001) *Perfection Salad: Women and Cooking at the Turn of the Century*, New York: Modern Library.

Sharpe, Peter Ernest Magnus (1968) *Sound and Vision: A Design Centre Publication*, London: Macdonald & Co. in association with the Council of Industrial Design.

Shepheard, Peter Faulkner (1969) *Gardens: A Design Centre Publication*, London: Macdonald & Co. in association with the Council of Industrial Design.

Shumway, David R. (1998) 'Something Old, Something New: Romance and Marital Advice in the 1920s', in *An Emotional History of the United States*, ed. Peter Stearns and Jane Lewis, New York: New York University Press, 305–318.

Sillitoe, Alan F. ([1971] 1973) *Britain in Figures: A Handbook of Social Statistics*, second edition, Harmondsworth: Penguin.

Simonds, Wendy (1992) *Women and Self-Help Culture: Reading Between the Lines*, New Brunswick, NJ: Rutgers University Press.

Singleton, Andrew (2004) 'Good Advice for Godly Men: Oppressed Men in Christian Men's Self-Help Literature', *Journal of Gender Studies*, vol. 13, no. 2: 153–164.

Sinnema, Peter W., ed. (2002) 'Introduction', in Samuel Smiles, *Self-Help; With Illustrations of Character and Conduct*, World's Classics edition, Oxford: Oxford University Press.

Sivulka, Juliann (2001) *Stronger Than Dirt: A Cultural History of Advertising Personal Hygiene in America, 1875 to 1940*, Amherst, NY: Prometheus Books.

Sklar, Kathryn Kish (1976) *Catharine Beecher: A Study in American Domesticity*, New York and London: W. W. Norton and Co.

Sleeper, Catherine and Harold Sleeper (1948) *House For You to Build, Buy, or Rent*, illus. by Henry Diamond and Lombard C. Jones, New York: J. Wiley.

Smiles, Samuel ([1859] 2002) *Self-Help; With Illustrations of Character and Conduct*, World's Classics edition, Oxford: Oxford University Press.

Smith, Caroline J. (2005) 'Living the Life of a Domestic Goddess: Chick Lit's Response to Domestic-Advice Manuals', *Women's Studies*, vol. 34, no. 8: 671–699.

Smith, Delia ([1971] 2008) *How to Cheat at Cooking*, London: Ebury Press.

Smith, F. Seymour (1956) *Know-How Books: An Annotated Bibliography of Do It Yourself Books for the Handyman and of Introductions to Science, Art, History and Literature for the Beginner and Home Student*, London: Thames & Hudson.

Snyder, Katherine (1998) 'A Paradise of Bachelors: Remodelling Domesticity and Masculinity in the Turn-of-the-Century New York Bachelor Apartment', *Prospects*, vol. 23: 247–284.

Spanier, Adrienne (1959) *Furnishing and Decorating in Your Home*, London: Arthur Barker Ltd.

Sparke, Penny (1995) *As Long as Its Pink: The Sexual Politics of Taste*, London: Pandora.

Sparke, Penny (2003) 'The "Ideal" and the "Real" Interior in Elsie de Wolfe's *The House in Good Taste* of 1913', *Journal of Design History*, vol. 16, no. 1: 63–76.

Sparke, Penny (2005) *Elsie de Wolfe: The Birth of Modern Interior Decoration*, ed. Mitchell Owens, New York: Acanthus Press.

Spigel, Lynn (1990) 'Television in the Family Circle: The Popular Reception of a New Medium', in *Logics of Television: Essays in Cultural Criticism*, ed. Patricia Mellencamp, Bloomington and Indianapolis: Indiana University Press, 73–97.

Spigel, Lynn (1992) *Make Room for TV: Television and the Family Ideal in Postwar America*, Chicago, IL: University of Chicago Press.

Spillers Flour (n.d., ca. 1950) *How to be a Good Hostess*, London: Spillers Flour Limited, foreword by Anna Neagle.

Spock, Dr Benjamin ([1946] 1967) *Baby and Child Care*, New York: Pocket Books [first published as *The Common Sense Book and Baby and Child Care*].

Spring, Joel (2003) *Educating the Consumer-Citizen: A History of the Marriage of Schools, Advertising, and Media*, Mahwah, NJ: Lawrence Earlbaum.

Spry, Constance and Rosemary Hulme (1956) *Constance Spry Cookery Book*, London: J. M. Dent & Sons (reissued London: Pan Books, 1972 and 1979).

Spry, Constance and Rosemary Hume (1961) *Hostess*, ed. Anthony Marr, London: J. M. Dent & Sons.

Spurlock, John C. (1998) 'The Problem of Modern Married Love for Middle-Class Women', *An Emotional History of the United States*, ed. Peter Stearns and Jane Lewis, New York University Press, 318–332.

St. George, Andrew (1993) *The Descent of Manners: Etiquette, Rules and the Victorians*, London: Chatto & Windus.

Starker, Steven ([1989] 2002) *Oracle at the Supermarket: The American Pre-Occupation with Self-Help Books*, New Brunswick, NJ: Transaction Publishers.

Stead, Jennifer (1983) 'Quizzing Glasse, or Hannah Scrutinized', *Petits Propos Culinaires*, no. 13: 9–24; no. 14: 17–30.

Stearns, Peter M. (1998) 'Consumerism and Childhood: New Targets for American Emotions', in *An Emotional History of the United States*, ed. Peter Stearns and Jane Lewis, New York: New York University Press, 396–413.

Stearns, Peter N. (2003) *Anxious Parents: A History of Modern Childrearing in America*, New York: New York University Press.

Steele, Jeanne R. and Jane D. Brown, (1995) 'Adolescent Room Culture: Studying Media in the Context of Everyday Life', *Journal of Youth and Adolescence*, vol. 24, no. 5: 551–576.

Stewart, Edith Helen Vane Tempest, Marchioness of Londonderry ([1933] 1938) *Retrospect*, London: Frederick Muller Ltd.

Stewart, Martha (1982) *Entertaining*, New York: Clarkson Potter.

Stewart, Martha (2009) *Martha Stewart's Dinner at Home: 52 Quick Meals to Cook for Family and Friends*, New York: Clarkson Potter.

Stone, Lawrence (1977) *The Family, Sex and Marriage in England 1500–1800*, London: Weidenfeld & Nicolson.

Stopes, Marie (1918) *Married Love*, London: A. C. Fifield.

Strange, Julie-Marie (2001) 'The Assault on Ignorance: Teaching Menstrual Etiquette c. 1920s to 1960s', *Social History of Medicine*, vol. 14, no. 2: 247–265.

Strasser, Susan ([1982] 2000) *Never Done: A History of American Housework*, New York: Henry Holt and Company.

Strong, Roy, Marcus Binney and John Harris, [with contributions by] the Duke of Bedford and others, (1974) *The Destruction of the Country House, 1875–1975*, London: Thames & Hudson.

Sutherland, Douglas (1978) *The English Gentleman*, London: Debrett's Peerage Ltd.

Sykes, Sydney A. (1990) *The Country Diary Book of Decorating: English Country Style*, Exeter: Webb and Bower.

Tapsell, Florence A. (1913–1914) *The Little Housekeeper*, 4 vols. Leeds: E. J. Arnold.

Taylor, Frederick Winslow (1911) *The Principles of Scientific Management*, New York and London: Harper & Brothers.

Taylor, Patrick, ed. ([2006] 2008) *The Oxford Companion to the Garden*, Oxford: Oxford University Press.

Teen Voices (2011) 'Make-Up, Models and Materialism', http://www.teenvoices.com/2009/03/03/makeup-models-and-materialism/. Accessed 10 May 2011.

Tester, Keith (1999) 'The Moral Consequentiality of Television', *European Journal of Social Theory*, vol. 2, no. 4: 469–483.

Thompson, Jane and Alexandra Lange (2010) *Design Research: The Store That Brought Modern Living to American Homes*, San Francisco, CA: Chronicle Books.

Tickell, Jerrard, ed. (1938) *Gentlewomen Aim to Please, Edited from Victorian Manuals of Etiquette by J. Tickell. Nicolas Bentley drew the pictures*, London: G. Routledge & Sons.

Tiersten, Lisa (1996) 'The Chic Interior and the Feminine Modern: Home Decorating as High Art in Turn-of-the-Century Paris', in *Not at Home: The Suppression of Domesticity in Modern Art and Architecture*, ed. Christopher Reed, London: Thames & Hudson, 18–32.

Tiger Aspect (1999–2002) *Country House*, 3 series, BBC 2.

Tinkler, Penny (1995) *Constructing Girlhood: Popular Magazines for Girls Growing Up in England 1920–1950*, London: Taylor & Francis.

Tomes, Robert (1872) *The Bazaar Book of Decorum: The Care of the Person, Manners, Etiquette, and Ceremonials*, New York: Harper & Brothers.

Tonkovich, Nicole (1995) 'Advice Books', in *The Oxford Companion to Women's Writing in the United States*, ed. Cathy N. Davidson and Linda Wagner-Martin, Oxford: Oxford University Press.

Townsend, Dr John (2006) *Boundaries with Teens: When to Say Yes, How to Say No*, Grand Rapids, MI: Zondervan.

Troubridge, Lady Laura ([1926] 1958) *The Book of Etiquette*, Cedar Special no. 55, Kingswood, Surrey: The World's Work, reprinted 1962, 1965, 1968, 1979.

Troubridge, Lady (1939) *Etiquette and Entertaining*, London: Amalgamated Press.

Trustees of the National Trust (2011) 'Board of Trustees Report for 2010/11', National Trust Annual Report 2010/11, 4.

Turnbull, Annmarie (1987) 'Learning Her Womanly Work: The Elementary School Curriculum, 1870–1914', in *Lessons for Life*, ed. Felicity Hunt, Oxford: Basil Blackwell.

Turner, Bryan S. and Roland Robertson (1991) 'How to Read Parsons', in *Talcott Parsons: Theorist of Modernity*, ed. Roland Robertson and Bryan S. Turner, London: Sage.

Turner, E. S. (1962) *What the Butler Saw: Two Hundred and Fifty Years of the Servant Problem*, London: Michael Joseph.

UK Council for Child Internet Safety (2012) http://www.education.gov.uk/ukccis/. Accessed 1 October 2012.

Veblen, Thorstein ([1899] 1970) *The Theory of the Leisure Class: An Economic Study of Institutions*, with an introduction by C. Wright Mills, London: Unwin Books.

Ventura, Viviana (1983) *Viviana Ventura's Guide to Social Climbing: Including (of Course) Photographs by Richard Young*, London: Macmillan.

Vollmer, John L., Pamela A. Schulze and Janice M. Chebra (2005) 'The American Master Bedroom: Its Changing Location and Significance to the Family', *Journal of Interior Design*, vol. 31, no. 1: 1–13.

Wagner, George (1996) 'The Lair of the Bachelor', in *Architecture and Feminism*, ed. Debra Coleman, Elizabeth Danze and Carol Henderson, New York: Princeton Architectural Press, 183–219.

Waites, Bernard (1987) *A Class Society at War: England 1914–1918*, Leamington Spa: Berg.

Walker, Nancy A. (2000) *Shaping Our Mothers' World: American Women's Magazines*, Jackson: University Press of Mississippi.

Walsh, John (2001) 'Half a Century of Cultural Caviar', the Books Interview, Weekend Review, *The Independent* (16 June): 9.

Walter, Dawna (2003) *The Life Laundry: How to Stay De-Junked Forever*, London: BBC Books, 2003.

Walter, Dawna and Mark Franks (2002) *The Life Laundry: How to De-Junk Your Life*, London, BBC Books.

Ward, A. W. and A. R. Waller ([1907–1921] 2000) *Cambridge History of English and American Literature*, New York: Bartleby.com [New York: G.P. Putnam's Sons].

Ward, Mary and Neville Ward (1978) *Home in the Twenties and Thirties*, London: Ian Allen Ltd.

Warde, Alan (1997) *Consumption, Food and Taste*, London: Sage.

Washington, George ([1747] 1926) *Rules of Civility and Decent Behavior in Company and Conversation*, ed. Charles Moore, Boston, MA and New York: Houghton Mifflin Company.

Watt, Ian ([1957] 1987) *The Rise of the Novel*, London: The Hogarth Press.

Weaver, William Woys (1983) 'Additions and Corrections to Lowenstein's Bibliography of American Cookery Books, 1742–1860', *Proceedings of the American Antiquarian Society*, vol. 92, no. 2.

Weber, Max ([1947] 1991) *From Max Weber: Essays in Sociology*, trans., ed. and with an introduction by C. Wright Mills and H. H. Gerth, London: Routledge.

Weber, Max (1964) *The Theory of Social and Economic Organisation*, trans. A. M. Henderson and T. Parsons, New York: Free Press.

Weber, Max (1968) *Economy and Society: An Outline of Interpretive Sociology*, ed. Guenther Roth and Claus Wittich, trans. Ephraim Fischoff *et al.*, New York: Bedminster Press.

Weber, Sandra and Shanly Dixon, ed. (2007) *Growing Up Online: Young People and Digital Technologies*, London: Palgrave Macmillan.

Weber, Sandra and Claudia Mitchell (2008) 'Imagining, Keyboarding, and Posting Identities: Young People and New Media Technologies', in *Youth, Identity, and Digital Media*, ed. David Buckingham, Cambridge, MA: MIT Press, 25–48.

Webster, Doris and Mary Alden Hopkins (1930) *Mrs. Grundy is Dead: A Code of Etiquette for Young People, Written by Themselves*, New York: Century.

Weisman, Steven R. (1973) 'Nancy Mitford, Author, Dead; Satiric Novelist and Essayist', *New York Times* (1 July), http://www.nytimes.com/learning/general/onthisday/bday/1128.html.

Wharton, Edith and Ogden Codman Jr. (1897) *Decoration of Houses*, first edition, New York: Charles Scribner's Sons.

Wheeler, Candace (1903) *Principles of Home Decoration, with Practical Examples*, New York, Doubleday, Page & Company.

Whelen, Christine (2004) 'Self-Help Books and the Quest for Self-Control in the United States, 1950–2000', PhD dissertation, Oxford University.

Wiener, Martin J. (1981) *English Culture and the Decline of the Industrial Spirit, 1850–1980*, Cambridge: Cambridge University Press.

Williams-Ellis, Amabel (1951) *The Art of Being a Woman*, London: The Bodley Head.

Wilson, Judith (2007) *Teen Zone: Stylish Living for Teens*, photography by Winfried Heinze, London and New York: Ryland, Peters and Small, Inc.

Winship, Janice (1987) *Inside Women's Magazines*, London: Pandora.

Wolf Tony and Suzanne Franks (2002) *Get Out of My Life – But First Take Me and Alex into Town*, London: Profile Books.

Wolff, Kurt H. ed. (1950) *The Sociology of Georg Simmel*, Glencoe, IL: Free Press.

Woman (1938) *Every Woman's Book of Home-Making*, London: The Amalgamated Press Ltd.

Woman ([1949a] 1950) *Woman Week-End Book: A Selection of Popular Short Stories, Many Interesting and Instructive Hints on Beauty, Housewifery, and*

Personal Problems, Cookery, Knitting, and Useful Things to Make, London: Odhams Press Ltd.

Woman ([1949b] 1950) *Woman Week-End Book Number Two*, London: Odhams Press Limited.

Woman's Own (1967) *Woman's Own Book of Modern Homemaking*, London: George Newnes Ltd.

Woodham, Jonathan (1996a) 'Managing British Design Reform I: Fresh Perspectives on the Early Years of the Council of Industrial Design', *Journal of Design History*, vol. 9, no. 1: 55–66.

Woodham, Jonathan (1996b) 'Managing British Design Reform II: The Film *Deadly Lampshade* – An Ill-Fated Episode in the Politics of "Good Taste"', *Journal of Design History*, vol. 9, no. 2: 101–15.

Worsley, Giles (2002) *England's Lost Houses: From the Archives of 'Country Life'*, London: Aurum Press.

Wouters, Cas (1995) 'Etiquette Books and Emotion Management in the 20th Century: Part One – The Integration of Social Classes', *Journal of Social History*, vol. 29: 107–124.

Wouters, Cas (2007) *Informalization: Manners and Emotion since 1890*, London: Sage.

Wright, Erik Olin (1979) *Class, Crisis and the State*, London: Verso.

Wright, Mary and Russel Wright ([1950] 1954) *Guide to Easier Living*, new revised edition, New York: Simon & Schuster.

Yerbury, Francis W. (1947) *Modern Homes Illustrated*, London: Odhams Press Ltd.

Yorke, F. R. S. (1934) *The Modern House*, London: Architectural Press.

Young, Mary (1962) *In Search of Charm*, designed and illustrated by the Peter Hatch Partnership Ltd., Leicester: Brockhampton Press.

Young, Michael (1954) 'The Planners and the Planned, the Family', paper to the Town Planning Institute, April 1954 in *Journal of the Town Planning Institute* (May): 134.

Young, Michael and Peter Willmott ([1957] 1992) *Family and Kinship in East London*, Reports of the Institute of Community Studies, Berkeley: University of California Press [London: Routledge & Kegan Paul].

Zuckerman, Mary Ellen (1998) *A History of Popular Women's Magazines in the United States, 1792–1995*, Westport, CT: Greenwood Press.

Index